REAL AND IMAGINED WOMEN

Real and Imagined Women explores a number of fascinating and important theoretical questions for feminists by offering a challenging mode of 'reading resistance', set against the stereotyped and sensationalist image of the 'third world woman' as victim.

Real and Imagined Women reconceptualizes this overdetermined subjectivity in separate but related essays that explore the practice and representation of sati, the issues around rape and wife-murder and the official and media construction of the 'new' woman as these relate to the situation of women in colonial and post-Independence India. In addition, an essay on the 'case' of Indira Gandhi identifies, at the other end, the elite female subject, the woman-as-leader, and seeks to reclaim her for a feminist politics. The central and repeated concern of these essays thus emerges as the (re)constitution of female subjectivity in the interests of a feminist praxis.

Rajeswari Sunder Rajan reads the cultural representations of women through a wide and varied range of texts – from the classical Tamil epic *Silapaddikaram* to recent film, popular fiction, commercial advertisements, legal texts and journalism – and by this means raises the issue of how the postcolonial situation frames the contest between 'real' and 'imagined' women.

Rajeswari Sunder Rajan lectures in English at the University of Delhi. She has edited a collection of essays entitled *The Lie of the Land: English Literary Studies in India* and her work on feminist theory and politics has appeared in *Signs: Journal of Women in Culture and Society* and *The Yale Journal of Criticism*.

D0061103

Frontispiece Arpana Caur, *Home Sweet Home* (1981)

REAL AND IMAGINED WOMEN

Gender, culture and postcolonialism

Rajeswari Sunder Rajan

London and New York

First published 1993
by Routledge
11 New Fetter Lane, London EC4P 4EE

Simultaneously published in the USA and Canada
by Routledge
29 West 35th Street, New York, NY 10001

Typeset in 10/12 pt Baskerville by Selwood Systems, Midsomer Norton

Printed and bound in Great Britain by T J Press (Padstow) Ltd, Padstow, Cornwall

British Library Cataloguing in publication Data

A catalogue record for this book is available from the British Library

Library of Congress Cataloging in Publication Data
Sunder Rajan, Rajeswari.
Real and imagined women: gender, culture, and postcolonialism/
Rajeswari Sunder Rajan.
p. cm.
1. Sex role–India. 2. Feminism–India. 3. Suttee. 4. Women–India–History. I. Title.
HO1075.5.I4S86 1993
305.42' 0954-dc20   93–6923

ISBN 0–415–08503–9 (hbk)
0–415–08504–7 (pbk)

To
Sunder
and
Kaushik

CONTENTS

FIGURES

ACKNOWLEDGEMENTS

I have had the support, friendship and critical advice of many friends and colleagues whom I take this opportunity to name and thank: Rimli Bhattacharya, Vivek Dhareshwar, Margaret Higonnet, Sharada Jain, Ania Loomba, Tejaswini Niranjana, Judith Plotz, Arvind Rajagopal, Venkat Rao, Amrit Srinivasan, and Kamala Visweswaran.

Dr G.K. Das, Director of the South Campus of the University of Delhi, graciously gave me permission to use the library at the South Campus.

To those who helped me cope with the mysteries of the computer – R. Chandramouli, R. Parthasarathy, V. Krishnamoorthy and A.K. Ghosh – my heartfelt thanks.

My editors at Routledge have been unfailingly helpful.

My parents, my brothers, my sisters-in-law and my niece were everything that only a family can be during a time of crisis; this acknowledgement of my gratitude is only a meagre return for all that they have given me. My son Kaushik typed, criticized and relieved the tedium of my work: he has been an invaluable ally.

I could not have written this book without my husband's support, encouragement and love. It is therefore jointly dedicated to him and our son.

INTRODUCTION
Subjectivity, representation and the politics of postcoloniality

I

This collection of feminist critical essays is an attempt to map the space of the postcolonial female subject. Written over the past three years, largely in response to suggestions and invitations from US feminist colleagues in the academy editing journals and anthologies, but from within the physical and intellectual space of the Indian university – with all that this implies of the material conditions and the political affiliations of such a location – these essays are already hybrid in their genealogy and address. There is the further hybridity of matter (history, issues, themes) and method (theory, language) that is a function of postcolonial intellectual production. Negotiating with this hybridity as both a historical determinant and an intellectual identity, I have sought to reach through to an understanding, which I think of as 'theoretical', about issues of gender in the contemporary Indian nation-state.

Intellectual work produced under the sign of global feminism and theory but over the signature of the postcolonial academic is open to charges of inauthenticity, dubiousness of politics, academic mileage, alienated modernism and native informancy. The activity of reading 'under western eyes' becomes a fraught and almost disablingly self-conscious exercise. Nevertheless, the dialogue with western feminists that such writing seeks to initiate, while it acknowledges our similarity of political motivation, also stresses the differences in the questions confronting us. Thus the comparative perspective both feeds into and provokes the articulation of sameness and difference that is such a necessary function of contemporary critical enquiry. It may also be argued that the sole allegiance we have heretofore acknowledged to historicist or culturalist explanations and empirical 'case'-studies has needlessly inhibited the scope of postcolonial intellectual work. The attempt to be politically correct without sterility, and to intervene creatively into the situation of theory without being irresponsible, is admittedly an enterprise that risks failure in both directions. But theoretical endeavour and speculation would still be worth undertaking even if – at the very least – they only set off theoretical quarrels, thus reclaiming questions of theory and method as integral to our politics.

1

My sense of the risk and challenge of academic work in the present Indian context, and especially that of feminist cultural studies, is conveyed in a review I wrote of Susie Tharu and K. Lalitha's anthology *Women Writing in India*, a work of stupendous research, scholarship and critical energy.[1] I quote from my review at some length in order to set out what seems to me the broad problematic of all postcolonial feminist criticism, including my own work.

'I turn to two issues that this volume throws up (among many others) that seem to me especially worth identifying and exploring further: the opposition between *politics* and *aesthetics* in the feminist critical enterprise; and the problem of subaltern, specifically gendered, *resistance*, in relation to writing.

'One of the most insistent beliefs that informs this project is the declaration that the recovery of women's writing, feminist literary criticism, and writing by women itself, are political rather than aesthetic activities. The unrelenting opposition that the editors maintain between the aesthetic and the political as separate cognitive structures plays not only into the opposition dominant/ subaltern, but also into other oppositions between form and content, scripts and life-stories, literary conventions and reality, art and experience, even "writing" and women, which are made to correspond to it.

'Now, while the reminder that feminist scholarship and criticism are political activities is necessary and even crucial for our reading practices, and while one understands and sympathises with the editors' anxiety not to see their work offered up at the altar of "literary studies" (especially that of the English "canon"), the domain of the aesthetic is surely neither as separately clear-cut nor as dominant as Tharu and Lalitha designate it. Further, their recognition that "women's writing", both as a critical activity and as an "object" of knowledge ("gynocritics"), has been pioneered by western feminism, creates a bind/bond that requires complex acknowledgement and dissociation. This leads to the long – disproportionately long, it turns out – discussion in the introduction, of western, chiefly American, feminist criticism, its chief practitioners, its assumptions, and its weaknesses (pp. 12–31). It is not only a tortuous way of making the point that there is a misfit between western feminist theories of women's writing and women's writing in India, but also one that makes reductive, in the process, the scope and the actual heterogeneity of American feminist criticism.

'Another result of the opposition the editors have set up between the political and the aesthetic is the apparent irrelevance of critical judgements – and of pleasure itself! – to our reading "politically". There is a strain of self-righteous puritanism in the concluding warning that they issue: "There will be few gratifications here to replace these domestic fires burning in polished hearths, few testimonies of liberation, or bugle calls that herald the nation or the revolution" (p. 35). This disclaimer is fortunately belied by their own abundant enjoyment in the literary text, the criteria they employ in their selections, and the actual masterpieces they have brought together. Nevertheless, one wishes

2

that there could have been a stronger sense of the infusion of the aesthetic into the political in the critical commentary.

'In stressing the political *fact* of women's writing, with all its attendant dangers and difficulties, at the cost of neglecting the *achievement*, there is a danger also of replicating Samuel Johnson's pronouncement upon a woman speaking in public (which he likened to a dog walking on its hind legs): the question is not whether it is well done or ill done but that it is done at all. Surely women's writing must be viewed within, and as an aspect of, social practice as much as without it and as a form of resistance to it. Paradoxically, therefore, the attempt to stress the political in women's writing results in its divorce from historical everydayness and in its attainment to the status of a heroic exceptionality.

'This debate is closely linked to the larger issue of reading resistance in subaltern historiography. Having successfully argued that gender is a constitutive element in literary production, Tharu and Lalitha also want to establish it as always and essentially resistant, a claim that not only is more problematic, but also uneasily contradicts the other implicit item on the political agenda of feminist criticism: which is that one must *read* resistance.

'Again and again Tharu and Lalitha place before us instances of women's writing that have been offered by traditional literary historians as works operating *within* formal conventions, and in terms of closure and resolution: the Therigatha of Buddhist nuns, the *atmanivedan* of Bahinabai, the erotic court poetry of Mudupalani. It is their defining mission, and their strength as critics, to read against the grain. While arguing that women's writing, in spite of their subsumption within "the ideologies that shape their worlds", are still "different", Tharu and Lalitha define the politics of feminist criticism in terms of learning "to read [them] ... in a new way ... to read them not for the moments in which they collude with or reinforce dominant ideologies of gender, class, nation, or empire, but for the gestures of defiance or subversion implicit in them" (p. 35).

'There are at least three problematic areas that they stumble over in carrying out this programme: the category of "experience", the legitimacy of the role of the subaltern/ feminist historian/ critic, and the related issue of the "invention of a tradition".

'Not that Tharu and Lalitha are naive about the category of experience (see especially pp. 23 and 34). But they are nevertheless obliged to privilege something that has to be designated as "women's experience" – even the experience of ideology – as the invariant "other" of male history, literary tradition, form, and ideology, in order to make women's writing resistant by definition.

'The discovery of resistance in women's writing also requires the investment of *our* desires and the acknowledgement of *our* politics as women/feminists reading. I must confess to finding this among the most intelligently self-conscious and bravely political assertions in this book. The bonding that Tharu and Lalitha create between the writer Mudupalani in the eighteenth century, the critic and publisher Nagaratnamma in the early twentieth century, and themselves as

3

translators and editors of Mudupalani's *Radhika Santwanam* in the late twentieth century, reading this as an "allegory" of the "enterprise of women's writing and the scope of feminist criticism in India", is a stunning example of critical sisterhood. It is an alliance that announces itself on other occasions: in their reading, for example, of Lalithambika Antherjanam's "The Goddess of Revenge" (1938).

'But is the subversion of women's writing to be located within the work/the act of writing, or in the critical reading that disengages it for us? Tharu and Lalitha imply that it lies latent in women's writing: an argument not unlike the American critics Gilbert and Gubar's reading of nineteenth-century women's novels as coded works whose secret messages in invisible ink they so ingeniously disclose in their *Mad Woman in the Attic*. We can have nothing against such an argument except that it elides the more problematic issues of power and privilege that inform the critical function, what the critic Benita Parry (describing the work of Gayatri Spivak) has called the "exorbitation" of the intellectual's self-assigned role of postcolonial critic as one who must undertake "to give the subaltern a voice in history". In spite of their care and solicitude for "their" writers, Tharu and Lalitha can never entirely avoid appearing as impresarios, never entirely abstain from speaking "for" (other) women.

'This is a larger question, of course, one that has to do with all feminist academic work. But at a more trivial level it also has to do with *tact*. At a rough computation over a third of the book consists of critical exegesis and editorial paraphernalia of various kinds – biographical headnotes, textual commentaries, historical background, bibliography, etc. – and while these serve admirably to historicize women's writing, one often feels a sense of disproportion between work and outworks. For example, ten pages of fascinating background information about *Radhika Santwanam* and its reception are followed by three tantalisingly short extracts, each less than twenty lines long, from the poem itself. The critical attempt to control the reading and reception of women's writing is at times a case of overkill.

'The problem does not disappear in the case of the more explicitly feminist works of the later nineteenth century, such as Mokshadayini Mukhopadhyay's *Bangalir Babu*, or Tarabhai Shinde's *Stri Purush Tulana*. The astounding feminist pamphlet written in Marathi by Tarabhai Shinde in 1882 is a particularly fortuitous example, since Tharu and Lalitha's recovery of this forgotten work coincides with the Cambridge historian Rosalind O'Hanlon's recent essay on her (in Douglas Haynes and Gyan Prakash's *Contesting Power: Resistance and Everyday Social Relations in South Asia*); and the difference in approaches helps me to exemplify the problem of the historical interpretation of gendered resistance.

'In contrast to Tharu and Lalitha's elaboration of Tarabhai's feminism, O'Hanlon – locating her reading in the context of the contemporary historiography of the "marginal and the dispossessed", which is often tempted to "celebrate their sheer defiance and their apparent autonomy" – seeks to emphasize, instead, the "ways in which resistances also enter into the processes by which structures of domination persist or renew themselves". In the case of Tarabhai the *cost* of resistance was "precisely the reproduction, in an inverted form, of some of patriarchy's own forms of sexual essentialism, belittlement and contempt".

'Admittedly, if there is a danger of making resistance too "autonomous", there is also that of making the dominant too monolithic. In the methodological impasse that this issue poses, whether the subaltern historian/feminist critic celebrates resistance or privileges the ultimate authority of the dominant will depend largely on the stragetic, political or corrective purpose that underlines her interpretation and intervention. Tharu and Lalitha are impelled by the force of their conviction that women's writing is "constantly contestatory", to stress the former. But the case for women's writing, while it has by no means been won, has been fought for a while now. Hence it is time for a judicious review of the politics of women's writing – one which recognizes that it is not always resistant, and which historicizes its conformism scrupulously.

'There is another poignant political dilemma that is played out in *Women Writing in India*: the contradiction between, on the one hand, the desired enterprise of "inventing" a "tradition" of women's writing, and on the other the subaltern nature of all "minority" literature. Susie Tharu sees the first activity as "violent" and hegemonic since we must "violate" the past in order to construct the future we desire. "Can we create a tradition that will not then require a hegemony for the tradition we are creating?" she asks (*Journal of Arts and Ideas*). The negotiations that Tharu and Lalitha have to constantly chart between the claims of the aesthetic and the political in reading women's writing, between recognizing women's individual achievement and their historical subalternity, between critical assertion and abdication, exemplifies the attempt to resolve this difficult question.'[2]

Many of the methodological and critical problems that Tharu and Lalitha foreground in their work are those of their location and politics, i.e. of postcolonial feminism, whose contours are briefly sketched below.

II

The six chapters that make up this volume are varied and loosely connected. Nevertheless – as I perceive largely from the retrospective vantage-point provided by writing an introduction after the event – the central and repeated concern of these essays is the (re)constitution of female subjectivity in the interests of a feminist praxis. If my interest in gender leads primarily to reflections about female subjectivity, my cultural analysis necessarily focuses on representation as the process by which the female subject is constructed in response to a variety of ideological imperatives. The broad context within which these writings are located is most succintly identified as postcoloniality, a condition that describes a specific historical identity, politics and method.

If there are certain broad features that postcolonial nations may be said to have in common as a result of their shared experience of colonialism these lie in the following: the central role of the state; inequalities in social structures; the contrary pulls of nationalism and regionalism (or centralization and federalization); and the conflicts between 'tradition' and 'modernity'. The particular consequences of this history as they impinge upon gendered issues are remarkably similar.

In all postcolonial nations the state, envisaged as the guarantor of rights to its citizens, has invariably emerged instead as a major perpetrator of injustices – whether as a function of military power or, as in India, as an aspect of political parties' electoral calculations. In such a context the women's movement ends by both forming alliances with the state – typically in the form of seeking the recourse of its laws in instituting legal reform or enacting new laws on behalf of women – as well as resisting the state's control, which is precisely a consequence of the powers vested in it.[3] Some of the complexities of such a contradictory functioning of the postcolonial state, and feminist negotiations with it, are explored in my essays on sati, rape and wife-murder.

'Developing' countries are also characterized by severe inequities in class, caste, community and gender relations which generate the endemic violence characteristic of their social structures. The reality of 'uneven development', as Indian feminists observe, 'both shapes and draws on gender relations', and thereby affects the nature of women's struggle for change. When dominant – chiefly majoritarian – groups fail in their attempts at hegemony, i.e. at 'politico-ideological control', they turn violence into their chief instrument of control.[4] The resistance of oppressed groups, including women, takes place on several levels of response, ranging from non-violent collective struggle, as in anti-dam and ecology struggles, to armed insurgency, as in several secessionist movements. The subjectivities of women, as victims of violence and agents of resistance, are constituted through the negotiations of these situations, as I try to show in these essays.

The postcolonial nation-state is riven also by the conflicts between the imperative of 'nationalism' as ideology on the one hand, and the reality of the multiple regional, caste, linguistic and religious divisions within its geographical boundaries, on the other. In this contest, the state attempts to assert the forces of homogenization and centralization against the various secessionist or federalizing movements for autonomy and control initiated by regional groups. Women, to whose allegiances grounded in one or other identity appeals are frequently directed, are more often the sites of such contests than participants in them. The conflict between 'tradition' and 'modernity' in various spheres also feeds into the problematic, and a similar fraught but passive subject-position is created for women. Chapter 6 subjects this problematic to extended scrutiny.

Thus, although colonialism may have been only a portion of the histories of postcolonial nations, its impingement upon their present social, political, economic and cultural situation is not simply a matter of 'legacies' (in India often benignly identified as the parliamentary system, the railways and the English

6

language), but of active, immediate and constitutive determinations (or overdeterminations). It is true that often and too quickly this recognition is used to 'fix' the responsibility for many of the present evils in the country – such as environmental degradation, communalism, the rigid bureaucracy, the system of personal law – upon colonial administrative decisions. Typically, this 'politics of blame', as Edward Said terms it,[5] short-circuits investigation into and analysis of the contingent and actual shape of postcolonialism. On the other hand the recurrence and refurbishment in the discourse of the state, as well as its opponents, of certain tropes and conceptual moves that colonialism and imperialism had framed – one example is orientalism – will not allow us to represent them simply as regrettable 'events' in the past. Kumkum Sangari identifies some of the fields where the 'new' orientalism legitimizes the more regressive aspects of state and culture in India:

> First, there is the escalation of a communal politics and the growth of a chauvinist and fundamentalist social milieu where a major ideological prop is found in versions of an essentialist indigenism, in which descriptions of caste, gender, language *et al.* are offered as eternal verities even though they may not have taken shape earlier than the colonial period. In this respect the biases of the nineteenth century Indology have left their mark on colonial and nationalist historiography as well as on popular perception of an Aryan/Hindu culture. Second, there is an assertive state-sponsored display of Indian tradition and culture, especially of the classical, the folk and the tribal, intended as a saleable compensation for the lack of democratizing initiatives on its own part. For example, the tribal is represented as a self-congratulatory mark of the surviving pre-modern indigenous, even as the tribals themselves face, and struggle with, both social change and actual dispossession. The flip side of this 'internationalization', which is also a permutation of the old orientalism, are the often equally appropriative and essentializing western representations of Indian folk, tribal and classical forms (seldom contemporary urban forms), in which Indian state institutions often seem to have a collaborative stake. Third, there are attempts, usually from anti-Marxist, neo-Gandhian positions, to re-establish the difference between us and them (the west) by taking a stand against the values of the Enlightenment (reason, science, progress) using a rhetoric of anti-colonial indigenism; these then set out via a rehash of certain nationalist projects to rediscover an essentially *desi* India with its very own modes of cognition. Not surprisingly, such projects have often clustered around the most retrogressive events, e.g. widow immolation. Fourth, there is the appearance of an institutionalized 'thirdworldism' on the elite academic scene. This makes an attempt to re-annexe the colonial subject – now albeit somewhat fragmented and elusive – through the application of recent de-essentializing critical theories pitted against bourgeois, colonial, Enlightenment value systems.[6]

If colonialism as a 'legitimation system' then still 'imbricates' hegemonic discourse today, as Arjuna Parakrama puts it,[7] it does so, further, in ways that cannot always or simply be refused. For instance, the implications, in the present context, of rejecting the colonial problematic of sati as a 'women's issue', and embracing instead an earlier reading of it as an index of conjugal love and female heroism, can be fraught with dangerously regressive overtones.[8] In chapter 2 I therefore argue the need to recognize the epistemelogical break that occurs with the advent of what is regarded as 'modernity'.

We are forced to concede that a 'non-colonialist (and therefore non-contaminated?) space remains a wish-fulfilment within postcolonial knowledge production'.[9] If the postcolonial intellectual position dictates the implicit deployment and critique of western sciences of knowledge, the wrestling with the problems of discovering a viable 'indigenous' theory − which will not at the same time be complicit with various regressive forms of nativism, fundamentalism or reaction − is a constant accompaniment of such intellectual enquiry. 'Indigenous', as Sarah Joseph points out, is a problematic description since, referring as it does to 'no more than the intellectual and cultural products which have emerged within a geographical space and which have escaped alien influences', a simple 'nationality test' may be imposed on them to see if they 'belong'. But 'nation' too is 'a highly contested term'; and this recognition only leads to 'the modified view that not one but many indigenous social sciences are possible'. The further stage, that of assuming a natural fit between indigenous theory and third world 'matter', is equally problematic.[10] Even an indigenous literary theory 'applied' to the reading of Indian literary texts on this assumption can become a misleading critical enterprise if such application is not historically validated (as I argue in chapters 3 and 5).

At the same time, I am aware of displaying a less than rigorous allegiance to 'theory' from the west, whose limits are betrayed − rather than systematically explored − at the points where they break down as explanatory models.[11] Thus Elaine Scarry's invaluable dissertation upon *The Body in Pain* serves both as a deliberately 'alien' documentary of the phenomenonology of sati in chapter 1, as well as the distinctive historical and cultural 'other' of its subject.[12]

'Theory' has here become the contracted domain of the western 'sciences of knowledge', as in much contemporary postcolonial intellectual discussions of epistemology. A theory that seems to be mobile, territorially expansive, and appropriative, both immanently as well as on account of the global hegemony of the western academy, is critically contained, as contributors to a forum on 'Traveling Theory/Traveling Theorists' have suggested, when questions of the theorist's location are inserted into it.[13] Location, however, is not simply an address. One's affiliations are multiple, contingent and frequently contradictory. Thus as a postcolonial feminist academic in India I undeniably have an institutional status that affiliates me with the academy in the west; at the same time I do not have a share in all the privileges of that 'other' place − especially, and above all, that of the distance that provides the critical perspective of 'exile'.[14] My intention is not to claim for myself 'marginality' – it is a dubious privilege in any case – but to show that location is fixed not (only) in the relative terms of centre and periphery, but in the positive (positivist?) terms of an actual historical and geographical contingency.[15]

The heterogeneity of postcolonial intellectual identities therefore needs to be acknowledged, as a matter of more than simple 'influences'. It has seemed to me worth while to insist upon the specificity of the configurations of the contemporary Indian social and political situation in describing the postcolonial intellectual's predicament. Thus chapter 1, on sati, grew out of the highly localized dilemma of Indian feminists' attempts to counter the claims of religious traditionalists on behalf of the sati's 'voluntary' death. On occasion it has seemed to me useful also to distinguish between 'native' and 'diasporic' (i.e. resident and non-resident) Indian intellectuals who, while sharing a common identity, do not inhabit the same historic space: questions of politics and method therefore impinge upon and compel 'same' identities in significantly different ways.[16]

III

The impact of colonialism on colonial and postcolonial societies has been predominantly investigated, as several postcolonial critics and historians have recently observed, in terms of economic and political policies and effects rather than of culture and ideology, an emphasis that they are all agreed now needs shifting.[17] But cultural analysis must proceed from the theoretical dilemma that the 'ontology' of culture poses: is 'culture' a circumscribed domain set apart from other domains like, say, society, that therefore creates this other space as a vantage point outside it from which it may be studied; or is it an envelope that wraps us around and constructs our very 'reality'? Implicitly this dilemma leads to an engagement in these essays with the major theoretical debates about the relationship between culture and society, the 'imagined' and the 'real', language and the world, discourse and materiality, as the somewhat crude polarity of the title of this book, borrowed from chapter 6, also emphasizes. Subscribing to the first position diminishes the force of culture so comprehensively as to suggest that the strategy of ideology-critique will suffice to demystify its hegemony. But, as Bruce Robbins has argued, 'the demystificatory cutting edge is blunter than we had thought', since it is based upon our ignoring 'our own historical and rhetorical positioning'.[18] The second becomes rarefied into a new determinism that effectively paralyses any political praxis.

The concept of 'representation', it seems, is useful precisely because and to the extent that it can serve a mediating function between the two positions, neither foundationalist (privileging 'reality') nor superstructural (privileging 'culture'), not denying the category of the real, or essentializing it as some pre-given metaphysical ground for representation. This is the reason why feminism, for instance, as Jacqueline Rose shows, has found it so productive to engage with representation as a 'domain with its own substantial political reality and effects'.[19] Our understanding of the problems of 'real' women cannot lie outside the 'imagined' constructs in and through which 'women' emerge as subjects. Negotiating with these mediations and simulacra we seek to arrive at an understanding of the issues at stake.

Culture then, viewed as the product of the beliefs and conceptual models of society and as the destination where the trajectory of its desires takes shape, as well as the everyday practices, the contingent realities, and the complex process by which these are structured, is the constitutive realm of the subject. As a result, culture appears as the chief matter and consequence of dominant ideological investment, powerfully coercive in shaping the subject; but since it is also heterogeneous, changing and open to interpretation, it can become a site of contestation and consequently of the reinscription of subjectivities. Therefore cultural analysis both calls forth the critique of ideology, and – given the crucial function of representation in the dialectic of social process – enables political intervention, scenarios of change, theoretical innovation and strategic reinterpretations.

IV

What we might describe as a convergence – not entirely fortuitous – of the itineraries of political (i.e. feminist, postcolonial, black) and theoretical (i.e. poststructuralist, postmodernist) criticisms upon a critique of essentialism, has had important consequences for the understanding of subjectivity. The displacement of the subject – the individual (bourgeois white male) subject of western humanism whose centrality had elided questions of class, gender and racial differences – has created a vacant space at the centre of humanist thinking, whose political consequences have been perceived in opposed ways. The important debates in feminism centre upon the gains and losses of theory's problematization of the 'subject', and are rehearsed by Judith Butler and Joan Scott in a recent collection of essays on the issue.

On the one hand, theory, in 'unfixing' the subject, has enabled the feminist 'analysis of the political construction and regulation' of the category 'women'; on the other hand, it has also led to the apprehension that 'without an ontologically grounded feminist subject there can be no politics'. Again, if poststructuralist criticisms of identity have enabled women of colour to theorize 'the split or multiple "subject" of feminism', equally there is black feminists' anxiety that post-structuralism 'deprives women of the right to be included in a humanist universality' at precisely the point when they are beginning 'to become subjects in their own right'. A further conflict is found between the problematization of the political construction and deployment of the 'real' in post-structuralist theory, which appears to 'forbid recourse to a "real body" or a "real sex"', and the

10

feminist conviction that 'such recourse is necessary to articulate moral and political opposition to violence, rape and other forms of oppression' if we are not to end up in 'positions of moral relativism and political complicity'.[20]

Butler offers a persuasive theoretical reconciliation of the oppositions that proposes that, though 'there are no necessary political consequences for such [an anti-foundationalist] theory', 'it can be used as part of ... a radical agenda', i.e. it contains the possibility of a useful 'political deployment'.[21]

One of the ways in which such a political appropriation may take place is by installing in the space vacated at the centre (of history, society, politics) a resisting subject – one who will be capable of the agency and enabling selfhood of the 'active' earlier subject, while at the same time acknowledging the politics of difference. The cleared site of the subject must provide the grounds of (new) gendered subjectivities that will enact more contingent, varied and flexible modes of resistance.

It is this that has prompted me to explore, in this book, the historically victimized – and, in the one instance, the 'elite' – female subject as the site for the constitution of 'alternative' subjectivities. Thus, in the first two chapters, both on sati ('The Subject of Sati' and 'Representing Sati'), I seek to displace the traditional construction of the subjectivity of the 'sati' (the widow who dies upon her husband's funeral pyre) in terms of one who chooses to die/is forced to die, first, on to questions of the *embodied* subject (the subject of pain), and then onto the (precolonial) literary and historical representations of the widow who chooses to *live*. In the first instance I endorse certain examples of feminist agitprop that succeed in forging an idiom of pain, escape and action for the female subject. Chapter 3, 'Life after Rape', privileges some recent fiction (my focus is on a short story in Tamil, 'Prison') that subverts narrative determinism itself by offering post-rape accounts of survival for the raped subject, in place of the classic trajectory that situates rape at the centre of novelistic structures. The possibilities of life after rape are able to shape a different subjective status for the raped woman from the traditional quiescence, apathy and death offered to Richardson's Clarissa or Forster's Adela Quested, both raped heroines of western 'master'-texts. In 'Prison' the raped woman calls upon her resources – in her case, her superior caste-identity – as a result of and in order to survive the (imagined) annihilation of self wrought by rape. In chapter 4, on the murdered wife, 'The Name of the Husband', I analyse the 'plot' of the wife's killing of the husband in recent popular Indian culture as being a fearful and guilt-ridden response to the widespread real phenomenon of bride-burning. What is the feminist potential of the scenario of this 'return of the repressed', the wife's revenge? Chapter 5, on Indira Gandhi ('Gender, Leadership and Representation: The "case" of Indira Gandhi'), identifies the limits of the contemporary representations of the woman leader in terms of 'motherhood' – regarded either as service or as tyranny – that have defined our understanding of the Indian Prime Minister. More frankly speculative than the earlier chapters, 'Indira Gandhi' proposes the theorization of the collective female subject-in-power as a 'solution' to feminism's refusal to endorse the woman leader's hegemonic individual female subjectivity. In the last chapter in the volume, 'Real and Imagined Women', my attempt is to show how the construction of a 'new' Indian woman in the hegemonic and official discourse of commercial advertising and media is subverted and appropriated by the voices of Indian women in the other texts of culture.

The spatial metaphor of displacement and occupation that I have had recourse to in my theoretical justification of this enterprise, not only makes transparent its contestatory nature but also marks the operation of desire, and perhaps of power, in such a project. Will the space overdetermine the function – reduce it to sameness? Or will a genuine revolutionary model of subaltern agency emerge from the very terms of the problematic?

The danger of overdetermining the 'solution' in the very terms of posing a problem is one to which we must remain alert. A liberal framework that proceeds from absolute moral values and irreducible moral positions (law, democracy, human rights) can impatiently foreclose upon a solution in its own terms, both reducing the complexities of the problem and refusing a consideration of it in its specific context. But while one can and must therefore defer the construction of a solution, one cannot, finally, evade it. The production of solutions is not merely an obligation the critic must recognize, but also a political opportunity, as Bruce Robbins puts it, to undertake 'myth-making' and to explore 'the possibility and imperative to fashion alternative narratives [and an] alternative rhetoric that will work in the circumstances where we find ourselves'.[22]

In many instances, it will be observed, I locate such 'resistances' within the scene of cultural production itself. Resistance is not always a positivity; it may be no more than a negative agency, an absence of acquiescence in one's oppression. The act of reading it as resistance can be an important political recognition especially in a context, as in sati, where it is the widow's acquiescence in her death that traditionally constitutes her (exalted) subjectivity. Nevertheless I am aware that the positing of resistances, as in this book, *without* a specific endorsement of 'agency' in the traditional sense – with its attributes of both action as well as intention – is a somewhat problematic claim. But not only have I wished to avoid the romantic fiction of 'resistance' – however politically well-intentioned such a fiction may be; I have also sought to redefine individual resistance itself in terms of its social function rather than its performative intentionality. As historical method too, such a construction has the advantage of making resistance more easily ascertainable as 'evidence'.[23]

Further, my assignation of what might seem a minimal or merely reactive agency to the female subject – in the 'Subject of Sati', for example, I suggest that the subject's experience of pain is itself a sufficient condition for the move towards 'no pain', and that such a reactivity must be read as a form of resistance to death by burning – would be politically trivial if it were not for the *abjectness* of the subject-status of the female victim, of widowhood, rape, or wife-murder, in popular as well as, even, sometimes in feminine perception. It is in the light of this victim-status, a condition which not only gives the female subjects of oppression no role except that of passive suffering, but also renders acutely problematic the role of those feminists who speak 'for' them, that my tentative constructions of resistant subjectivities must find their defence.

NOTES

1 Susie Tharu and K. Lalitha, eds, *Women Writing in India*, vol. I, Delhi, Oxford University Press, 1991.

2 Rajeswari Sunder Rajan, review of *Women Writing in India*, *Book Review* XVI, 3 May – June 1992, pp. 16 and 17. I have referred in this quotation to the following: Sandra Gilbert and Susan Gubar, *Madwoman in the Attic: The Woman Writer and the Nineteenth Century Literary Imagination*, New Haven and London, Yale University Press, 1979; Benita Parry, 'Problems in Current Theories of Colonial Discourse', *Oxford Literary Review* 9, 1–2, 1987, pp. 27–58; Rosalind O'Hanlon, 'Issues of Widowhood: Gender and Resistance in Colonial Western India', in Douglas Haynes and Gyan Prakash, eds, *Contesting Power: Resistance and Everyday Social Relations in South Asia*, Delhi, Oxford University Press, 1992, pp. 62–108; and Susie Tharu, 'Women Writing in India', *Journal of Arts and Ideas* 20–1, March 1991, pp. 49–65, esp. pp. 50 and 52.

3 The Indian feminist journal *Manushi* has taken a sustained position against state intervention. See, for instance, the statement of its editor, Madhu Kishwar, in 'Why I am not a Feminist', on her opposition to the anti-pornography law:

> My reservations were not related to a lack of commitment to women's equality but to my mistrust of the state machinery and of attempts to arm the state with even more repressive powers than it already has in the name of curbing pornography.

Similarly, she has opposed the death penalty for wife-murderers because of her objection to 'legitimising killing by the state machinery, even when the pretext may be protection of women'. See *Manushi* 61, November–December 1990, pp. 2–8, esp. pp. 7–8.

4 These formulations appear in the 'theme note' for a forthcoming volume tentatively entitled *Postcoloniality and the Construction of Feminist Politics*, eds U. Kalpagam, Rajni Palriwala, and Vibhuti Patel.

5 Edward Said, 'Intellectuals in the Post-Colonial World', *Salmagundi* 70–1, Spring – Summer 1986, pp. 44–64, esp. p. 45.

6 Kumkum Sangari, 'Introduction: Representations in History', *Journal of Arts and Ideas* 17–18, June 1989, pp. 3–7, esp. pp. 3–4.

7 Arjuna Parakrama, *Language and Rebellion*, London, Katha, 1990, p. 13.

8 Such an earlier 'reading' may, of course, well actually be, as Sangari has argued, the product of colonial discourse.

9 Parakrama, *Language and Rebellion*, p. 13.

10 Sarah Joseph, 'Indigenous Social Science Project: Some Political Implications', *Economic and Political Weekly*, 13 April 1991, pp. 959–63, esp. p. 960.

11 By way of contrast, one of Gayatri Chakravorty Spivak's purposes in examining 'a woman's text from the third world' ('Stanadayini') is to 'wrench it out of its proper context and put it within alien arguments', and thereby 'show us some of ... [the] limits and limitations' of western feminist theories. See 'A Literary Representation of the Subaltern: A Woman's Text from the Third World', in *In Other Worlds: Essays in Cultural Politics*, New York and London, Methuen, 1987, p. 241.

12 Elaine Scarry, *The Body in Pain*, New York and Oxford, Oxford University Press, 1985.
13 James Clifford and Vivek Dhareshwar, volume eds, *Traveling Theories: Traveling Theorists, Inscriptions* 5, 1989, Special Issue.
14 See Edward Said, 'Secular Criticism', in *The World, the Text and the Critic*, London, Faber & Faber, 1983, pp. 1–30, esp. pp. 5–8, for a discussion of the virtues of 'exile' as critical location.
15 For a discussion of marginality and postcoloniality see Gayatri Chakravorty Spivak, 'Poststucturalism, Marginality, Postcoloniality and Value', in Peter Collier and Helga Geyer-Ryan, eds, *Literary Theory Today*, Cambridge, Polity Press, 1990.
16 In this connection see Rashmi Bhatnagar, Lola Chatterjee and Rajeswari Sunder Rajan, Interview with Gayatri Spivak in *Book Review* XI, 3, May – June 1987, pp. 16–22. Our question to Spivak raised the distinction between the 'native' and the 'diasporic' intellectual – a distinction which she resisted – in the following terms: 'What we write and teach has political and other consquences for us that are in a sense different from the consequences, or lack of consequences, for you' (p. 16). This interview ('The Post-Colonial Critic') has been reprinted in Gayatri C. Spivak, *The Post-Colonial Critic: Interviews, Strategies, Dialogues*, ed. Sarah Harasym, New York and London, Routledge, 1990, p. 68.
17 See especially Edward Said ('Intellectuals in the Post-Colonial World', p. 63), Lata Mani ('Multiple Mediations', *Inscriptions* 5, 1989, pp. 1–23, esp. pp. 13–14), and Susie Tharu ('Thinking the Nation Out: Some Reflections on Nationalism and Theory', *Journal of Arts and Ideas* 17–18, June 1989, pp. 81–9, esp. p. 85).
18 Bruce Robbins, 'The Politics of Theory', *Social Text* 18, Winter 1987/8, pp. 3–18, esp. p. 15.
19 Jacqueline Rose, 'The State of the Subject (II): The Institution of Feminism', *Critical Quarterly* 29, 4, Winter 1987, pp. 9–15, esp. p. 12.
20 Judith Butler and Joan W. Scott, eds, *Feminists Theorize the Political*, London and New York, Routledge, 1992, pp. xiv–xvii.
21 Butler, 'Contingent Foundations: Feminism and the Question of "Postmodernism"', in Butler and Scott, p. 8.
22 Robbins, 'The Politics of Theory', p. 15.
23 An earlier essay, 'Shahbano', exemplifies this reading more fully. See Zakia Pathak and Rajeswari Sunder Rajan, 'Shahbano', *Signs: Journal of Women in Culture and Society* 14, 3, Spring 1989, pp. 558–82, esp. p. 571. See also Parakrama for the argument that 'radically other paradigms ... sensitive to subaltern agency' must be formulated which will question 'traditional criteria of narrow intentionality and hierarchical organization' (p. 4).

1

THE SUBJECT OF SATI

Pain and death in the contemporary discourse on sati

I

A woman burns to death in a village in the state of Rajasthan in India. The news makes it to the front page of the *New York Times* – as had some years earlier the news that a woman had been stoned to death for adultery in a Middle East country.[1] The 'monolithic "Third World Woman"'[2] as subject instantaneously becomes an overdetermined symbol, victim not only of universal patriarchy but also of specific third world religious fundamentalism.

The stereotypical and merely sensational aspects of these 'events', isolated from their context, have tended to overwhelm not only the much greater complexity of the issues actually involved, but the equally significant protest mounted by local women's groups and other sections of the population; the continuing and persistent role of the 'west' in post-colonial gender issues; and the theoretical considerations that are of relevance to the issue of female subjectivity in general. It is some sense of these other aspects of sati in contemporary India that I attempt to communicate in the first section of this chapter. The next section explores, tentatively, how a western meditation on the subject of the body in pain may be appropriated for and contested by a specific historical and feminist project in the interests of the female subject as agent.[3] A survey of the representations of sati created upon various discursive sites – the formulations of the anti-sati legislation of 1987, the journalistic media, visual (iconic and photographic) productions, documentary films, cinema and fiction – which follows in the last section, reveals how the politics of representation crucially intersects with the procedures of subjectification of the sati in India today.

If my reading of the 'social text' of sati highlights its discursive dimension, it is because this dimension has been so crucially interwoven with the material reality of the phenomenon. (I bear in mind here the caution issued by Benita Parry: 'discourses of representation should not be confused with material realities.')[4] One index of the widespread recognition of its importance is that the new anti-sati legislation extends its scope to prohibit not only the 'commission' but also the 'glorification' of sati, a glorification achieved primarily through representations of women who commit sati. The opposition between the discursive and the 'real' has admittedly been a contentious one in feminist issues, corresponding as it does to the opposition between academic/theoretical projects on the one hand and activist interventions 'in the field' on the other; but it is not an opposition that has developed into an absolute one in the aftermath of the recent sati. A notable feature, therefore, of the recent debate on sati, a debate I recapitulate in the opening section, has been its public dimension. The fact that religious scholars, philosophers, jurists and writers have expounded their views at public meetings and conferences and interviews in the mass media and that academic historians, sociologists, psychologists and political scientists have published widely in newspapers and mass-circulation journals is indicative of the breakdown of the isolation of these spheres. In this discourse on sati one also notices the quick appropriation of academic research for interventionary purposes, and the corresponding theorizing that takes place from experiences 'in the field'.

In the analysis that follows I attempt to promote such dialectical infusion methodologically by making Elaine Scarry's subtle academic dissertation on 'the body in pain', along with popular art forms and a variety of other representations of the burning woman, converge upon the subject of sati.

II

On 4 September 1987, 18-year-old Roop Kanwar, married only seven months, died on her husband's funeral pyre in Deorala village, about two hours from Jaipur, the capital of Rajasthan. The event was reportedly witnessed by hundreds of people. The state government did not react to the news although sati is an illegal practice. The massive media interest and the concerted action of women's groups eventually led to the issue of an ordinance banning not only the commission but the glorification of sati. Nevertheless, over 300,000 people attended the *chunari mahotsav*, the function marking the thirteenth day after the sati. Huge pro-sati rallies in Jaipur protested the government's interference in the Rajputs' practice of their religious rites. The village of Deorala has now developed into a prosperous pilgrim centre. Several of those arrested after the sati have been released under political pressure, and no one has yet been convicted. In January 1988 new legislation was enacted in Parliament (The Commission of Sati (Prevention) Act, 1987) replicating the chief features of the Rajasthan State ordinance.

It was not for the first time that the government at the centre found itself under pressure both from fundamentalist forces, this time those of a large Hindu community (constituting a sizeable vote bank), and from the liberal press, women's rights groups, civil rights organizations, left political parties and world opinion to prevent the erosion of women's rights.[5] The state's commitment to secularism, interpreted as the protection of the freedom of religious practice,

16

conflicts with another constitutional guarantee, that of the right of life (in addition to all other equal rights) to women. Compromising between its legal and liberal commitment on the one hand and political expediency on the other, it therefore in this instance passed the required legislation without actively attempting to enforce it.

Sati was prohibited by law in Bengal in 1829 by a British governor, William Bentinck. It is assumed to have declined in frequency thereafter. In post-Independence India, stray cases of sati have been reported, about forty in all, chiefly in some northern states. In the past decade, the phenomenon has seen a significant increase; a number of sati attempts have been prevented by police intervention, but four or five have been successfully carried out.

But what worries women's groups is not an epidemic of sati — sati defenders mock the triviality of the issue in terms of its numbers — but the disturbing implications of the recent phenomenon of the glorification of sati through temples and annual fairs. Rich businessmen, for the most part belonging to the Marwari community, have deified centuries-old satis by building temples to them all over Rajasthan and nearby Delhi; these centres attract thousands of devotees and rake in huge donations. Annual fairs bring prosperity to villages that have been sites of past and recent sati. As is clear, religious sanction, political complicity and economic benefits have combined to encourage a cult of sati in a climate of overall oppression of women.

The issue of sati in India today is not a simple one, but in essence it has resolved itself into a series of binary oppositions subsumed into the larger categories, 'tradition' and 'modernity'.[6] Defenders of or sympathizers with sati are purportedly on the side of 'tradition': for them sati is a venerated ritual which gains its sanction from the Vedic scriptures;[7] it is also a practice written into the history of the Rajputs and hence serves as an index of a glorious martial civilization. Belief in sati is in this view expressive of the simple and idealistic faith of India's rural masses[8] — so that the ban on sati and its celebration pits the state against the community, the colonial or westernized rulers and elites against the 'native' Indian subject.[9] The negative identity of 'modernity' — as an elite, high bourgeois and alienated 'westernization' — can be and is, by the same token, thrust upon those who take the stand of opposing sati.[10] To repudiate ancient scripture as a basis for modern practice is to invite the charge of alienation; to designate sati as crime rather than ritual, and by such designation seek to intervene through legislative prohibition, is to merely replicate the move of the colonial ruler;[11] to highlight the plight of the woman is not only to be insensitive to the identity of the Rajput community (which is defined by her act),[12] but also to be selective and hypocritical in the women's issues that one champions — and have one's bona fides questioned.[13] It is within the problematic of 'tradition' versus 'modernity' that the opponents of sati have had to negotiate their position even as they seek to call the very terms into question. By historicizing the practice of sati, and by plotting the social, economic and political configurations of the scenario of its contemporary version, the notion of a timeless and virtually platonic sati is combated.[14] Historians conclude on the basis of regional variations in the number of satis in Bengal in the nineteenth century that the practice of sati was legitimized by local custom rather than by authoritative and invariable religious prescription.[15] The vocal and organized proponents of sati today, other investigations reveal, are not the simple rural masses, but the landed gentry and the urban business classes; the 'State' is not a nameless adversary but is made up of politicians, policemen and other functionaries deeply entrenched in regional politics; the glorification of sati through temples and fairs is a commercial reality and an entirely 'modern' phenomenon; the enactment of modern sati derives its features from popular cinema and political meetings rather than hallowed ritual.[16] When they choose to, supporters of sati may themselves claim that the issue is not the opposition between tradition and modernity, but rather 'the ironing out of the contradictions between the two'[17] – such as is displayed in the case of Roop Kanwar, a 'modern' girl in many respects, 'choosing' to commit sati in spite of her affluent background, her school education, etc. Thus the categories 'tradition' and 'modernity' are invoked and contested in a significant way in the struggle for self- and other definition between the two sides.

Nevertheless, the problematic remains insidiously coercive in framing the issue of female subjectivity. In the representations of sati in contemporary India that I shall be discussing shortly the subjectivity of the woman who commits sati remains a crucial issue; female subjectivity has in its turn hinged on the questions: Was the sati voluntary? Or was the woman forced upon the pyre? These stark alternatives were posed as an aspect of British intervention in the issue in the late eighteenth and early nineteenth centuries[18] and still retain their force when played into the series of oppositions that categorize the problematic of tradition versus modernity. For defenders of sati today all satis are voluntary, and for its opponents all of them are coerced. But when the individual woman's subjectivity is read in terms of intention, intentionality can only be a matter of conjecture and, finally, ideological conviction.

It is revealing, nevertheless, to see how transparent such intention can appear to be when read back from the initial premise that sati is suicide. In the first place there is the assertion that 'sati was never a system, it is not one now, it will not be one in the future. It is a case of an *individual decision*' (emphasis added).[19] The establishment of sati as individual decision permits the investment of the woman with the fullest integrity of free will: the analogies to the event are drawn with male heroic suicides, the religious martyr, the soldier, the ascetic monk, and the recent political activist, Gandhi or Vinobha Bhave. These equations then mark the woman as exceptional and singular.[20] Finally, a triumphantly circular argument can claim that evidence of coercion establishes only that certain satis are 'inauthentic'. The pamphlet issued by the Sati Dharam Raksha Samiti (the Committee for the Protection of the Sati Faith) in Jaipur on 15 October 1987 claimed that satis in Rajasthan have always been voluntary, unlike satis in nineteenth-century Bengal.[21] By these successive procedures of subjectification – the establishment of sati as 'individual decision', the comparison of sati-as-suicide with other socially valorized male acts of self-annihilation, the arguments that sati is the exceptional rather than the routine option exercised by the Hindu widow and that voluntarism alone bestows authenticity upon the sati – the woman who commits sati reaches the transcendent subjective state, deification.

The most thorough demystification of these procedures undertaken by anti-sati crusaders consists of the exposure of sati as murder. Their assertions that satis are coerced are not to be understood as conceding by implication that voluntary satis are therefore permissible. Coercion has been established by such evidence as the 'haste [with which sati is performed], family pressure, opiates, photographs of women imprisoned by wood and coconuts in a neck-high pyre'.[22] But even where they allow that the widow may have complied with the decision, her 'suicide' is regarded not as true 'choice' but merely as an option that is preferred to life as an ill-treated widow, or one which results from 'false consciousness' and ideological indoctrination. In any case, they have refused to grant that wanting to die is a sufficient reason to die. However, if one subscribes to a liberal ideology of the freedom of choice one must sometimes grant sati the dubious status of existential suicide. To refuse to do so is to find oneself, as feminists have done, in another bind, that of viewing the sati as inexorably a victim and thereby emptying her subjectivity of any function or agency.

The choice for the concerned feminist analyst in this predicament, if formulated as Gayatri Spivak does, as one between subject-constitution (i.e. 'she wanted to die') and object-formation (i.e. 'she must be saved from dying'), is a paralysing one.[23] Roop Kanwar is one in a succession of individual women who have emerged into the public limelight in India in the past decade, around whom issues out of all proportion to their individual stature have gathered.[24] For feminists these women cannot be regarded as mere counters in the larger play of power struggles, or as cautionary examples, as indeed they have been treated; but neither can they be aggrandized into individualistic figures of heroism or tragedy. It is in the context of this methodological crisis that the issue of conceptualizing female subjectivity as agency gains its political imperative.

Hence the necessity, as I see it, for a reconsideration of subject-status itself and of its constituents – for effecting that shift from 'concerns about the subject and consciousness to concerns about embodied subjects and personification' which Mark Seltzer has identified as a significant aspect of the contemporary discourse of 'a logistics of realism'.[25] In the case of sati, this involves shifting the emphasis from sati-as-death (murder or suicide, authentic or inauthentic) to sati-as-burning, and investigating both the subjective pain and the objective spectacle that this shift reveals.

III

Though positioned within a historical and cultural materialism, Elaine Scarry's phenomenology of pain is nevertheless being invoked here to counter the transcendence of pain that is claimed as a reality in the contemporary arguments in defence of sati. By insisting upon the existential, the brute reality of pain, the sheer aversiveness of it, its gratuitousness, and its investment in the isolated individual body, Scarry creates out of pain the very condition of the human subject. It is this insistence that is of relevance and value for my purpose. The 'radical subjectivity' of pain, as Scarry calls it, referring to its essential privacy and incommunicability,[26] can also serve as the basis of subjectivity in the sense in which I invoke it here, that of the constitution of the identity of the self/subject. I claim, in other words, that the condition of pain can serve adequately to define the human subject in certain contexts.

Scarry's notion of the radical subjectivity of pain, however, creates an absolute 'other' of the subject in pain; for her the operation of sympathy is found only in certain heroic and exceptional areas of human endeavour, whereby pain is brought into the area of a shared public discourse. But the procedures by which the knowledge of pain is produced, which make possible the deliberate infliction of pain by one set of human beings upon another (in torture, war and violence of all kinds), are equally based upon the universal experience of pain. It is the shared knowledge/experience of pain that unites sufferer, torturer and helper.

Outside this circuit of sympathy are ranged those who regard others' pain as ontologically different from their own, and act accordingly. It is among these that the defenders of sati must be placed. In the contemporary debate over sati the subject of pain figures only in the language of the defenders of sati, who speak with authority about the absence of pain felt by the sati (thus they are humane), or the transcendence of pain achieved by her spirit (thus they are reverent). The common reassurances run as follows: the sati does not feel pain as you and I do – what is fire to us is water to her; she smiles as she sits within the fire; she counts the duration of pain as a mere few minutes, against an eternity of bliss; she feel her pain as pleasure; the *sat* (truth) has entered her, making her immune to pain. Ritual pain is regarded as a discipline, a yogic submission, both abject and heroic.[27]

Such attribution of separateness is facilitated also by the absolute otherness of woman as subject-of-pain through the mystique built around sexual difference. The labour of childbirth, for instance, is frequently treated as both natural for women and selflessly, even heroically, submitted to; since men can have no experience of it they are willing either to valorize women's experience through mystification or naturalize it through acceptance of anatomical difference. 'They are not like us' is an explanation for the forms of oppression practised by those not naturally sadistic.

It is important to recognize that the coercion of a woman towards the act of sati cannot be simply regarded as an infliction of pain. Though the phenomenon

20

of sati as a spectacle is an important consideration — as I shall be claiming later — its affect is not to be equated with that of blood sports. That is why supporters of sati cannot be located within Scarry's scenario. It is also why the most frequent explanation offered by feminist analysts, that the prevalence of sati is an index of the 'devaluation' of women, like bride-burning and female infanticide, is also off the mark. In the glorification of sati the facts of pain and death have to be granted, since it is their transcendence, or at the very least endurance, by the woman that becomes the signifier of value. An initial dichotomy of body and spirit is the basis for postulating the superiority of spirit over flesh, as in all forms of asceticism, heroism and martyrdom. The subjectification of the sati demands, not a devalued 'body for burning', but a body invested with exceptional physical properties.

In the discourse of the anti-sati position, however, while pain is undeniably everywhere present, it is nowhere re-presented. Certain empirical 'facts' about a sati — such as the woman's drugged condition or her screaming and jumping off the pyre — which can be deployed equally in arguments about her 'will' or about her pain, are invoked invariably on behalf of the former.[28] Since the reasons for the reluctance to construct the gendered subject as embodied pain in this instance are formidable ones, I wish to explore them in some detail before risking the dangers of such a project myself.

There is, in the first instance, Scarry's basic premise, that of pain's resistance to language. While I am unwilling to concede this as an essential attribute of pain, it is true that there are fairly widespread cultural inhibitions about representing pain. A certain fastidiousness of response is a natural reaction to the obscenity of pain. The very materiality of pain — it is so incontestably and self-evidently *there* — obviates the need to represent it. There is a major problem in countering pain discursively except by denouncing it. The sentimental and moral force of any recognition of pain, within discourse, seems to direct it towards the language of polemic, rather than towards an analytic or theoretical articulation. The first major difficulty in developing a politics and ethics of pain is the absence of such articulation.

In the second place, the body/mind dichotomy is so firmly in place in theoretical discourse, religious as well as philosophical, that any invocation of the body as *ground* for human subjectivity inevitably appears reductive. The dangers of grounding gendered subjectivity thus are doubly present since the female subject has been so facilely created already through the hierarchically inferior attributes of binary oppositions such as mind/body, reason/sentience, culture/nature. Moreover, recent appropriations of the body in western theory — for inscribing technologies of power and resisting pleasures in Foucault, for liberating female sexuality in radical feminism — have been carried out in the service of anti-humanist projects.

Scarry's own book, in spite of its unique preoccupation with the phenomenology of pain, and its invaluable moral and sentimental force, exemplifies certain other theoretical and political problems. To see pain in such consistent opposition to language, the world and 'making' as she does only results in its fixation, a reified condition that, paradoxically, virtually makes it ontologically autonomous, independent of the suffering human subject. There is also a certain fatalistic totalization in conceptualizing pain as essentially unrepresentable, ontologically anti-discourse, definitionally that which is not language, which concedes the battle not only to chaos ('unmaking'), but to those who have a well-developed language for the trivialization of pain. To attribute pain's resistance-to-representation to the essential nature of pain itself is to ignore the cultural, historical, gender-specific and generic variations in the representation of pain. Mark Seltzer has noted another consequence of Scarry's methodological binarism: 'the tendency to oppose stories of Third World torture and pain to lyrical accounts of the domestic intimacies of the "civilized" world'.[29] For the third world writer to endorse Scarry's discourse on pain totally would be to embrace this well-established alterity.

As Scarry also makes clear, the interventionary force of a contemporary politics of pain has also been provided largely by the western institutions of medicine, law and human rights.[30] It is not surprising that contemporary anti-sati arguments have failed to respond to the discourse of no-pain, given the linguistic, theoretical, strategic and political difficulties of the phenomenology of pain in this context.

The language of pain that does exist theoretically, and existing representations of pain, are not invariably a suitable paradigm for the subject in anti-sati discourse. Representation of pain in western art and literature have by and large served as objects of contemplation. Sensitivity to others' pain – 'sympathy' – has also served as an index of cultural, even racial, superiority and as an absolute signifier of 'difference'. It is this that made possible the propagandistic use of the pain of satis in missionary discourse in nineteenth-century Bengal. As Lata Mani has argued, the work of proselytism, and indirectly of colonial intervention, was facilitated when missionaries in their public addresses, by widely evoking the screams of the burning sati, berated Indian villagers for their barbarity and displayed their own contrasting religious pity.[31] In the USA today, pro-life campaigns of the right have developed an elaborate rhetoric of pain on behalf of the foetus ('the silent scream') that is displayed in anti-feminist campaigns.[32]

To invoke the subject in/of pain on behalf of a feminist theory and politics requires great caution (as what contemporary feminist project does not?). The subjectivity of pain, it is important to stress, needs to be conceptualized as a dynamic rather than passive condition, on the premise that the subject in pain will be definitionally in transit towards a state of no-pain (even if this state is no more than a reflexivity). While the affect produced by a body in pain – pity, anger, sympathy, identification – is an important consideration in formulating a politics of intervention, it is important also to recognize that an inherent resistance to pain is what impels the individual or collective suffering subject towards freedom. It is therefore as one who acts/reacts, rather than as one who invites assistance, that one must regard the subject in pain. Nor do I mean to suggest that pain is a perennial or definitional attribute of the subject; the sati is understood not psychologically, in terms of a predisposition to or a disregard of pain, but as a contingent self.

In an important observation Scarry discovers that 'physical pain is exceptional in the whole fabric of psychic, somatic and perceptual states for being the only one that has no object ... in the external world; ... pain is not "of" or "for" anything – it is itself alone'.[33] This observation is of relevance in a project of subject-constitution since it draws our attention to the fact that the subject in western philosophy has traditionally been recognized through projections or extensions of the self: through voice, i.e. language, consciousness, reason (Descartes), desire (Freud), or possessions (materialism). The immanence of pain, on the other hand, seems to circumscribe the self rather than to extend it. As I have pointed out earlier, even in much post-humanist theory, as well as, paradoxically, in Scarry's, the body becomes what one *has*, rather than what one *is*. An analysis by Teresa de Lauretis of the 'rhetoric of violence' reveals the implications of the alienation of the body for the female subject in pain. She contests Lévi-Strauss's reading of a Cuna incantation performed by a shaman to facilitate difficult childbirth: 'the incantation aims at detaching the woman's identification or perception of self from her own body. It seeks to sever her identification with a body which she must come to perceive precisely as a space, the territory in which the battle is waged. ... The effectiveness of symbols ... would thus effect a splitting of the female subject's identification'.[34]

It seems necessary, in other words, to prevent this conceptual split between body and consciousness in arguing that pain constitutes subjectivity, as well as to reiterate that the necessary consequences of such holism are to see pain as a stage rather than a state and to regard the subject in pain as a dynamic being rather than a passive 'space'.

By abandoning the commitment to construct the subjectivity of the woman who performs sati in terms of her motivation we may be enabled to break out of a methodological impasse. Since those who claim that the sati embraces death do not also claim that she embraces pain, but instead argue that she knows no pain, it is necessary and possible to contest the latter argument. We need, however, to develop both a phenomenology of pain and a politics that recognizes pain as constitutive of the subject. In my next section I survey a few of the significant sites of the recent discourse of sati in India to mark how the subjectification of the sati occurs in terms of her consciousness and/or her pain.

IV

The subjectivity of the woman who commits sati is a major preoccupation in the contemporary discourse on the phenomenon that I survey below. It will shortly become apparent that it is her 'consciousness' or 'will' that continues to feature as the major component of this subjectification. My attempt to identify the place of pain in such representations and to locate it within the ambit of the discursive structure of sati, might seem both to be redundant and to carry relatively little political charge when the pain of burning is so incontestably there as a fact of the 'real' event. But feminist theorists have persistently argued the importance of acquiring a 'language', an 'enunciative position' and 'power apparati' to speak of women's experience.[35] As Teresa de Lauretis goes on to point out, the 'social' has a 'semiotic, discursive dimension', so that it was, for instance, the expression 'family violence', invoked by feminist sociologists, that crystallized the concept of family violence so keenly experienced by women.[36] By a similar paradoxical inversion it may be that the discursive recognition of pain in subject-constitution will propel it into 'reality'.

The discursive situation I analyse is still fluid. The law, newspapers and mass-circulation magazines, popular iconic representations and photographs, documentary films, 'art' cinema and magazine fiction form a collage of texts that are heterogeneous, multi-levelled, and ideologically uneven.[37] Nor is this an exhaustive survey. My selection is merely intended to reflect 'a section of the social text, in however haphazard a way'.[38]

The Commission of Sati (Prevention) Act has come into being, as stated earlier, to provide 'more effective measures to prevent the commission of sati and its glorification', since the provisions of the existing laws were deemed not 'deterrent enough to prevent the commission of such practice'.[39] The new act reveals its ambivalence towards determining sati as either suicide or murder and seems inclined on the whole to view it as a joint act for which the woman herself and those who 'abet' her are together responsible. Where a sati has been foiled, the woman will be tried for 'the offence of attempt to commit sati'. Here her motivation is considered ascertainable and hence assessable by the same criteria as suicides. As in suicide, the court must 'take into consideration the circumstances leading to the commission of the offence, the act committed, the state of mind of the person charged of the offence at the time of commission of the act, and all other relevant factors' before conviction. Though the language of the act would appear sceptical of any deliberate willingness on the part of the woman, since 'in most cases the widow or the woman is compelled to commit sati and invariably she will not be in a fit state of mind or will be labouring under a state of intoxication or stupefaction or other cause impeding the exercise of her free will', one might argue, as does Vasudha Dhagamwar, a feminist legal expert, that 'in effect they [Sections 3 and 4] treat all sati as voluntary. That is why the woman [who attempts sati] is punished and that is why those who kill her are punished for abetment, and not for murder.'[40]

If sati is not-quite suicide it is also not-quite-not suicide. The possibility that the woman may have been coerced is never explicitly articulated although the punishment for abetment is identical with that for murder, namely death or imprisonment for life. 'Abetment' is defined in terms of 'inducement to a widow or woman to get her burnt or buried alive', 'making a widow or woman believe that the commission of sati would result in some spiritual benefit', 'encouraging a widow or woman to remain fixed in her resolve to commit sati and thus

24

instigating her to commit sati', 'aiding the widow or woman in her decision to commit sati by taking her along with the body of her husband or relative to the cremation or burial ground', etc. All of these terms suggest the secondary or supplementary role of others while at the same time characterizing the woman herself as naive, superstitious and susceptible. The real force of the ambivalence about the role of the woman is seen in Section 4(2)(c) of the Act: 'encouraging a widow or woman to remain fixed in her resolve to commit sati and thus instigating her to commit sati'. The 'resolve' of the one party and the 'instigation' of the other do not have opposed purposes, but are both directed towards the same end! The initiative of a woman in resisting sati (or her response to the pain of burning), as well as the possibility of coercion, is recognized in only one instance, Section 4(2)(f), where abetment is defined also as 'preventing or obstructing the widow or woman from saving herself from being burnt or buried alive.'

Since the transactions between the woman who commits, or attempts to commit, sati and those who 'abet' her are treated as crucial in determining the seriousness of the crime, and since these transactions are treated primarily as contests or collaborations of will rather than as struggles between weakness and force, the consciousness of the woman, whether derived from her own testimony or from those of witnesses, remains a crucial area in the legal discourse. The ambivalence, if not outright contradictions, that characterize the representation of this consciousness in the formulations of the new act only reflect, as we may expect, the pull of the tradition-versus-modernity (ritual-versus-crime) dichotomy in characterizing sati that has resulted from colonial formulation of the law.[41]

The procedures and protocols that operate in the legal, as also in the journalistic, production of 'knowledge' confront inherent difficulties while negotiating the sati event. In confronting any event both are motivated by the need to know 'what really happened' and are consequently frustrated by the impossibility of knowing. Such knowing depends centrally on seeing. The act empowers officials both to prevent sati and to investigate cases of sati, i.e. to exercise control over pre- and post-sati events; but the sati itself is only the negative space of what 'never-will-happen' or 'has-already-happened'. The relations of power inscribed in seeing, when the 'natural machinery of bodies'[42] is deployed as spectacle, are a very real aspect of the dynamics of sati: a sati, by virtue of being a publicly witnessed event, is at once a 'production', here the staging of a 'miracle', a show of strength by believers, and a defiance of the state as repressive 'other'. Therefore, the recent law against sati had in one sense no option but to outlaw the spectacle; but it has thereby deprived itself too of the powers of surveillance. The special provisions of this act place the burden of proof upon the accused; so elaborate alibis have to be produced by them to establish absence at the site of sati and presence elsewhere.[43] No one can report a sati participant without logically having to submit himself to examination as well. Modern sati has rendered itself at once spectacular and secret.

25

The absence of reliable and authoritative eyewitnesses to Roop Kanwar's and other recent satis is in contrast to the elaborate official surveillance of satis in Bengal prior to the passing of the abolition act in order to ensure their legitimacy.[44] To define the woman's subjectivity as her willingness or reluctance to commit sati, to interpret that 'decision' from her behaviour and speech at the sati site, to base that interpretation upon objective 'seeing' was, logically, to demand surveillance in order to sanction suicide or punish crime. Now when a woman dies, by a 'collective amnesia'[45] her death never occurred.

Newspapers, which also rely centrally upon eyewitness reporting, have instead been able only to quote unidentified and therefore unreliable sources while reconstructing accounts of the sati event. Most accounts of Roop Kanwar's sati are based on rumour, which surfaces after passing through a chain of communications with no verifiable source.[46] Though the sensational press on this basis has not hesitated freely to dramatize the sati as murder or miracle, mainstream press reports have had to be more constrained. The media has been hamstrung by official censorship as well. Police harassment of journalists, the ban on photography and tape recording, and the hostility of villagers towards reporters continue in Deorala.

But the interest in 'knowing' Roop Kanwar has been a persistent one in the journalistic media. Her life and beliefs have been investigated as having explanatory potential for the act of sati. Newspaper reports, like the official police investigations, have also been delving into the nature and circumstances of her husband's illness and death, the role of the doctor who treated him, the responses of the natal family, and a host of other related 'mysteries'. As in much traditional realist fiction, a minute and extensive accumulation of details about family and environment gives substance to the individual 'self'. In many cases, however, the contradictions between the 'self' and her death have caused puzzlement: how could a favoured younger daughter from a well-to-do family, with ten years of schooling, brought up in an urban milieu, married into a 'good' family where the father-in-law was headmaster of a school, the husband a college student, in a prosperous village with several schools, television, a regular bus service, a medical dispensary, having lived with her husband a bare few weeks in seven months of marriage, have 'chosen' to commit sati – or have been forced to? The evidence of her devoutness to the Rani Sati deity at the temple in the lane in which she lived, and the significance of Deorala as the site of three previous satis are other facts which seem to throw some light on her 'predisposition' to commit sati.

The complex construction of Roop Kanwar's subjectivity through such extensive procedures of research and analysis has served an important purpose, that of questioning the standard explanation that sati is a belief and practice characteristic of 'superstitious' individuals in 'backward' villages. Nevertheless the assumption underlying the project, that the 'answer' to such a complex mystery is to be sought in knowing the sati herself, leads all too often to a closure of analysis, her death creating a condition of definitional unknowability.[47]

The visual representations of sati are numerous and varied, and I examine only a few of them below.[48] One of the most commercially successful products of Roop Kanwar's sati was a photograph of her seemingly actually immolating herself, a clever photomontage made up with pictures of the bridal couple at their wedding cut and pasted to show the bride in all her finery, smiling straight into the camera, with her husband's body laid in her lap; her red veil as backdrop simulates flames (fig. 1). In another, more dramatic composition, she holds him up amidst the flames in a stark naturalistic landscape of bare trees and hills with a temple behind her, while a small figure of a goddess hovering in the heavens sends down the magic ray that lights the fire (fig. 2). This iconography is a composite of several art forms: the generic sati 'deity picture', the studio photo, calendar art kitsch, cinema posters and a kind of comic strip popular art. Not only are these easily consumable and ideologically powerful images; they also fulfil a narrative purpose for a largely illiterate populace.

Along with the innumerable photographs of the actual Roop Kanwar that flood the market and dominate the media, various traditional symbols are deployed as iconography. There is an ensemble created at the *chunari mahotsav* which stands upon a platform erected at the sati spot: a red and gold veil draped over the three-pronged spear or *trishul*, symbol of Siva. In appearance this structure resembles a veiled bride. Medieval satis have left imprints of their hennaed palms upon the walls of countless palaces in Rajasthan, icons which are preserved, embellished and venerated (fig. 3). In the new sati temples the sati goddess is generally represented by a fierce face, or by the trishul, both iconographically derived from Durga or 'Shakti'. Symbols are both synecdochic and significant, at once reductive and excessive. The body in pain is dissolved to give place to representations of its parts, invested with transcendent value.

Newspaper photographs would be expected, on the other hand, to provide the most 'authentic' expressions of bodily mutilation. But in the absence of eyewitnesses to the sati event, most media pictures have only reproduced and given currency to the photomontage and the draped veil. In general, the burnt bodies of women (common enough in the news in bride-burning cases) do not make good photographic subjects; burning erases the identity of the victim and makes her remains gruesome to behold. One understands why the photographic lie is necessary to represent the burning sati. The fact of pain has no aesthetic dimension. In contrast, one of the most arresting and well-known visuals of the past year in the Indian media is a photograph of three sisters in Kanpur who hanged themselves from a ceiling fan, driven to despair over their father's having to provide dowries for all of them if they married.[49] The photograph is a poignant and powerful one and stirred strong feelings of anger and pity all over the country. But its currency has something at least to do with its aesthetic quality: the composition of the three bodies gracefully swinging outwards from a central point, one girl facing obliquely away from the camera, her beautiful face drooping like a flower broken on a stalk, the expression calm, tragic: painless (fig. 4).

Figures 1 and 2 Photomontages of Roop Kanwar's 'sati'.

Figure 3 Palm prints of queens who became satis, Bikaner Palace, Rasjasthan. From
Manushi: A Journal about Women and Society (1987) 42–3.

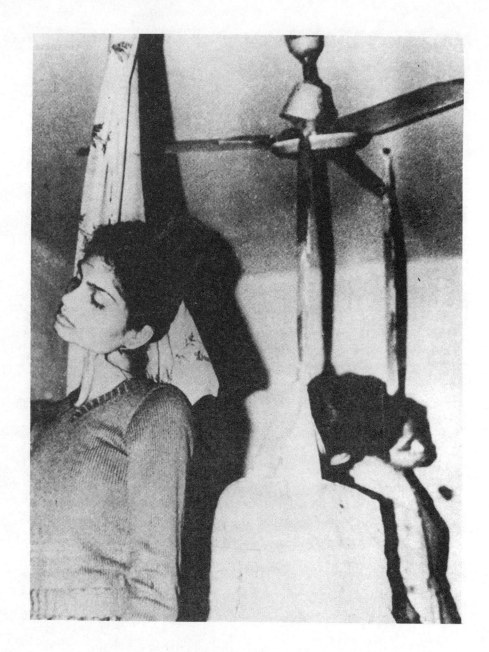

Figure 4 Suicide of three sisters, Kanpur. UNI Photo.

Finally we may look at a poster issued by an anti-sati activist group which does assert the facticity of a woman's body.[50] The graphic is a simple and powerful line drawing of a woman writhing upward from the flames (the standard figure of the recumbent male corpse is a silhouette), at once that of a being in pain and one protesting against it (fig. 5). There is no naturalistic insistence on the mutilation of burning, but the posture and expression of the figure, though stylized, capture the essence of pain. The sati is not a dead woman, but a burning woman seeking to escape, not a spectacle but the subject of action and agency.

The documentary film *Burning Embers* attempts consciousness raising in the same way. It was made by a group of women students at a film institute, operating outside the circuit of official and commercial film-making.[51] It includes a number of interviews with politicians, religious leaders and activists and has some banned footage of the *chunari mahotsav* and the Jaipur rally; but embedded within this material are clips of a street play on sati, one of a number of such plays performed extensively through the countryside. In the film the woman speaks from inside a red cocoon, representing both veil and fire, expressing her anguish and denouncing her oppressors; other women sing and dance in chorus. Individual militancy and female solidarity are offered as important correctives to the passivity and isolation that characterize typical representations of the sati.

I am therefore obliged to endorse, admittedly in a certain idealizing and prescriptive way, the forms of agitprop representations in theatre, film and posters as bringing us closer to the 'reality' of sati than does either the liberal discourse denouncing it or the popular and religious discourse glorifying it. It is not naturalistic or symbolic images, but a certain specific mode of stylization that points to the idiom for pain.

If official discourses have no idiom for pain, and if media representations are governed by censorship, decorum and the requirements of the aesthetic to avoid its representation, one might expect that the mimetic mode of realist narratives would succeed better in replicating pain. There will also be in such representations an equal pressure to establish subjectivity through exploring the consciousness of the protagonists. It is with these expectations that one turns to cinematic and literary representations of sati.

My two representative texts are not directly related to the recent Roop Kanwar sati; both were produced before her death. Nevertheless, they are recent works created in full awareness of and in response to the reality of contemporary sati. The Bengali film *Antarjali Jatra* (Death by Drowning), made by Gautam Ghosh in 1987, focuses on a young woman who is married off to a dying old man especially in order that a sati may be performed, in the years immediately following Bentinck's anti-sati legislation in Bengal.[52] The Tamil short story 'Anaippu' ('The Embrace'), by Anuradha Ramanan, first published in a weekly magazine in 1980, explores the consciousness of a modern, urban, middle-class woman so ill-treated by her husband and his family that she commits suicide by burning.[53] While it is true that nineteenth-century sati, bride-burning, and

सवाल है नारी की पहचान का
सवाल है नारी के सम्मान का

क्या नारी को
समाज का सम्मान
पाने के लिए
चिता की भस्म
बनना पड़ेगा ?

क्यों हम एक सामाजिक कुप्रथा को
महिमा मंडित करना चाहते हैं ?

धर्म व जाति के नाम पर हो रहे
अत्याचारों की हम निन्दा करते हैं।

हम हैं – नारी के जीवन और सम्मान के समर्थक
जागरूक नागरिक व महिला संगठन

राज्य इद्वारा, राजस्थान प्रौढ़ शिक्षण समिति द्वारा प्रकाशित

मुद्रक : कुमार एण्ड कं., जयपुर

Figure 5 Graphic from anti-sati poster, issued by the Rajasthan Adult Education
Committee. The poster, in part, reads: 'The question is one of women's worth. ... Why
must women burn to achieve social equality?'

modern sati cannot be simply collapsed into identity, we may usefully claim, as Spivak does, that in this narrative they are 'displacements on a chain of semiosis with the female subject as signifier'.[54]

In *Antarjali Jatra* Gautam Ghosh does not make his young heroine's subjectivity inhere wholly in her 'will', her choice to live or die, although such a choice is inevitably part of the drama. Instead, it is the female body, responding almost reflexively to pleasure and pain, that dominates the film. The obsessive male gaze directed by the husband, the lover and the film-maker himself at the female body is inevitably sexual; but it insists also upon the woman's destiny, which is to burn. The keeper of the *ghats* (the *chandal*) is given to diatribes and harangues which do not spare the susceptibilities of the woman, Yashobati, to pain and fear. In a brief but stunning moment in the film the woman imagines her sati in a waking nightmare: her hair is streaming, there are crowds at her feet, the flames leap, and she is screaming and terrified. The angle of the camera is tilted to seem as if she and the crowds are sliding on a ship's deck and are about to capsize. But both female subject and male film-maker quickly avert their gaze from this scene of terror and pain, and it may be that the limits of the visual imagination are inexorably drawn at this point. Authorial authority intervenes to spare the female subject pain in the controversial conclusion as well, in which a flood washes away the bodies of husband and wife in what seems to be an ironic fulfilment of the sati prophecy. Viewers of the film were rightly critical of the ideological ambivalence of such an ending. But what interests me is that the chosen authorial mode of death for the woman is the benignity of water and natural calamity instead of the fierceness of fire and patriarchal tyranny.[55] (The possibility of escape, although always retained in the discourse of the film, is nevertheless unsatisfactorily foreclosed by a kind of grim naturalistic fatalism.)

The ending of Anuradha Ramanan's 'The Embrace' is also fraught with questions. The burning woman launches herself upon her husband and holds him in a close embrace as they both die. Is it her impulse of love or of revenge that prompts her to embrace her husband? Is she staging a reverse sati? Or is it a sati? We do not know who dies first, and who after. The sati connotations of this common newspaper occurrence[56] are enhanced by the fact that Bhuvana is a widow who has remarried, a transgression that has led to her problems in her second marriage. Ascetic widowhood and sati are the two prescribed options for the widow in the religious texts. Bhuvana has already violated the taboo against remarriage, and she plays out the second option in an ironic fulfilment/reversal of the prescription. But at the end of a long and naturalistic account of her hardships, including intimate access to her inner states, we find complete authorial reticence about both her pain and her motivation at the moment of death.

In both film and story this flinching from the female subject in her apprehension of pain is marked. I believe that these points in the narrative signify, even when they do not represent, the crucial areas of female subjectivity.

What this quick survey leads me to conclude is that an exclusive focus on choice and motivation in constructing the subjectivity of the sati in some representations leads either to mystification or to cognitive closure. I have tried to identify the polemic and imaginative force of those representations in which, on the other hand, it is the woman's experience of pain that is apprehended as subject-constitutive. The demystification of sati would seem to require, therefore, the acknowledgement of the subject of/in pain within discourse, and thus would open the way for effective intervention.

V

The high visibility of Roop Kanwar's sati in the media and other popular forums, the improved legal status of women, and the impact of women's groups[57] are some of the factors that have centralized the issue of women's subjectivity in contemporary discourse and created a context for the exploration of female subject-constitution significantly different from that of nineteenth-century Bengal under East India Company rule.[58] So where women in the colonial discourse on sati were not 'subjects' or even 'objects', but 'rather the ground of the discourse', as Mani has argued,[59] their subjectivity has tended to be more systematically foregrounded in the contemporary discourse. Nevertheless, the debate has become mired within the enterprise of 'knowing' the subject of sati. But in view of the extensive 'knowledge' about her that contemporary reports have amassed,[60] it is not possible, either, to conclude of her as Spivak does of the Rani of Sirmur, 'there is no "real Rani" to be found'.[61]

The enterprise of reading the contemporary social text has therefore made necessary the project of radically reconstructing the subjectivity of the woman who commits sati, on the premise of the pain of the body that burns. It is of course another question whether a feminist politics can be generated from a conception of female subjectivity generalized from the inherence of pain in the female body in certain specific contexts. In view of the association of pain with suffering, oppression and physical subjugation, it would seem to propose a view of the female subject as victim, a description increasingly resisted by feminists as an aspect of the self-representation of women, especially women of the third world.

I admit the force of such resistance, especially when articulated by such feminist analysts as Chandra Mohanty and Lata Mani from their location in the western academy.[62] What Mohanty labels the 'colonialist' move in a certain 'western' feminism is the same procedure Mani identifies in historical colonialism: the identification of third world women as 'victims' of 'native' patriarchal structures as a first diagnostic, or analytic, step, followed by benevolent intervention as a second (political) move.

It is therefore necessary to repeat that 'pain' must be circumscribed in its connotations, just as 'victimhood' must be seen as a differentiated ontology. I have tried to claim pain as a specific, gendered ground for subjectivity, even as I have admitted that it is a 'universal experience': thus it identifies the subject historically (or transitionally) rather than ontologically (or psychologically). Sati, rape and genital mutilation, for instance, are forms of oppression different in kind (if not in degree) from wearing the veil or getting a divorce: questions of choice may be inserted in our understanding of the female subject and her social context in the latter instances, when to do so in the former would be regressive as feminist politics.

To conclude, while I am sympathetic to a feminist politics that seeks to resist intervention, I am also anxious, like many feminists in this part of the globe, to discover what might make intervention possible.[63] If 'victim' and 'agent' are adopted as exclusive and excluding labels for the female subject, and if, further, victimhood is equated with helplessness and agency with self-sufficiency, all feminist politics will be rendered either inauthentic or unnecessary. To view the 'victim' as subject in my argument about sati (to anchor the argument once again within its specific social and historical context) is to maintain that pain is the very condition of a move towards no-pain, without, at the same time, obviating the need for the operation of sympathy.

Ultimately the limits – and limitations – of any theoretical speculation can be tested only after it has been risked abroad. The female subject of/in pain stands now in need of such contestation.

NOTES

An earlier version of this chapter was presented at a colloquium on 'Representations of Death' sponsored by the George Seferis Chair of Modern Greek Studies at Harvard University in November 1988. I am grateful to Margaret Alexiou and Margaret Higonnet for inviting me, and to the other participants for their responses. To Kamala Visweswaran, for her extended involvement in my project at every stage, and in particular for help with key theoretical portions of this chapter, I owe a special debt. Professor Sharada Jain (Women's Studies Unit, Institute of Development Studies, Jaipur) gave generously of her time and ideas when I was revising this chapter. I am also grateful to Ruth Vanita, co-editor of *Manushi*, for providing me with material on file on sati. More special debts to several other people who generously assisted me are acknowledged in the notes.

I have used 'sati' to refer, as in Hindi (and as recognized by the Oxford English Dictionary), both to 'the Hindu widow who immolates herself on the funeral pile with her husband's body', and to 'the immolation of a Hindu widow in this way'.

1 Edward Said, *Covering Islam: How the Media and the Experts Determine How We See the Rest of the World*, New York, Pantheon, 1981.
2 The phrase is Gayatri Spivak's. See 'Can the Subaltern Speak? Speculations on Widow-Sacrifice', *Wedge*, Winter/Spring 1985, pp. 120–30, esp. p. 120.
3 Elaine Scarry, *The Body in Pain: The Making and Unmaking of the World*, New York and Oxford, Oxford University Press, 1985.
4 Benita Parry, 'Problems of Current Theories of Colonial Discourse', *Oxford Literary Review* 9, 1–2, 1987, pp. 27–58, esp. p. 35.
5 The most well-known recent controversy arose out of the victory of Shahbano, a divorced Muslim woman, in the Supreme Court of India in the issue of maintenance. Her victory was followed after a year by the passage of the Muslim Women (Protection of Rights in Divorce) Act, 1986, which ruled that divorced Muslim women would be

covered by Muslim personal law and hence no longer entitled to maintenance under the common Criminal Procedure Code.

6 For a critique of this problematic, see Madhu Kishwar and Ruth Vanita, 'The Burning of Roop Kanwar', *Manushi* 42–3, September–December 1987, pp. 15–29; Sujata Patel and Krishna Kumar, 'Defenders of Sati', *Economic and Political Weekly*, 23 January 1988, pp. 129–30.

7 See Niranjan Dev Teerth, Shankaracharya (Hindu religious head) of Puri, in an interview with Anuradha Dutt, *The Illustrated Weekly of India*, 1–7 May 1988, pp. 26–9.

8 Ashis Nandy, 'The Human Factor', *The Illustrated Weekly of India*, 17–23 January 1988, pp. 20–3 esp. p. 22.

9 Inderjit Badhwar, 'Militant Defiance', *India Today*, 31 October 1987, pp. 38–41, reports a number of Rajput responses of this kind: '[Rajiv Gandhi, the Indian Prime Minister] is a parsi, married to a foreign woman, who is insulting the Hindu religion' (p. 39).

10 Nandy, 'The Human Factor'; also 'Sati in Kaliyuga', *Economic and Political Weekly*, 17 September 1988, p. 1976; Patrick Harrigan, 'Tyranny of the Elect? Bringing Bharat Mata Up to Date', *Statesman*, 5 November 1987.

11 Veena Das, 'Strange Response', *The Illustrated Weekly of India*, 28 February–5 March 1988, pp. 30–2. Das seems to suggest that the modern Indian state uses intervention in the sati issue to 'inferiorise small groups', much as the British used it to argue 'that Indians were not fit to rule themselves' (p. 32).

12 See, for instance, Kalyan Singh Kalvi, Janata Party leader, in an interview with Inderjit Badhwar, *India Today*, 31 October 1987: 'To build temples to [satis] is part of Rajput culture which believes that sati and shakti (power) are identical. ... In our culture, we worship the motherland, dharma (faith), and nari (woman). We are ready to die for any of them' (p. 41).

13 Nandy, 'The Human Factor', p. 23.

14 Kumkum Sangari and Sudesh Vaid, 'Sati in Modern India', *Economic and Political Weekly*, 1 August 1981, pp. 1284–8.

15 Lata Mani, 'Production of an Official Discourse on Sati in Early Nineteenth Century Bengal', *Economic and Political Weekly*; *Review of Women Studies*, 26 April 1986, pp. 32–40; also Prahlad Singh Shekhawat, 'The Culture of Sati in Rajasthan', *Manushi* 42–3, September–December 1987, pp. 30–4.

16 Kishwar and Vanita, 'The Burning of Roop Kanwar'.

17 Kumkum Sangari, 'There Is No Such Thing as Voluntary Sati', *The Times of India*, 25 October 1987.

18 Lata Mani, 'Production of an Official Discourse'.

19 Kalvi, interview.

20 The frequent argument that 'satis happen extremely rarely' (Kalvi) is intended defensively to make the point that widows are not routinely burnt. But we also realize that the spectacular value of sati would only be trivialized by its frequency – even as we are covertly reminded that power is a power to withhold death as well as to deal it.

21 Nandy also develops the distinction between authentic and inauthentic sati, in 'The Human Factor', p. 22.

22 Sangari, 'There Is No Such Thing as Voluntary Sati'.

23 Spivak, 'Can the Subaltern Speak?' p. 127.

24 Some examples are Shahbano, whose legal battle has been briefly described in n. 5; Phoolan Devi, a woman dacoit who surrendered to the police after committing a series of killings, who is now serving a sentence in jail; Vibha Mishra, an actress who was seriously burnt, but recovered, and who acquitted her arrested lover of all guilt

in the burning; Indu Arora, a woman arrested for the death of her two children, who was discovered to be involved in an adulterous relationship; the three Kanpur sisters (see p. 38, n. 49).

25 Mark Seltzer, 'Statistical Persons', *Diacritics* 17, 3, Fall 1987, pp. 82–98, esp. p. 87.

26 Scarry, *The Body in Pain*, p. 50

27 The invocation of the Rigveda relating to sati includes the line 'May fire be to them as cool as water.' See Bhismadutt Sharma, 'What Do the Hindu Dharmashastras Have to Say about the Sati Ritual?' (Hindi), *Gokul*, February 1985, pp. 20–5 and p. 42. There is also widespread popular faith in the power of the sati's curse. Sudesh Vaid reports the legend that grew around the sati of Taradevi in Madhav-ka-kas in 1954: 'Taradevi's mother in a dream asked her daughter how she could have borne the pain of live burning. The daughter replied with serenity that she had not suffered at all, the fire was like bathing in water.' See 'Politics of Widow Immolation', *Seminar* 342, February 1988, pp. 20–3, esp. p. 23.

28 Mani, 'Production of an Official Discourse', points out that even colonial arguments in favour of prohibiting sati 'were not primarily concerned with its cruelty or "barbarity"' (p. 35).

29 Seltzer, 'Statistical Persons', p. 88.

30 An indigenous discourse on *ahimsa* (non-violence) is part of the Buddhist scriptures and was subsequently appropriated by Mahatma Gandhi as part of the strategy of *satyagraha*. But as far as I know it does not include a phenomenology of pain; non-violence is prescribed as a moral, and political, way of life from what might, in a sense, be called an ecological point of view, i.e. an interest in the balance of forces in the universe.

31 Lata Mani, 'Early Missionary Discourse in India: The Journals of Carey, Marshman and Ward', unpublished MS.

32 I am grateful to Phyllis Palmer (Director, Women's Studies Program and Policy Center, George Washington University) for pointing this out to me, and for convening the GWU Feminist Theory Faculty Seminar where this discussion took place.

33 Scarry, *The Body in Pain*, pp. 161–2.

34 Teresa de Lauretis, 'The Violence of Rhetoric: Considerations on Representations and Gender', *Semiotica* 54, 1/2, 1985, pp. 11–31, esp. p. 25.

35 Ibid., p. 18.

36 Ibid., p. 13.

37 This stands in contrast to the hegemonic colonial and Brahminic discourses analysed by Lata Mani and Gayatri Spivak in their essays on sati.

38 Spivak, 'Can the Subaltern Speak?' p. 129.

39 Earlier, anyone who attempted sati was tried under Section 309 of the Indian Penal Code; a forcible or coerced sati was tried as murder or culpable homicide under Sections 299 and 300 of the Code; abetment of sati was tried under Section 306 as abetment of suicide. There were only three laws in force in the states, including the Rajasthan Sati (Prevention) Act, 1987, the Bengal Sati Regulation, 1829, and the Tamil Nadu Sati Regulation, 1830. My quotations in the text are from The Commission of Sati (Prevention) Act, 1987 (Act No. 3 of 1988).

40 Vasudha Dhagamwar, 'Saint, Victim or Criminal', *Seminar* 342, February 1985, pp. 34–9, esp. p. 38.

41 Spivak, 'Can the Subaltern Speak?' p. 122.

42 Michel Foucault, *Discipline and Punish: The Birth of the Prison*, trans. Alan Sheridan, New York, Vintage/Random House, 1979, p. 156.

43 Roop Kanwar's father-in-law, Sumer Singh, has produced questionable evidence to show that while the sati was being performed he was in hospital in a state of shock following his son's death.

44 Mani, 'Production of an Official Discourse', esp. pp. 33–5.

45 Sangari, 'There is No Such Thing as Voluntary Sati'.

46 Gayatri Chakravorty Spivak has discussed rumour as a 'subaltern means of communication', its power 'deriving from its participation in the structure of illegitimate writing'. See 'Subaltern Studies: Deconstructing Historiography', in Ranajit Guha ed., *Subaltern Studies IV: Writings on South Asian History and Society*, Delhi, Oxford University Press, 1985, pp. 351–4.

47 Inderjit Badhwar's report in *India Today*, 1 October 1987, carries this typical statement: 'Roop Kanwar's real thoughts, her secrets, are burnt with her' (p. 105). Similarly, Shiraz Sidhva's report in *The Sunday Observer*, 20 September 1987, concludes that 'no one will really know' whether Roop Kanwar was coerced or chose to commit sati.

48 Shri Vijender Singh (Jaipur) provided me with numerous pictures of Roop Kanwar's as well as previous satis, and with information about local sati-worship. My grateful thanks to him.

49 The situation, ironically, reverses every element of a sati: the girls are unmarried, not widowed; the suicide is pragmatically motivated, not gratuitous; the 'beneficiary' is the father, not the husband; the act is secret and private, not public; elaborate suicide notes make public the reasons for the girls' decision, in the place of the 'unknowability' of the sati's death; and, finally, in this 'co-death', the partners are women (sisters), not the conjugal couple. Overriding these differences is the common social perception that links both acts: to be without a husband (whether unmarried or widowed) is to be a 'burden' on the family, to lack *raison d'être*.

50 The poster is issued by the National Front of the Rajasthan Adult Education Committee.

51 The group calls itself 'Mediastorm', and had earlier made a documentary video film on the Muslim Women (Protection of Rights in Divorce) Act, entitled *In Secular India*.

52 The film is based on a Bengali novel of the same name by Kamal Kumar Majumdas published in 1965. I record with gratitude my indebtedness to Manikuntala Dar Bhowmik, who translated parts of the novel for me and explained its tantric philosophy.

53 First published in the Tamil weekly magazine *Kungumam*, 15 June 1980, and included in *Sirai* (The Prison), a collection of short stories (Madras, Kanimuthu Pathippagam, 1984).

54 Spivak, 'Can the Subaltern Speak?' p. 129.

55 The visual impact of this contrast is striking. The entire action takes place at a single locale, the banks of the Ganges. The scenic beauty of the broad, invariably placid, river is a backdrop to the turmoil of human events. For a different reading of 'death by drowning', see Sushmita Dasgupta (Centre for the Study of Social Sciences, Jawaharlal Nehru University, New Delhi), 'The Counterfinality of "Sati": A Study of "Antarjali Jatra"', unpublished paper presented at Gender Workshop: The Female Body and Gender Identity, Jawaharlal Nehru University, in January 1989. Dasgupta points out, 'As opposed to the sanctity of death by fire, drowning has an inauspicious connotation. ... [It] is considered to be very shameful and is often a cultural form of suicide for the so-called unfulfilled woman.' She goes on to argue that Yashobati's death, however, also resembles the immersion of the Durga idol in the Ganges, and therefore suggests her eventual 'resurrection'.

56 In a postscript to the story, Ramanan ironically turns it into a distorted newspaper report: 'Husband tries to save wife, dies. While trying to put out the burning sari of his wife, a man's clothes caught fire, and the two died together. This tragic incident took place in Madras yesterday.'

57 For an account of the intervention of women activists in the Deorala episode, see Sharda Jain, Nirja Misra and Kavita Srivastava, 'Deorala Episode: Women's Protest

in Rajasthan', *Economic and Political Weekly*, 7 November 1987, pp. 1891–4. The views of rural women in Rajasthan on the Deorala sati are recorded by members of the Women's Studies Unit, Institute of Development Studies, Jaipur, in 'Rural Women Speak', *Seminar* 342, February 1988, pp. 40–4.

58 I refer here primarily to the work of Lata Mani and Gayatri Spivak, to which I am profoundly indebted. In addition to the works already cited, see also Mani's 'Contentious Traditions: The Debate on Sati in Colonial India', *Cultural Critique* 7, Fall 1986, pp. 119–56; and Spivak's 'The Rani of Sirmur: An Essay in Reading the Archives', *History and Theory* 24, 3, 1987, pp. 247–72.

59 Mani, 'Contentious Traditions', p. 152.

60 Lata Mani has welcomed the 'analytical sophistication' of contemporary reports, arguing that it has resulted in a greater 'complexity' of the 'model of victimisation'. See 'Sati in the Media: Then and Now', *Indian Post*, 25 October 1987.

61 Spivak, 'The Rani of Sirmur', p. 271.

62 See Chandra Talpade Mohanty, 'Under Western Eyes: Feminist Scholarship and Colonial Discourse', *Boundary 2*, 12, no. 1, Fall 1984, pp. 333–58.

63 This brief account may illustrate the views of some feminists in India: at the Second Subaltern Studies Conference in Calcutta in January 1986, Julie Stephens presented a paper entitled 'Feminist Fictions: A Critique of Feminist Studies of Third World Women, with Special Reference to India'. Stephens's critique is similar to Mohanty's, though more sweeping and condemnatory of most analyses (including Indian feminists') of Indian women. In a report on the conference, David Hardiman concludes that 'the women present rejected Julie Stephens's paper in a remarkably united way'. Some of the arguments opposing her critique were that 'feminism was not a discourse to be analysed, but a method for bringing about social change'; that the writings in question were by no means homogeneous; that the category of 'experience' questioned by Stephens has to be preserved since 'the experience of the subjugated is central to any feminist writing'. See David Hardiman, '"Subaltern Studies" at Crossroads', *Economic and Political Weekly*, 15 February 1986, pp. 288–90 esp. pp. 288 and 289.

2

REPRESENTING SATI
Continuities and discontinuities

I

As 'the woman who dies', the sati eludes full representation.[1] The examination
of some texts of sati that I propose to undertake in this chapter leads to the
realization that it is, ironically, through death that the subject-constitutive 'reality'
of woman's being is created at certain historical junctures. The construction of
the Hindu widow's subjectivity in terms of sati that these texts propose is a
foreclosure of her existential choices; but to identify the woman as 'widow' is
already to have defined her proleptically. Around the subject-position that is
thus cleared for her in terms of death – her own, her husband's – various other
positions, dictated by ideology and politics, irresistibly come to range themselves.
I trace in this chapter the intertwining of death, gender and the politics of
representation as it shapes the subject of sati.

My focus will be on some texts of colonial and contemporary (post-
Independence) India, which map out the discursive field of sati, having in
common, as I shall try to show, the following features: the identification of sati
as a gendered issue; hence the definition of the widow as, exclusively, the subject
of sati (conceptualized only as one who chooses to die or is forced to die);
and, finally, a pronounced ambivalence towards the practice.[2] It is necessary,
nevertheless, to mark within this discursive field the gradual but significant
changes from colonial history to the postcolonial present, especially as they
relate to the question of female subjectivity; and to note the divergences between
British (or, broadly, European) attitudes to sati and the indigenous, mainly
liberal/reformist adoption and adaptation of these.

In the concluding part of the chapter I offer, by way of contrast, an analysis
of the classical Tamil epic, the *Shilapaddikaram*, to point to what seems to me the
entirely different ideological investments that are made in indigenous, precolonial
representations of sati – so that it is possible to suggest that a major paradigmatic
shift occurred at the point where a specifically colonial discourse on sati began
to emerge and then gain ground.[3] The identification of sati as a women's issue
(i.e. as a practice that reflected women's status in society), and the consequent

focus upon the sati's subjectivity only in terms of her willingness or reluctance to die, may be historicized as an aspect of the colonial and postcolonial discourses of sati. This occurs when we are able to recognize that, in contrast, in precolonial periods and cultures (i.e. in ancient, medieval or Islamic 'India'), sati – while always an act of suicide specific to women – subsumed gender within other social categories, such as class, community, region, or nation, in which women were included as representative members. In this construction of the widow's subjectivity, every act of sati is an expression of choice on the part of the woman (but such representations have also, invidiously, informed recent Hindu fundamentalist defences of sati). More crucially, the woman who does *not* commit sati is equally, if often implicitly, expressing choice – an aspect of 'choosing' that nowhere figures in later representations.

Since I have risked an oversimplified contrast in the interest of foregrounding a thesis, several clarifications and qualifications are in order. In the first place, the 'precolonial past' of India is by no means a single homogeneous period: it comprises several millennia of civilization, within which sati (which some scholars attribute to Dravidian cultures that predate the Aryan invasion of India) has had widely differing manifestations at different times and in different places. So any single notion of 'sati in precolonial India' is only a broad generalization about a conceptual paradigm rather than an indication of invariable or pre-scriptive ritual.

In the second place, it is not my intention to read the various representations as unmediated reflections of different 'realities': such a reading would lead one to the invidious distinction between 'authentic' (voluntary) and 'inauthentic' (forced) sati that nationalist and contemporary fundamentalist social scientists and religious leaders in India postulate, which corresponds to the distinction between sati in an early 'Golden Age' of Hinduism and sati in 'Kaliyuga' or the fallen age of the recent past. Such an idealized history is in danger of validating the concept of sati while condemning only its practice, and thereby reinforcing its ideological valorization. I must therefore repeat that by 'representations' I mean not 'representations of reality', but autonomous and paradigmatic conceptual structures.

Finally, I do not undertake here a history of sati. Such a history is yet to be written. The dialectical relationship between 'reality' and its representations, between history (itself a text but not reducible to it) and the 'texts' of sati, remains unexplored here. Outside the circuit of ideology-narrative representations that I trace here lies – we cannot escape the reminder – the 'reality' of a woman's death, which they both occlude and deploy in different ways. Colonial representations of sati, for instance, acquired force and materiality when they shaped colonial policy – precisely because they were offered as representations *of reality*. Therefore 'history' is the always-present subtext of my argument, and the readings of the handful of representative texts that I propose here are intended as a contribution to the historical enterprise.

My discussion in the following sections begins with an exposition of three exemplary ideological paradigms that structure the texts of sati in the nineteenth and twentieth centuries; it then offers a historical 'placing' of contemporary feminist critiques of the colonial discourse on sati; and concludes with some tentative observations on the representations of women in precolonial indigenous literatures, focusing on the *Shilapaddikaram*.

II

The abolition of sati in 1829 was the first major legislation of the East India Company's administration in India. That it – like the series of laws that were subsequently enacted on behalf of women – served as the moral pretext for intervention and the major justification for colonial rule itself, does not have to be argued further.[4] What is of concern here is how the colonial imagination seized upon and ordered the self-representation of such an administrative procedure: not merely, as Gayatri Spivak has succinctly formulated it, as a case of 'white men … saving brown women from brown men',[5] but as an actual narrative scenario of a single white man saving a brown woman from a mob of brown men. In other words, it is the trope of chivalry that provides the contours of the scenario.

Whether the institution of chivalry in medieval and renaissance Europe had an actual material basis, or was nothing more than a literary invention, historians seem to agree that the ideology of knighthood was profoundly influential in constructing and sustaining actual structures of power based on class (ruler and vassal, as in feudal society), gender (lady and knight, as in the courtly love tradition), or religion (the church and its followers, as in the Crusades against Islamic 'infidels'). It created reciprocal bonds of duty and obligation between the two parties that mediated relations of power and dependence. Further, chivalry, even while it formed and authorized the class, gender and racial/religious superiority of the knight, also provided the young male of an aspiring lower aristocracy with the means of upward social mobility at a historically transitional period; in other words, it was both a birthright and a career.[6] How eminently transferable such a concept is to the context of colonization is obvious. Large numbers of British young men, in the administrative, judicial, military, trading and education services of colonial rule, or in missionary orders, found themselves unexpectedly authorized in the exercise of power. But they also discovered that they had to undergo rites of initiation into it. For the colonizer's racial superiority, however flagrant skin colour or the appurtenances of power may have rendered it, had also to be demonstrated by acts of valour and authority.[7] It was this expectation that made intervention in the custom of sati both a test and a legitimization of British rule.[8]

The two texts I invoke here, Jules Verne's adventure tale *Around the World in Eighty Days* (1873) and M.M. Kaye's novel *The Far Pavilions* (1978), reproduce the ideological contours of the trope of chivalry in their representation of British

India. Jules Verne's popular story is the account of an eccentric English clubman, Phineas Fogg; and in the portion of the narrative that covers his journey across India, from Bombay on the west coast to Calcutta on the east, Fogg manages to rescue a young princess from sati in the jungles of central India. In conformity with what had by then developed into a stereotype, the widow is young, beautiful and a princess; the dead husband is old, ugly and a king; the other villains are a bloodthirsty mob and a cabal of scheming Brahmins; and the rescue itself is an act of chivalry, combining daring adventure with the humanitarian gesture.

Sati, as one can see from the example of this late-nineteenth-century French novel, continued to exercise the European imagination long after it was legally abolished by the 1829 Act. It could continue to be regarded as one of the 'realities' of 'India' because the division of the country into 'British' India and the princely 'native' states meant that sati's legal abolition could be officially enforced only in the former. Hence the necessity for heroics in the 1872 escapade of Fogg and Co. With the growing dominion of British rule (India was taken over by the Crown in 1858), the native states were reduced to mere pockets which were regarded as backward ('medieval') and decadent, in contrast to the provinces of 'enlightened' British rule.[9] The sati in *Around the World* is planned by the natives as a consciously transgressive act, a horrible ritual, to be performed in a clearing in the jungle of a native state; and the 'heart of darkness' is penetrated by the band of adventurers, who then emerge from it into light, the railways, British-administered provinces, and safety, with the rescued Indian princess in tow.[10]

The same demarcation of two worlds is emphasized in *The Far Pavilions*, whose hero, Ashton Pelham-Martyn, is a conflict-ridden product of the two cultures. But these opposed worlds are not only those of 'Britain' and 'India', but also of 'British' India (the North-West Frontier provinces) and 'native' India (the kingdoms of Gulcote and Bhither); and Pelham-Martyn's constant crossings over from one to the other are intended to emphasize the contrast between the two. One is the area of light, the other an area of darkness; the one is represented by the club and the army barracks, the other by labyrinthine palace interiors; within the first world the hero is able to develop uncomplicated homoerotic relationships, with a British Army fellow-officer, as well as a Pathan 'subedar', whereas in the other he is caught up in a frustrated romantic affair with a half-caste Indian princess; his British life is the 'open' life of war and heroism, his 'native' experiences involve him in intrigue and treachery; and, most strikingly, the position of women is marked differently in each world: the English belle, Belinda, is a flirt (hence a 'free agent'), while the Indian princesses are forced into first marriage and then sati.

The Far Pavilions spans the years between and describes two major historical events, the Indian Mutiny of 1857 and the Second Afghan War of 1878. The 'scene' of sati and the rescue is one of the climaxes of the book, the one that concludes the hero's involvement in native India with marriage to the princess Anjuli whom he has rescued; the other climax is the storming of the Residency in Kabul, after which he makes his own 'separate peace' to wander off into the sunset in search of the no man's land of the 'far pavilions'. We must not forget that *The Far Pavilions* is a product of the late 1970s post-empire, pre-Thatcher Britain, a book that has both marked and in a sense even inaugurated the whole complex cultural phenomenon now labelled 'Raj nostalgia'. Such a book would not have been complete without a scene of sati; but it would also have been expected to display a self-conscious liberal rectitude about the imperialist mission – which it does.

This is why the clear outlines of the scenario of 'rescue' are somewhat blurred. The 'rescue' is preceded by a brief history of sati, its origins and practices, provided by Ashton's Indian friend, Sarji. With this friend Ashton also engages in a debate about sati, and Sarji's 'native' views are allowed space: for the Indian nobleman death is a matter of little consequence, conjugal love is admirable, the women wish to die, faith is not to be mocked – and did not the west have its own witch burnings? But the last word is allowed to Ashton: 'Well, if we have done nothing else, at least we can mark up one thing to our credit – that we put a stop to that particular horror.'[11]

The rescue itself is in one sense not that: the princess Anjuli whom Ashton sets out to rescue is finally saved not from death but from blinding and incarceration (the rumour of her sati turns out to be a false one); while the queen, her half-sister Shushila, who actually wishes to die, is in fact not saved but only shot dead by Ashton at Anjuli's insistence so that she may be saved the horror of death by fire. Ashton's heroism is thus complicated by issues of morality and by considerations of the pragmatic costs of the enterprise. The first is indicated by his guilt over the killing of Shushila (which is compared with the mercy-killing of his wounded – and much-loved – horse Dagobaz): 'But then Shushila was not an animal: she was a human being, who had decided of her own free will to face death by fire and thereby achieve holiness: and he, Ash, had taken it upon himself to cheat her of that' (p. 778). The second is conveyed by his sorrow over the loss of his three loyal Indian friends, Sarji, Manilal and Govind, who die while escaping.

The analogy between the sati-'rescue' and knight-errantry is explicitly drawn, but is ironically repudiated immediately after (p. 780). British officialdom, whose assistance Ashton invokes at first to prevent the satis, is, finally, impotent and lacking in political will; so that the friends who in the end help Ashton to effect the rescue are Indian. In spite of these complexities, the ideological core of meaning remains intact. *The Far Pavilions* retains the main structural aspects, and the ideologemes they encode, that we notice in *Around the World in Eighty Days*: the same actors; the discrediting of woman's conjugal love as a possible motive for the sati; the suggestion of an actual or potential romance between the rescuer and the rescued; the representation of the rescue action as individual enterprise ('adventure') rather than official intervention; the establishment of a disinterested good through the act in a climate of benightedness. Ashton's scruples and his partisanship towards Indians therefore only embellish his knighterranty, exemplifying both *noblesse oblige* and chivalric love.[12]

These texts record the progressive consolidation of what has come to be an essentially fixed British attitude to sati. By foregrounding Hindu women as passive and unresisting victims of Hindu patriarchy, as these texts do, it could be established beyond argument that the women were in need of saving.[13] However, the possibility that some widows might have wished to die as an act of conjugal love persisted as a doubt, and gave rise to other views. This possibility is given some cursory credence in Ashton's self-questioning:

> [H]e had interfered in something that was a matter of faith and a very personal thing; and he could not even be sure that Shushila's convictions were wrong, for did not the Christian calendar contain the names of many men and women who had been burned at the stake for their beliefs, and acclaimed as saints and martyrs?

> (p. 778)

It is no idle question. In the next section I examine how the conceptual paradigm of Christian martyrdom accommodated the unsettling possibility that the widow 'chose' her death.

III

The positive view of sati – with its flip underside – had popular currency, as this mid-nineteenth-century jingle advertising 'Maspero' Egyptian cigarettes suggests:

> Calm is the early morning
> Solace in time of woes,
> Peace in the hush of twilight,
> Balm ere my eyelids close.
> This will Masperos bring me,
> Asking naught in return,
> With only a Suttee's passion
> To do their duty and burn.[14]

The jingle is accompanied by an illustration of a burning cigarette in an ashtray: appearing in the swirls of smoke rising from the cigarette is the shrouded figure of the sati, suggestive simultaneously of a Christian martyr and of a genie from a magic lamp awaiting orders. The commodification of the sati's self-sacrifice effectively eclipses her subjectivity.

Even as the Indian widow's death with her husband is elevated to fit into the more recognizable paradigm of religious martyrdom, it was also, less admiringly, trivialized as a form of feudal – or 'native' – subservience, an act of unthinking, if not actually deluded, loyalty. Therefore the two views of the sati – as a woman forced to die and as a woman who chooses to die – did not necessarily have to collide.[15] The perception that Hindu women were victims was the basis for the establishment of sati as a women's issue, as I noted earlier; it provoked an implicit comparison of their devalued social position with the freedom and privileges of British women – thus offering further proof of the superiority of British civilization.

But the British women's movement was gaining ground at home even as British rule was being consolidated in the colonies – and its members were denying the superior advantages ascribed to their status in British society. It is in the fact of this conflict that the powerful ideology of the family as the 'woman's sphere' was assiduously developed on behalf of women.[16] Within this ideological structure the Indian widow as *subject* of sati could be selectively admired as exemplifying chastity and fidelity – important components of the model of behaviour that was being constructed for the Englishwoman at 'home'. Thus sati, whatever subject-position was assigned to the Hindu widow, could be usefully fed into different ideological conjunctures.

These procedures of subjectification are less transparent in the literary text. A complex and suggestive ambivalence towards the sati can be located in the following passage from Charles Dickens' *Dombey and Son* (1848), which serves as my exemplary text in this section.

Susan Nipper, Florence Dombey's personal maid, is seen upbraiding Mr Dombey for his ill-treatment of Florence; and she describes thus her own courage and determination in confronting the formidable man:

> I may not be an Indian widow Sir and I am not and I would not so become but if I once made up my mind to burn myself alive, I'd do it! And I've made up my mind to go on.[17]

In this startling metaphor, Susan's simultaneous disavowal and embrace of the act of sati is characteristically ambivalent: however *like* an Indian widow Susan may be, she 'would not ... become' one; but at the same time the qualities of determination and courage that motivate Susan are attributed to the Indian widow as well. Susan's allusion suggests that sati could be raised above its cultural and gender specificity to express, in popular usage, any kind of excessive zeal. Susan had earlier sought another analogy to convey her loyalty: 'she's the blessedest and dearest angel is Miss Floy. ... the more that I was torn to pieces Sir the more I'd say it though I may not be a Fox's Martyr' (p. 703). This conflation of sati with Christian martyrdom is a familiar cognitive procedure.

But the invocation has other implications in this narrative. For *Dombey and Son* is a profound study of marital discord, and one which is remarkably sympathetic to the wronged wife. Dickens's discomfort about the particular form that Edith Dombey's disloyalty towards her husband eventually takes – sexual infidelity – is well known (so much so that he does not permit actual adultery to take place: Edith defends her honour at knife's point!). The allusion to sati, occurring at the precise juncture in the narrative when she is planning her elopement with Carker, is a brilliant irony. Susan's own blindness to this application of her metaphor – which she has displaced from conjugal love to feudal loyalty – is no less striking.[18] Between the actual English wife of the narrative (who plans to leave a living husband) and the figurative Indian widow, transiently evoked as a trope in its discourse (and who will burn with a dead husband) – between these two female subjects an implicit contest of conjugal loyalty is set up, and cultural relativism (racial otherness) is effectively elided.

Two feminist critics have recently carried further the analysis of the ideological uses to which the interracial 'contests' between women, around the subject of sati, are put. Nancy Paxton has astutely diagnosed how, in Flora Annie Steel's *On the Face of the Waters* (1897), 'the sexual politics of colonial life in India' drive the British heroine, Kate Erlton, into emulation of and rivalry with her Hindu maid-servant, Tara. Ultimately, 'Kate concedes the contest of purity to Tara, accepting her assertion of the absolute cultural differences that separate the English and the Indian woman.' After her husband dies, Kate marries again; it is Tara who 'triumphs' by dying a sati-like death in the fires of war while helping Kate to escape.[19]

Steel's novel has a special significance because it is set in 1857, the year of the Indian Mutiny. This was an event in which the British women in India, because of the indignities and danger they publicly suffered at the hands of the native sepoys in the attack, became the objects of British men's protection. Thus they briefly came to occupy the same position as the women who committed sati, their Indian sisters, becoming, like them, both public spectacles and objects of salvation. Steel uses this historical irony to bring about a confrontation of the two women's worlds.

Such confrontations are of course stage-managed by an interested patriarchy. But an emergent feminist individualism could also deploy the 'native' woman towards its own ends, as Gayatri Spivak has brilliantly demonstrated through her reading of three women's texts of the nineteenth century. She shows how another kind of struggle between the women of the two cultures may also have been the price paid for an 'imperialist project cathected as civil-society-through-social-mission'.[20] In such a situation the emergence of the feminist individualist in the West cannot be an isolated development, but is, instead, achieved through an imperialist project (that of 'soul making') in which the 'native female' must play a role. Spivak is talking of *Jane Eyre* (1848); and to counter the temptation to 'see nothing there but the psychobiography of the militant female subject [Jane Eyre]' (p. 245), she invokes Jean Rhys's *Wide Sargasso Sea* (1966), whose 'powerful suggestion' is that '*Jane Eyre* can be read as the orchestration and staging of the self-immolation of Bertha Mason as "good wife"' (p. 259). *Jane Eyre* must be read in conjunction also with the history of sati in British India for such a reading to carry conviction. Given such a perspective, we might also be able to see how Tara's death in Steel's *On the Face of the Waters* is directly the cost of Kate's escape and of the Englishwoman's eventual 'liberation' of consciousness from the excesses of martyrdom.

To sum up: in the colonial encounter the Hindu 'good wife' is constructed as partiarchy's feminine ideal: she is offered simultaneously as a model and as a

47

signifier of absolute cultural otherness, both exemplary and inimitable. She is also, as Spivak points out, both indispensable (the justification for the imperialist project itself) and eminently dispensable (the sacrifice offered to an emergent western feminist individualism). The colonial ambivalence towards sati was, in any case, productive for the achievement of the diverse goals of imperialism.

IV

The three Indian texts I identify in the following discussion – Henry Derozio's long poem, *The Fakeer of Jungheera* (1826), Rabindranath Tagore's short story, 'Saved' (1918), and Gautam Ghosh's film (1987) based on Kamal Kumar Majumdar's novel of the same name, *Antarjali Jatra* (1986) – are representative of what I shall call briefly, for the sake of convenience, the male indigenous reformist/liberal position on women's issues. The abolition of sati, as well as other colonial laws on behalf of women in nineteenth-century India, was considerably aided by the growing spirit of reform among the increasingly western-educated, male, elite of India. The reform movements on behalf of women tied in with other issues relating to caste, education and, later, nationalism. In the texts listed above, therefore, while sati is undeniably viewed as a 'women's issue', its abolition is also located within a matrix of broadly reformist ideals.

Within the constraints of narrative what is retained in these texts is the paradigm of rescue, shorn no doubt of its trappings of European chivalry, but exploiting several of its other significant structural elements. As in the colonial texts of imperialism described earlier, the *dramatis personae* are stereotyped, and their triangular relationship persists.

The break with the past that we associate with 'modernity' is never a clean one. Among the indigenous reformers, a sentimental affiliation to indigenous 'tradition', the early stirrings of nationalism, and an acute recognition of the resistance of social forces to change, created a complex inheritance which considerably complicated the ideological stance towards issues relating to women. Thus while sati could be condemned on both humanitarian and religious grounds, the prescribed alternative for widows, ascetic celibacy, was not so easily opposed. Therefore the remarriage of widows, long after it was made legally permissible, was a practically non-existent practice.

It is this conflict of allegiances between 'tradition' and 'reform' that modifies the narrative paradigm of 'rescue' that structures these texts. The crucial feature common to all of them is that, in spite of not submitting to sati, the woman dies. The inhibition about representing the rescued widow with an after-life of romantic/sexual fulfilment with her rescuer is striking. What her death also implies is the impotence of her rescuer, an inability to work out her salvation that accurately reflects the perceived difficulties of social change (as opposed to the facility of official intervention). The failure also reflects an internalization of the notion that the colonized male was not 'man enough' to protect his womankind. Ashis Nandy has suggested that the sudden and major changes brought about by colonial rule produced effects of alienation in the Hindu male; and the strong defence of sati advanced by some members of the indigenous male elite was an attempt to recover their identity by enforcing traditional patriarchal norms.[21] Finally, what these texts also offer is a more complex construction of the subjectivity of the heroine than the polarities of 'damsel in distress'/'martyr' (i.e. she was forced to die/she chose to die) scripted by the text of imperialism. Nevertheless, these are texts that are historically divergent, and we must plot their interaction with the texts of imperialism differently.

Henry Derozio's *The Fakeer of Jungheera* (1826) runs to a thousand lines, but it has a simple enough plot: the young and beautiful widow Nuleeni is about to be burned with her dead husband, a rich old man whom she had been forced to marry. She is rescued from the sati site by her former lover, an outlaw masquerading as a holy man (a *fakeer*), and his band of robbers. They enjoy a brief idyll on his solitary island-rock Jungheera. Meanwhile, Nuleeni's distraught father approaches the Muslim ruler, Prince Soorjah, and with his help raises an army to fight the Fakeer and avenge his daughter's 'dishonour'. The lovers are forced to part. The father kills the lover in a fierce battle. Nuleeni finds her slain lover on the battlefield, and dies of heartbreak in his arms.

Henry Vivian Louis Derozio (1809–31) was the first Indian poet of any note to write in English. He was a precocious East Indian youth (of mixed Portuguese-Indian and English blood) who produced most of his poetry, including the *Fakeer*, before he was 20. Derozio's role in what came to be called the Young Bengal movement has been recognized by historians to have had a significant impact on the later Bengal 'Renaissance', itself a forerunner of nationalist struggles. Among the 'superstitions' of religion that Derozio attacked was sati, which was, in the 1820s, the decade preceding its abolition, an issue of intense debate and division among the indigenous elite as well as between its members and the colonial administration.

But if we expect *The Fakeer of Jungheera* to be an anti-sati tract we shall be disappointed. There is little or no comment on the cruelty of sati, or on the social debasement of women that it reflected. Instead, as the epigraph to the first canto makes clear, it is loveless marriage that Derozio condemns, and romantic love that he extols in its place. Romantic love as the only valid basis for marriage was, of course, a radically westernized notion; and it is disconcerting to find an argument in its favour in the context of a widow's imminent death. Almost it would seem as if for Derozio sati would be tolerable if the wife had married the husband for love in the first instance. And in fact to die of love is to die of a recognized western disease. It is *this* death that Derozio devises for his heroine at the end of the poem.

Derozio is constructing a romantic tale, and it is the formal thrust of the genre that determines its message, rather than a social critique of women's oppression. The poem is actually a pastiche of several English poetic forms, a medley of inset ballads, songs and madrigals within a larger narrative in rhymed couplets.[22] At the same time, Derozio exploits many of the features of self-conscious 'exoticism': the set-piece iconic sati-scene (resembling the scene of religious martyrdom), the elaborate nature descriptions, and the fervent invocations to Vedic gods (Surya). But for all its formal derivativeness, the poem is still significant for our argument when we recognize that Nuleeni, the heroine, is granted a measure of selfhood: she submits to her sati not because she is coerced or deluded but because she is willing to die (not, however, on account of her dead husband, but because of the loss of her lover). And she is totally daring in expressing her love for a man other than the one she is married to and one who, further, belongs to a class and caste so different from her own (the outlaw is a Muslim, and Derozio makes a passing point about true love breaking caste barriers). The union of the lovers is, of course, frustrated. Nuleeni's death is sanctioned by the conventions of romantic poetry, and the social status quo is preserved by the cautionary deaths of both the lovers. However heroic the rescuer's death, it defeats the purpose of the rescue.

Rabindranath Tagore's short story, 'Saved', could not be more different. While Derozio uses large contrasts of love and war, 'nature' and 'society' virtually to swamp the human characters, Tagore stages a small (five-page) domestic drama, and tells the story of a frustrated wife, a jealous husband and a *swami* (ascetic monk) to whom the wife turns for religious consolation. The *swami* begins to see himself in the role of rescuer, and finally makes an assignation to meet Gouri and take her away: 'I will with god's help rescue his handmaid for the holy service of his feet.'[23] Gouri hides the letter in the loops of her hair, 'as a halo of deliverance' (p. 211). But it falls into the husband's hands. Gouri finds him struck down in his room, dead of apoplexy, the letter clenched in his fist. Gouri discovers that the *swami*'s real intention was to seduce her. She then kills herself. The story ends: 'All were lost in admiration of the wifely loyalty she had shown in her *sati*, a loyalty rare indeed in these degenerate days' (p. 212). It is a laconic ending, the last line packed with a multitude of ironies. The authorial free indirect speech transcribes the nostalgia for and idealization of sati that is characteristic of large sections of orthodox Hindu society, at the same time that it highlights the titillating sensationalism that the double death provides. Does the irony lie in society's conclusion that Gouri committed sati, when she died perhaps for quite other reasons than conjugal loyalty? Or is there irony in the extent of Gouri's reformation, the transformation from her hatred of her husband to the guilt, remorse and expiation of her death? Is she indeed 'saved' by death – from her 'saviour'?

The notion of rescue is therefore itself framed for ironic examination. Gouri is beset and betrayed by both men, and when, finally trapped, she kills herself, it is to be apotheosized as a sati. Her terseness in communication has been marked all through the story ('she was a woman of few words'; 'his wife treated it [his jealousy] with silent contempt'); and so the reticence about her final motive is appropriate.

Tagore's privatization of the bourgeois family drama, and his psychological subtlety in probing the woman's consciousness, parallel his ironic manipulation of the typical sati-narrative. The figure of the 'rescuer' as outlaw is here unequivocally reduced to that of a would-be seducer; the *sanyasi* or ascetic monk is frequently a socially anomalous and displaced figure, treated either with veneration as a holy man or with suspicion as a charlatan. Gouri herself is given the responsibility for a number of the events of the story, and acts decisively and even rebelliously in various crises. The jealous husband is treated with a measure of sympathy, as a financially insecure and perhaps sexually impotent failure. Tagore diagnoses this tragedy as the product of a certain 'modernity' (characterized by scepticism, some mobility for women, the anomie experienced by the Bengal middle-class male under colonial administration), in conflict with residual orthodoxy (characterized by 'faith', purdah for women, and traditional patriarchal authority). The status and meaning of the widow's death serve as the focus of this ironic enquiry.

My third text representing a male liberal/reformist view of sati, like the first two, is marked by a failure to imagine a viable way out for the widow; at the same time, it renders the 'rescue' paradigm considerably more complex. *Antarjali Jatra* (Death by Drowning), directed by Gautam Ghosh, is a recent Bengali film. Set in 1832, immediately after the abolition of sati in Bengal, it narrates the story of Yashobati, a young girl hurriedly married off to a dying old man with her father's promise to the 'pundits' and the family that she will commit sati. She is left with her dying husband at the burning *ghats* on the banks of the river Ganga, with only the *chandal* (the untouchable *ghat*-keeper, the burner of the corpses) for company. The *chandal* urges her to escape; but she refuses, even though she dreads her death. Instead she tends her dying husband, who seems to revive under her care. The *chandal* pities her and reviles her fate. They are drawn together, and become lovers. One night the river floods, and the bier of the old man is swept away. Desperately, Yashobati swims out in search of her husband, finds only the empty bier, clings to it, but is drowned. The sati prophecy would appear to have been ironically fulfilled, but through death by drowning rather than fire. The *chandal* is full of rage and sorrow at her death.

While Ghosh retains the features of the 'rescue' paradigm, these are reworked to an almost unrecognizable degree. The characteristics of the chief *dramatis personae* – Brahmins, dying/dead husband, widow, rescuer – are versions of the stereotype. Thus the Brahmins, while they are identified as the chief 'villains', are also seen close up: Ananta, the chief Brahmin and astrologer, is at least partially motivated by the desire to defy the alien edict against an indigenous religious rite; the father of Yashobati, a poor Brahmin, is tempted by the prospect of marrying off his daughter without having to provide a dowry; the doctor, an 'enlightened' Brahmin with some access to modern systems of medicine, does protest on legal and humanitarian grounds, but is blackmailed into silence; the dying man, a *kulin* Brahmin, and his grown sons, welcome the glory and prestige of a sati in the family. This differentiated characterization makes it possible for Ghosh to probe the complex social phenomenon of sati.

The husband, dying and comatose for most of the film, is a grotesque caricature whose resurrection is a parody of lust for a new and nubile wife.

The heroine, too, is shown as young and beautiful: but not merely to highlight her vulnerability sentimentally. The fact is an aspect of this film's insistence upon the female *body* as what is at stake in sati. The obsessive male gaze, directed by the husband, the lover and the film-maker himself at the female body, is inevitably sexual; but it is equally a reminder that the body will burn. A single episode makes the point. The *chandal*, prohibited by caste restrictions from touching a living Brahmin, rakes Yashobati with his gaze in order to measure her for the pyre: a gaze which is necessarily enacted by the viewer as well, but with no such purpose to legitimize it. Yashobati's subjectivity includes the 'objectification' that is cinema's characteristic endowment; but it is also given the more familiar novelistic dimension of 'consciousness' through her 'choosing' to die. Her acquiescence, however, is made a matter more complex than that of faith. At one point she turns on the *chandal* and his incessant badgering; between him and those who wish her to die, she protests, she is made to feel a mere object. She seeks the realm of her true subjectivity outside the parameters of the question of her death – and her love-making with the *chandal* is one expression of this search.

The most complex rendering, finally, is that of the would-be rescuer, the *chandal*. His outsider status is not merely a romanticization of individualistic anti-establishment heroics: he is by class, caste and occupation the most outcast of society's members; and his helplessness to save Yashobati is a function of this social marginality. By allying these two subaltern figures, the *chandal* and the woman fated to die, Ghosh tries to make the most telling point in his film. Further, the *chandal* does not intervene from the outside: his habitation is the cremation grounds, he is part of the hierarchical social structure, and he asserts his *dharma* (social/religious obligation) by refusing to burn a living body. By making him an articulate and fearless spokesman for the oppressed, Ghosh compensates for the 'victim's' speechlessness. So we are forced to ask why, given this, as well as the desperation of the two characters, the frank sexuality of their relationship, and the pragmatic possibilities of escape (solitude, a moored boat), a different, happy ending was not envisaged for the film. Finally it seems to be only a grim naturalistic fatalism that forecloses it.

Antarjali Jatra is a contemporary film, and its relationship to its material is mediated by its historical distance from sati in Bengal 150 years ago. This distance makes possible a materialist analysis of sati based on contemporary historical and sociological researches.[24] Paradoxically, it also proceeds from an understanding of the contemporary phenomenon of bride-burning: the problem of providing dowry for unmarried daughters is so acute that their deaths may even be viewed as a 'solution' by their parents. Third, *Antarjali Jatra* reveals the attempt of the contemporary left to explore the possibility of an alliance between women, the working class and the lower castes, based on the similarity of their oppression and the commonality of their oppressors.

52

Finally, female sexuality and its social control are allowed to appear as dominant rather than recessive aspects of the phenomenon of sati in this narrative. The imperialist text covered over sexuality by discrediting conjugal love, and by sublimating chivalric love into disinterested justice or 'romance'; or, by elevating sati to an act of martyrdom, it represented it as transcending human, and merely sexual, affective bonds. In the indigenous liberal/reformist text the issue of female sexuality became a more overt factor in the social dynamics of marriage and widowhood, and consequently of sati. But while in *Antarjali Jatra* the woman's body is blatantly foregrounded, the potency and the potential anarchy of her sexuality are not let loose; the metaphoric flood instead ravages the land, while she herself dies. In this sense, Ghosh remains captive to his inheritance from the past.[25]

V

If I conclude this part of my analysis with a brief consideration of the work on sati in the colonial period produced by two Indian feminist scholars, Lata Mani and Gayatri Spivak, it is not to offer it as the culmination of a progressive narrative.[26] Rather, I see their work, identified dialectically as *critique*, as being representative of the present historical moment of postcolonial feminism. Their own self-conscious adoption of the stance of the postcolonial woman intellectual whose politics – anti-imperialism and feminism – is overt, makes such a representation possible.

Mani and Spivak operate within the boundaries of the earlier discourse of sati, but with two major breaks. In the first place, they radically interrogate the 'rescue' paradigm through fresh historical evidence (Mani), and through semiotic analysis (Spivak). Second, they reconceptualize and centralize the subjectivity of the sati as part of an explicitly feminist project.

In both cases, narrative intervenes significantly to structure their arguments. Though Mani, in fact, explicitly privileges synchronicity (discourse) over dia-chronicity (narrative), her 'legislative history of sati' is nevertheless chronologically traced.[27] It emerges as a powerful counter-narrative to the scenario of rescue which was the ideological translation of the colonial pretext for intervention. What Mani's researches restore is the long prehistory of abolition, a period of debate primarily concerning 'the feasibility rather than the desirability' of abolition, so that 'rather than arguing for the outlawing of sati as a cruel or barbarous act ... officials in favour of abolition were at pains to illustrate that such a move was entirely consonant with the principle of upholding indigenous tradition'.[28] The settlement of this issue was sought through appeal to Brahmin pundits who were to investigate the scriptural authority for sati. During this period (1789–1829), a number of circulars were issued to district officials on the basis of official interpretation of the pundits' *vywasthas* (rulings), and a meticulous surveillance of all satis was undertaken to ensure that they were 'legally' performed. In spite of this the incidence of sati rose. The two were even connected in some analyses: '[G]overnment attention had given "a sort of interest and celebrity to the sacrifice". . . . [The circulars] had a tendency "to modify, systematize, or legalize the usage" and made it appear as though "a legal sutte" was . . . better than an illegal one'.[29] This is a very different scenario from that of 'rescue'. At the same time, colonial reports on sati incidents assiduously circulated the stereotypes of cruel Brahmins, bloodthirsty mobs and, above all, the widow as victim, which found their way into the narratives of rescue.[30]

It is not my intention to offer Mani's reading of the archives as the 'correct', 'historical' version in opposition to a 'fabricated' colonial narrative construction. But neither do I subscribe to an extreme post-structuralist position that reduces history to narrative, and makes all truth indeterminate or relative. The truth-value of Mani's reconstruction of the 'production of an official discourse' seems to me inestimable. I merely refrain from positing these opposed versions as contests of truth. Instead, I emphasize Mani's historical location and the politics of postcolonial feminism as important constituents shaping the counter-narrative that she (re)constructs.

Gayatri Spivak is also obliged to frame a narrative in order to halt the woman as signifier from disappearing into 'a violent aporia' between (native patriarchy's) 'subject-constitution' and (imperialism's) 'object-formation'. In responding to indigenous partriarchy's 'constructed counter narrative of woman's consciousness' as 'woman's desire [to die]', Spivak is led to 'tabulate a psycho-biographical norm'.[31] She concludes with an 'example' to 'illuminate the social text', the case of a young girl, Bhuvaneswari Devi, who hanged herself (p. 129). In another essay in 'reading the archives', Spivak demonstrates that colonial intervention in the decision of the Rani of Sirmur to commit sati had little to do with 'saving' her: the Rani had to continue to rule 'because of the commercial/territorial interests of the East India Company'.[32]

Since Mani and Spivak undertake a reconstructive project in history, motivated by a concern to 'know' the subject of sati, both are frustrated by the unavailability of records of women's consciousness. 'One never encounters the testimony of the women's voice-consciousness';[33] 'precious little [is] heard from them; . . . one learns so little about them.'[34] It is, of course, this significant absence that engenders their powerful criticism of the British imperialist construction of the Indian woman as perennial victim (Mani), and of the native patriarchal endowment of her with a 'dubious' free will (Spivak). Their historical analysis is clinched when they reveal how such constructions legitimated colonial intervention.

The force of their attacks upon the partial and interested representations of the woman who committed sati has significant implications in the area of female subject-production. In Mani the reaction to 'the discourses of salvation' is the privileging of what Spivak has called 'the woman's unrepresentable willing subjectivity';[35] in Spivak, on the other hand, the hegemonic repression of the woman's consciousness results in her stress upon the abjectness of women's subject-constitution.[36]

The preoccupation with the sati as colonial female subject, which is a function of Mani's and Spivak's reiterated feminist concern with contemporary Indian women's issues in the postcolonial context, pushes them to further speculations which pounce upon absences in the text of history. For Mani, such partial and systematic subjectification 'precludes the possibility of a complex female subjectivity';[37] for Spivak, what is of 'greater significance' than the debate on sati is that 'there was no debate upon this exceptional fate of widows [i.e. celibacy] – either among Hindus or between Hindus and British', with the resultant 'profound irony [of] locating the woman's free will in self-immolation'.[38] The role of the postcolonial woman intellectual is then clearly but variously indicated: there are suggestions that Mani's project would be the restoration of 'full' subjectivity to the woman through more assiduous historical research. She counters, for instance, the 'infantilising' of the Hindu woman by offering statistical proof that 'a majority of *satis* were undertaken by women well past childhood'.[39] Spivak's lack of faith in such positivistic enterprises is well known. Noting that the archives have no records of the eventual fate of the Rani of Sirmur (who had announced her intention to commit sati and whom British officials had sought to dissuade), Spivak responds, 'I intend to look a little further, of course. . . . [But] to retrieve her as information will be no disciplinary triumph. . . . [T]here is no "real Rani" to be found.'[40] Since the subaltern 'cannot speak', it is she herself, through an 'exorbitation' of her self-assigned role as post-colonial critic, who must undertake to 'plot a story, unravel a narrative and give the subaltern a voice in history'.[41]

In attempting to locate both the genderization of the issue of sati and the subjectification of the woman who dies within a cognitive structure that is historically produced, it has not been my intention merely to subsume feminist critiques of imperialism and native patriarchy within the larger colonial/postcolonial discourse. These critiques advance the terms of the argument considerably, and promise an alliance between the project of feminism and the female victim-as-subject that is entirely new, and is both theoretically and politically challenging. At the same time it is important not to discredit the epistemological breakthrough achieved by the colonial establishment of sati as a 'woman question' – however suspect its politics – that has fed into the contemporary feminist analyses of the issue. An examination of some texts of precolonial India that I will undertake in the next section – which produce a different focus on the issue of self-immolation, and consequently a different subjectivity for the widow – makes retrospectively clear where the 'break' may be identified.

VI

The ancient epics and tales, the *Mahabharata*, the *Ramayana* and the *Bhaga-vadpuranas*, draw attention to the women who commit sati by celebrating their courage and devotion in panegyric verses. Such women are invariably the wives of warrior-heroes, kings, *rishis* (sages), 'great men' of one kind or other, and their act is therefore intended to serve as a reflection of/on the status of the men on whose behalf they die, rather than be read as a gratuitous act of self-willed heroism. The failure of a woman to commit sati never seems to call for corresponding comment of any kind, whether of censure or surprise; the four wives of the king Dasaratha (Rama's father, in the *Ramayana*), for instance, continue to live on after his death as revered dowager queens, leading the celibate life prescribed by the *shastras*. In the *Mahabharata*, both wives of the king Pandu (the father of the Pandavas) wish to commit sati at his death, and argue about who should exercise the privilege. Finally, Madri persuades Kunti, the senior queen, not to die since, because of her great love for her step-children as well as her own, she would be the better mother.

The three most famous of the legendary good wives, the eponymous 'Sati' herself (the goddess Parvati), Sita (in the *Ramayana*), and Savitri (in the *Puranas*), did not actually commit self-immolation as widows.[42] After the death of Savitri's husband Satyavan, she does battle with the god of death Yama himself, and journeys to the underworld to reclaim her husband; because of her penances she is able to win back her husband's life as a boon from Yama. I do not argue that these women are not, in anything but a literal sense, satis: the word itself means only 'good wife', and in all these cases the women must submit to trials of various kinds to establish good wifehood. But Savitri's 'death', her journey to the nether world, is a trial that is at least undertaken to some purpose: she not only reclaims her husband, but herself comes back to the living. While the widow's continuing concern (or obsession) is with the dead husband, her devotion may at least find expression in life rather than death.

The recourse to texts of the Indian past is of course a familiar move, and figured prominently in the debate on sati initiated in colonial India, and has been resurrected – within a different political framework – in recent times. I have no wish to reproduce their dubious idealization of the past, or of Hindu women's status in earlier societies.[43] My argument that the identity of the 'good wife' (sati in the original sense) is a broader framework for female subjectification than that of the widow who burns (sati according to later usage) is based on the observation that good wifehood has different manifestations, and some of these included the option of life rather than death. The representation of the female subject as good wife in the *Shilappadikaram*, which I examine next, occupies this larger space cleared for the widow who 'chooses' life over death.

Shilappadikaram (The Lay of the Ankle Bracelet) is one of the three surviving 'great poems' written in the third and last epoch of classical Tamil literature. Its author is Prince Ilango Adigal; and the date attributed to the main body of the work is the second century AD. The story is summarized in a Preamble to the book:

> In the ancient town of Puhar, immortal capital of the Chola kings ..., there lived a rich merchant named Kovalan. He dissipated his great wealth in the pleasure offered him by a dancing girl expert in her art. He had a wife named Kannaki. With her he went to Madurai, the capital of the celebrated Pandya kingdom. In need of funds, he wished to sell her beautiful ankle bracelet, and went into the main bazaar looking for a buyer. There he showed the ankle bracelet to a goldsmith, who said, 'Only a queen can wear such jewelry.' He suggested that Kovalan wait near his shop, and ran to the palace to inform the king that he had found the thief of the queen's gold bracelet. At that moment Kovalan's hour of destiny had come. The king ... did not bother to make an investigation, but simply ordered a guard to put the thief to death and bring back the queen's bracelet. The wife of Kovalan found herself abandoned and shed abundant tears. She tore away one of her breasts, adorned by a string of pearls. By the power of her virtue, she burned down the great city of Madurai and called down upon the Pandya king the anger of the gods.[44]

There are two major thematic aspects of this work, as the poet is at pains to point out: the domestic, or love (*aham*), and the political, or war (*puram*) (p. 204). Its drama is also of two kinds, the 'human tragedy' and the 'mythological play' (p. 144); and the precepts it illustrates deal with both justice and conjugal love (p. 209). Thus Kannaki is at once an instrument (of political, as well as divine justice) and an agent; she therefore simultaneously asserts her righteousness in burning down the city, and expresses sorrow and guilt at her crime; she must inflict punishment upon the king and queen and upon the entire polity, but also upon herself, as she tears out her left breast as a symbolic repudiation of her femininity.

These contradictions are resolved because Kannaki's virtue is conceptualized as a social trait, just as the Pandya king's injustice is a national shame. In other words, it is not individual motivation that prompts human action, but social roles. When Kannaki confronts the king it is as the representative of a city, a nation, a class and her sex, and as a subject. Kannaki claims that she cannot act otherwise than she does because she comes from 'Pukar, where these noble women with fragrant braids [whose stories she has narrated] live. If these stories are true, and if I am faithful, I cannot allow your city to survive' (p. 131). Here it is the community that dictates women's behaviour; the reverse of this, the invocation of the status or behaviour of women to define a community as backward or 'advanced', is a later argument, and one that has figured prominently in the debate on sati.

What is especially significant is that Kannaki is faced with choices as soon as she confronts Kovalan's corpse, between abject and helpless widowhood on the one hand, and death on the other. In an extended, fluently rhetorical passage, she repudiates the ways of widowhood (p. 122). But the vision of Kovalan appears, and advises her to stay: 'Beloved! Stay there, stay! Remain peacefully in life!' (p. 125). Kannaki takes this as an injunction to avenge his death: 'I shall not search for my husband [i.e. follow him in death] before he is avenged. I shall meet this inhuman king and ask for his justice against himself' (p. 126). After she has burned down the great city by the power of her curse, she leaves, wanders forlornly for fourteen days, and then dies 'naturally' to ascend thereafter to heaven with her husband.

We cannot deny that Kannaki emerges as a complex and tragic figure if she is read from the familiar perspective of western literary representation of character. But we must also recognize that within a different 'world view', that of the Tamil classical epoch, roles are prescribed for human beings by social expectation and divine arrangement (duty and fate). We see this in the comparison of Kannaki's action with that of another good wife's reaction to her husband's death. Kannaki's reproaches had shamed the king of Madurai so keenly that he died of heartbreak. His queen then, 'unable to bear her sorrow ... died, saying: "I must follow my king."' The question is posed: 'A virtuous woman lost her life because her husband died. Another wandered in anger through our kingdom. ... [I]n your judgement, which one should we admire?' And the answer is that while both are great, the queen wins her rewards in heaven, but Kannaki has become 'a new goddess of Faithfulness' who will be 'forever honored' here, in this kingdom (p. 158).[45]

The queen's death is a manifestation of sati, while Kannaki's curse is an expression of *shakti*, the powerful, ferocious, feminine cosmic principle. But it is the excess of sati, the ascetic virtue of good wifehood, that is converted into *shakti*.[46] These two generally opposed aspects of femininity in Hindu representations of the goddesses are linked in Kannaki, indicating that the source of feminine power lies in the virtue accumulated as a good wife.[47] And yet to envisage that such virtue can prove excessive – can overflow the domestic, conjugal relationship into the realms of history and polity – is to give another dimension to 'good wifehood'. In Kannaki's case 'the woman who burns' has more than one meaning.

If we seek a more radical repudiation of the entire syndrome of 'good wifehood' of which the act of sati is only an item, we shall find it in the lives and works of the women *Bhakta* poets of India.[48] These women – saints, mystics, poets – had to make life-choices: their devotion to god came into conflict with their sexuality and with the life of domesticity, both of which were normally regulated by the institution of marriage. They resolved this conflict by either bypassing marriage altogether, or, once married, opting out of marital commitment.[49] Here too we must be careful not to read their poetry as feminist credos. The ideological structure of the man–woman relationship is not itself displaced; the god of these women poets is male, cast as lover, husband, father, or child, frequently indeed the first two, so that a highly eroticized idiom is brought into play.[50] Nevertheless, as Madhu Kishwar has pointed out, *bhakti* did make a 'social space' available for women who 'outrageously defied what are ordinarily considered the fundamental tenets of *stri dharma* [women's duty] – marriage and motherhood'.[51]

The foregoing comparative exercise has not been substantial enough to prove absolute differences between two structures of representation, the one indigenous, the other characterized as colonial/postcolonial or British/European; still less does it seek to establish the superiority of one over the other.[52] The absence of any gendered perspective, and the ultimately deterministic framework of 'choice' in precolonial representations of women, prevent any easy sentimentalization of the indigenous cultures. On the other hand, the colonial perception of a collective gendered identity for the women who die sharply contradicts a focus on the individual female subject, the sati, who is framed for scrutiny.

The identification of differences serves to indicate only the newness of the discursive terrain explored by colonial rulers in response to new ideological pressures. In this discourse death came to define women's behaviour, not descriptively – as male heroism, martyrdom, or suicide do – but absolutely; the subject of sati came into being as the absent (dead) subject. But, of course, beyond the woman's death-in-life (burning alive) lay life-in-death, the (re)construction of her subjectivity: it is this paradox that I have tried to uncover in this chapter.

NOTES

I am grateful to Tejaswini Niranjana, Uma Chakravarty, and Kamala Visweswaran for their attempts to save me from errors, ambiguities and mistakes of fact and interpretation in this chapter. Those that still remain are my own responsibility. Grateful thanks also to Sarah Goodwin and Elisabeth Bronfen for their editorial guidance. This essay also appears in Sarah Webster Goodwin and Elisabeth Bronfen, eds, *Departures: Death and Representation*, Baltimore, Johns Hopkins University Press, 1993.

1 'Sati' is the self-immolation of a Hindu widow along with the corpse of her husband. The word is used here to refer both to the practice and to the widow who performs it.

2 The texts are, for the most part, narratives of various kinds, tales, long poems, short stories, novels, epics and a film. I am interested in the way narrative structures encode ideologemes, and, conversely, in the way ideological structures are accommodated within and expressed through narrative paradigms. See Fredric Jameson, *The Political Unconscious*, Ithaca, Cornell University Press, 1981, pp. 76, 87–8. There is an interesting argument here about the differences among the narrative genres in the production of specific ideological constructs, but I have allowed it to remain implicit.

3 Lata Mani has argued for the emergence of a specifically colonial discourse on sati. See 'Production of an Official Discourse on *Sati* in Early Nineteenth Century Bengal', *Economic and Political Weekly* 21.7, Review of Women Studies, 26 April 1986, pp. 32–40, esp. p. 32.

4 Robert Southey's *The Curse of Kehama* (1810), a poem now little read, but influential in its own day as the precursor of the exotic 'Eastern tale' made popular by the younger Romantics (especially Byron and Moore), represents the clearing of the ground for such intervention, at a time when the East India Company was engaged in large-scale territorialization in India. It narrates the story of Kehama, a despotic

REAL AND IMAGINED WOMEN

Indian prince who represents the debasement of Hindu rule. Two vivid set-pieces are provided to illustrate his unfitness to rule: the first, a scene where the victims are two young and beautiful Hindu princesses about to die with an old king, their husband; the second, a court scene where the king curses a peasant to a life of perpetual suffering. Thus a certain 'Hinduism', with the spectacular inequities of its class, caste and gender relations, provided the necessary pretext for the overthrow of 'native' rule; and Southey's poem creates the picturesque and narrative version of such cultural and civilizational decay.

5 Gayatri Chakravorty Spivak, 'Can the Subaltern Speak? Speculations on Widow-Sacrifice', *Wedge* 7–8, Winter/Spring 1985, pp. 120–30, esp. p. 121.

6 See, for instance, Roger Boase, *The Origin and Meaning of Courtly Love*, Totowa, NJ, Rowman and Littlefield, 1977; and Larry D. Benson, *Malory's Morte d'Arthur*, Cambridge, MA, Harvard University Press, 1976.

7 Often such acts involved big-game hunting. The most complex exposition of this 'white man's burden' is found in George Orwell's 'Shooting an Elephant'. See *Shooting an Elephant and Other Essays*, London, Martin Secker & Warburg, 1945.

8 My point will be clearer if I make a distinction between colonial self-representation and earlier interventions in the practice of sati in Islamic India. Muslim rulers had regarded sati as suicide and hence as illegal according to the *Sharia* (the Muslim code), but permitted it to Hindu women. The Moghul ruler Akbar took a strong stand against forcibly burning women, and passed an ordinance to prevent such deaths. According to contemporary historians, Akbar personally intervened to rescue a Rajput princess, widow of his friend Jai Mall, who refused to die as a sati. But her son Udai Singh forced her onto the pyre; Akbar sent his agents, who saved her when the pile was already lighted, and seized Udai Singh. See Romila Thapar, *History of India*, vol. I, Harmondsworth, Penguin, 1966, p. 292; G.B. Malleson, *The Emperor Akbar and the Rise of the Mughal Empire*, Delhi, Sunita Publications, 1986, pp. 164–6. The point is that the prohibition of sati did not become a strategic political move, and hence did not feature in the Moghals' self- and other-representation of the Islamic and Hindu communities. Sumit Sarkar has commented on the 'secularism, rationalism and non-conformity ... of pre-British Muslim ruled India', within which the issue of sati could be raised. See 'Rammohan Roy and the Break with the Past', in V.C. Joshi, ed., *Rammohan Roy and the Process of Modernization in India*, New Delhi, Vikas, 1975, p. 53.

9 Colonial historians like Edward Thompson could declare that, after the abolition of sati in British India, 'a practice which had caused the sacrifice of many hundreds of women annually was driven into the Native States'. Henry Laurence, the British Agent in Rajputana, boasted, in 1854, of effective law-enforcement even in the princely states, especially those under strong British supervision. See *The Reconstruction of India*, Delhi, Kaushal Rakashan, 1985, pp. 26, 28–9.

10 In Conrad's novella, in contrast, Kurtz is unredeemable. Not only is he guilty of 'unspeakable rites', but he also has a native woman.

11 M.M. Kaye, *The Far Pavilions*, 2 vols, New York, St Martin's Press, 1978, p. 618. All references are to this edition, and page numbers are indicated in parentheses within the text.

12 The after-life of the rescued widow remains vague. However, in both books the heroines have some European blood/education, a great deal of predisposition to adapt to European ways, and sufficient Eastern acquiescence to ensure that the new partnership will work.

13 See Mani, 'Production of an Official Discourse', for the establishment of such a view, esp. p. 32.

14 *The Bombay Times and Journal of Commerce*, date not given; reprinted in *The Times Magazine*, November–December 1988, p. 13.

15 See Lata Mani, 'Contentious Traditions: The Debate on SATI in Colonial India', *Cultural Critique* 7, Fall 1987, pp. 119–56; Mani points out that in annual reports of sati, 'women were cast as either pathetic or heroic victims'. In the former instance they were seen to be 'dominated by Hindu men', in the latter they were considered to be 'victimized by religion' (p. 129).

16 See Kumkum Sangari, 'What Makes a Text Literary?', paper delivered at a conference on English Studies in India at Miranda House, Delhi University, in April 1988.

17 Charles Dickens, *Dombey and Son*, Harmondsworth, Penguin, 1970, p. 704. All references are to this edition.

18 Susan makes the terms of her loyalty explicit: 'I take no merit for my service of twelve years, for I love her ... but true and faithful service gives me right to speak I hope' (p. 703).

19 Nancy Paxton, 'Unma(s)king the Colonial Subject: Subjectivity and the Female Body in the Novels of Flora Annie Steel and Anita Desai', paper presented at the MLA Convention, 1988. I am grateful to Nancy Paxton for making this paper available to me.

20 'Three Women's Texts and a Critique of Imperialism', *Critical Inquiry* 12.1, Autumn 1985, pp. 243–61, esp. p. 244. All page references to further quotations from this essay are indicated in the text.

21 Ashis Nandy, 'Sati: A Nineteenth Century Tale of Women, Violence and Protest,' in *At the Edge of Psychology*, New Delhi, Oxford University Press, 1982, pp. 7–8.

22 *The Fakeer* is closest in plot outline to Walter Scott's ballad 'Lochinvar'. In both, a dashing outlaw rescues his mistress dramatically in the nick of time. The differences – between death and marriage – are, of course, significant, but their elision even more so. See *Poems of Henry Louis Vivan Derozio: A Forgotten Anglo-Indian Poet* with an Introduction by F.B. Bradley-Birt and a new foreword by R.K. Das Gupta, New Delhi, Oxford University Press, 1980.

23 'Saved' is included in a collection, *Mashi and Other Stories*, Delhi, Macmillan, 1918. This quotation appears on p. 210. All further quotations are from this edition.

24 Among these, Nandy's essay, cited above, is an important one.

25 A slightly different version of this analysis of *Antarjali Jatra* appears in my 'Subject of Sati', *The Yale Journal of Criticism* 3.2, Spring 1990, pp. 1–28, included in this volume, pp. 15–39.

26 In addition to the works already cited, see also Gayatri Spivak, 'The Rani of Sirmur: An Essay in Reading the Archives', *History and Theory* 24.3, 1987, pp. 247–72.

27 Mani, 'The Production of an official Discourse', pp. 32–3.

28 Ibid., p. 32

29 Ibid., p. 34.

30 This paragraph summarizes part of Mani's long and intricate argument in 'The Production of an Official Discourse'.

31 Spivak, 'Can the Subaltern Speak?' p. 123.

32 Spivak, 'The Rani of Sirmur', p. 263.

33 Spivak, 'Can the Subaltern Speak?' p. 122.

34 Mani, 'Contentious Traditions', pp. 152–3.

35 Spivak, 'Can the Subaltern Speak?' p. 122.

36 These are only the implicit and perhaps merely logical corollaries of their theoretical positions. But they are given significant emphasis precisely through the disavowals they issue (such disavowals must surely be gratuitous, given the transparency of their political commitments): 'this criticism of the absence of women's subjectivity in colonial accounts is not to argue either that women died voluntarily or that I in any way endorse *sati*. From my perspective, the practice was and remains indefensible' (Mani, 'Contentious Traditions', p. 130); 'it should therefore be understood that the

example I discuss ... is in no weay a plea for some violent Hindu sisterhood of self-destruction' (Spivak, 'Can the Subaltern Speak?' p. 129).

37 Mani, 'Contentious Traditions', p. 152.

38 Spivak, 'Can the Subaltern Speak?' pp. 125–6.

39 Mani, 'Contentious Traditions', p. 130.

40 Spivak, 'The Rani of Sirmur', pp. 270–1.

41 The observation is made by Benita Parry, 'Problems in Current Theories of Colonial Discourse', *Oxford Literary Review* 9.1–2, 1987, pp. 27–58, esp. p. 35.

42 According to legend, Sati is so distressed by the exclusion of her husband, the god Shiva, from her father's court, that she dies. Shiva dances the *tandava* (the dance of destruction) with Sati's corpse carried on his shoulder. In the *Ramayana* Sita, wife of Rama, has to undergo an ordeal by fire in order to establish her chastity after she is rescued from Ravana, who had abducted her.

43 Romila Thapar comments on the status of women at various periods. Their changing features have to be understood within a specific historical context. For example, in the early Aryan civilization, she argues, 'the position of women was on the whole free' (pp. 40–1). Sati was only a symbolic act, and the remarriage of widows was common. But in a later age, from about AD 300 to 700, women developed 'a distinctly subordinate position' (p. 151). The practice of widow-burning appears to have begun at this time. The only women who had 'a large measure of freedom' were those 'who deliberately chose to opt out of ... the "normal" activities of a woman,' and became Buddhist nuns, or actresses, courtesans, or prostitutes (p. 152). Feudalism in the Rajput states (from about AD 800 to 1200) led to the glorification of military virtues, so that 'women ... were taught to admire men who fought well', and were themselves expected to commit sati when their husbands died (p. 247). During Muslim rule, from the thirteenth to the sixteenth centuries, the position of both Hindu and Muslim women of all classes was an inferior one (pp. 301–2). Women's seclusion (purdah) was the normal custom. There thus seems to be little grounds for celebrating the status of precolonial women – at least without careful qualification.

44 I have used a translation by Alain Danielou (New York, New Directions, 1965). According to Danielou's note (pp. 207–8), the Preamble is considered by the ancient commentators not to be part of the original text but a later addition. All references are to this edition.

45 The differences between the queen's passive behaviour and Kannaki's active response are, of course, functions of their class positions. The *Shilappaddikaram* presents a vivid picture of the wealth, power and aspirations of the rising mercantile class, of which Kovalan and Kannaki are members.

46 See Veena Das, 'Shakti Versus Sati: A Reading of the Santoshi Ma Cult', *Manushi* 49, November–December 1988, pp. 26–30, esp. p. 28.

47 Kannaki has been shown to be a 'good wife' in the first half of the book; she forgives Kovalan for his desertion of her, makes him a gift of her gold anklet to be sold, and uncomplainingly accepts the hardships of the journey to Madurai and of poverty with him.

48 *Bhakti* is a religious devotion which signals a different, more personalized and intimate, relation between the devotee and his or her god; the members of the cult were often, though not always, women, peasants, artisans, or untouchables. The movement began in the fifth or sixth century AD in the Tamil kingdom, and continued for well over a thousand years, spreading from region to region throughout the country. I am indebted to a special issue of *Manushi* 50–2, January–June 1989, on women *Bhakta* poets, for information contained in this paragraph; especially to articles by Madhu Kishwar, 'Introduction', pp. 3–8; A.K. Ramanujan, 'Talking to God in the Mother Tongue', pp. 9–17; and Uma Chakravarty, 'The World of the Bhaktin in South Indian Traditions: The Body and Beyond', pp. 18–29.

49 Chakravarty, 'The World of the Bhaktin', pp. 18–29. The Kannada poet Akka Mahadevi (twelfth century AD) writes:

> So my lord, white as jasmine, is my husband
> Take these husbands who die, decay,
> and feed them
> to your kitchen fires!
> (Trans. by A.K. Ramanujan, *Speaking of Siva*, Harmondsworth, Penguin, 1985)

And Mira, the Rajput princess-poet (sixteenth century) asserts:

> I will sing of Girdhar [the lord Krishna]
> I will not be a sati.

50 See Ramanujan, 'Talking to God', p. 14.
51 Kishwar, 'Introduction', p. 6.
52 My omission of any texts of Islamic India from this analysis reflects only the constraints of length and inadequacies of scholarship; it is not intended to exempt this period from colonial prehistory. Gauri Viswanathan has pointed out that in 'the relativized domain of history', where differences are attributed to 'the effect of historical change and movement', 'concepts like absolute truth have no place' – instead 'there is only formation, process, and flux'. See *Masks of Conquest: Literary Study and British Rule in India*, New York, Columbia University Press, 1989, p. 97. This of course does not prevent the diagnosis of the political imperatives underlying ideological constructs. In other words, my method offers an explanatory model.

3

LIFE AFTER RAPE
Narrative, rape and feminism

I

Texts lie not outside the circuit of sexual politics but implicated in them. It is this mode of implication, particularly as it results in the constitution of the sexed subject, that the feminist critical method uncovers. My investigation in this chapter bears on the issue of the raped woman as the subject *of* narrative and *in* feminism since rape is a term central to the poetics of narrative as well as a crucial area of feminist politics. How are rape, narrative structure and feminist politics imbricated? How may we contest the claims of universal/global validity advanced by feminists and narrative theorists on the grounds of rape/desire? A comparative approach, by indicating the historical and specifically contextual limits within which the terms operate in their mutually constitutive roles, serves as an empirical check and a reference point.

My exemplary text is 'Prison' (1984), a short story in Tamil by Anuradha Ramanan, which quickly and ironically plots the narrative of a raped Brahmin (upper-caste) woman. By setting up this 'third world' woman's text as a model against which the master-texts of 'first world' literature and their criticism can be measured, I exploit the resources of the comparative method. I invoke two canonical English novels, *Clarissa* (1748) and *A Passage to India* (1924), whose central episodes turn on the rape of the female protagonist. I also selectively draw upon Maya Angelou's *I Know why the Caged Bird Sings* (1971), Alice Walker's novel *The Color Purple* (1982), and Jonathan Caplan's film, *The Accused* (1988), to serve as representative contemporary American 'feminist' narratives of rape. The texts I choose are deliberately heterogeneous, occupying different historical, cultural, racial and gendered locations. This heterogeneity fosters the exploration of difference and sameness within a broad thematic, the representation of rape/the raped woman as the subject of narrative, and the different politics that they engender within feminism. In the concluding section, I draw together these scattered observations on the texts of rape to relocate it within the politics of feminism.

II

Anuradha Ramanan is a prolific writer of fiction, both short stories and novels, for popular mass-circulation Tamil magazines (published mainly in the state of Tamil Nadu, in South India). 'Prison' first appeared in one of these magazines, *Ananda Vikatan*, in 1984, as the prize-winning entry in a short story competition; it was subsequently filmed, and then included in an anthology of Ramanan's short stories.

'Prison' is a post-rape narrative concerned to show how the female protagonist, Bhagirathi, survives the fear and humiliation of her rape by a stranger and her subsequent abandonment by her husband. Bhagirathi comes to a small village in Tamil Nadu as the 18-year-old bride of the temple priest Raghupathi. She catches the eye of Anthony, the rich and rakish village landlord, who immediately plots to catch her alone. The story begins with his easy, insolent rape of Bhagirathi, in broad daylight, at a time when the priest is offering prayers at the temple.

Bhagirathi, shocked and frightened, seeks her husband's protection. He spurns her in anger, and walks out of the house, never to return. Bhagirathi wanders the streets, becomes a byword as a fallen woman.

She then comes to a decision. She goes to Anthony's house, announces that she is going to live there, and forbids him to touch her again even though he has already raped her once. Anthony is stunned and remorseful. At her insistence, he arranges for her to have her own living quarters and her own cooking utensils. After some years he remonstrates with her at her confined existence, and offers to find her husband for her. She mocks his naivety, and insists that he too must share her punishment – her continued presence in his house will be his bane.

They spend thirty years in this fashion, living in the same house, hardly talking to each other. She proudly goes every day to the river to fetch her own water, braving the villagers' taunts. Anthony leaves more and more of the management of his lands to her, and she is meticulous in her dealings. He is a Christian, and she a Brahmin. But she places flowers every day at his shrine of the Virgin Mary. Her presence in his house inhibits his drinking and womanizing.

Finally, Anthony lies ill. When he goes into a fit of coughing and gropes for a basin to spit into – there is no attendant – Bhagirathi hears him and offers him the basin, speaking her first direct words to him in all their years together. He is moved at her offer of service but considers himself unworthy of her attentions.

Anthony dies shortly thereafter. He has left her his house and enough money to live on comfortably. The rest of his wealth goes to orphanages. At his death, Bhagirathi realizes that he has cared more for her than the husband who made his marriage vows to her. She takes off her *thali* (the symbol of marriage worn round the neck), and places it on the butt of Anthony's gun. Better to live as the widow of Anthony than the wife of Raghupathi, she decides. She lies down weeping, to mourn him.

The question that irresistibly offers itself is: what impels Bhagirathi's social and sexual rebellion? If I choose to read 'Prison' as a feminist text it is in spite of a complete absence in the story of any feminist 'solution' to the issue of rape. Among the possibilities that the story ranges over on behalf of Bhagirathi – her vagrancy, her suicide, her return to her rapist, or her reclamation by her husband – there is, on the contrary, not even a suggestion of recourse to women's groups and their strategies of resistance. Ramanan does not consider that an activist women's group might have provided Bhagirathi with legal aid so that she might prosecute her rapist or seek out her husband to claim maintenance from him.[1] Nevertheless, a certain feminism (here, western liberalism and a 'liberated' sexual code) is implied in any attack on religious orthodoxy in the Indian social context. In this situation, Ramanan gives the initiative and resources for coping entirely to Bhagirathi though she is a product of a culture that largely negates any meritocratic individualism and envisages an entirely subordinate role for women. Needless to add, Bhagirathi's rebellious celibacy has little to do with modern sexual liberation. But destitute and socially outcast though she is, Bhagirathi still retains her identity as a superior caste-subject, and deploys it to intimidate her rapist, first into accepting her in his house, and then into leading a life of chastity with her.

There are two ironies here. The first is that a Brahmin is male by definition; a Brahmin woman is neither formally initiated into the rites of castehood, nor does she follow any separate practices of Brahminhood except as they relate to her connection with the male Brahmin. A Brahmin is born into his caste, a Brahmin woman is born his daughter. 'Brahmin woman' is a derived identity.

The second irony is that in today's Tamil Nadu, Brahminism has been stripped of virtually all its traditional material and political claims to power – the religious supremacy of the priesthood, and its monopoly over learning – in large part due to a vigorous Dravidian (non-Aryan) political and cultural movement in this century.[2]

Yet it is through laying claim to one of the standard practices of Brahminism – ritual purity – that Bhagirathi secures her safety. On the grounds that she would be contaminated otherwise, she commands her own living quarters and her own cooking utensils, and fetches her own water. She cows Anthony, more powerful than her in every other way, by asserting her superior caste-status. The semiotics of purity bear further scrutiny. We notice how within this situation Bhagirathi invokes one standard of purity (caste) to modify or displace another (female sexuality), by claiming for the former higher validity and broader social import. Taking into account the complexity of the social procedures by which both caste and female chastity are invested with power, Bhagirathi plays off one against the other.

Why and how does her strategy work? The most important of the reasons is the supremacy that 'Brahminism' as a cultural and ideological value still retains in contemporary Tamil Nadu. In spite of successfully curbing institutional

Brahmin influence in the region, the Dravidian political parties have not successfully forged a counter-culture. Their early ideological struggles for atheistic rationalism and a reformist language policy aimed at de-Sanskritizing the Tamil language, have in recent years largely lost their force. The upward class- and caste-mobility of non-Brahmin groups has instead been directed towards, precisely, Sanskritization.[3]

But where is the locus of these superior values? Not in the Brahmin male, marginalized in the economic and political spheres: it is precisely his emasculation that the rape of his wife emphasizes. Instead the Brahmin woman now assumes and deploys 'Brahmin' values in the context of an identity crisis. The separation, in 'Prison', of ideological value from political/economic power, and its correspondence to the separation of the Brahmin woman from the Brahmin male, dramatizes a crucial historical warp.[4] A realignment of gender positions is inscribed via the crisis in caste identity.

I wish to emphasize that only the configuration of Brahminism and femininity at this specific historical juncture allows Ramanan to grant Bhagirathi access to the power of asserting caste-status. Nothing in the traditional content of Brahminism – or Hinduism, broadly – would encourage Bhagirathi's negotiation with her sexual violation in this way. She ironically recalls the legendary figures of Ahalya and Sita from Hindu mythology, women raped or abducted, who are forced to establish their chastity through miraculous tests or prolonged ordeals.[5] As traditional narrative models, these legends propose purification for the violated woman through symbolic death (transformation into a stone, passage through fire) to resolve the crisis of rape or attempted rape. The social imposition of tests/ordeals through which women must pass in order to qualify for their re-entry into 'society' gives Bhagirathi no reason to suppose that she can defy sexual mores with impunity.

Nevertheless, the 'rewards' of these processes of sexual violation–test/ordeal– survival are great for the women who undergo them. Ahalya and Sita become triumphant and enduring cultural symbols of *pativrata*, or husband-worship; their legendary and heroic chastity has retained a powerful ideological hold on the Hindu imagination. Thus, in a narrative that is structured as a series of escalating shocks aimed at the Hindu bourgeoisie – first the woman's return to her rapist, then the Brahmin woman's cohabitation with a lower-caste Christian – the greatest blow lies in the story's ending, when Bhagirathi blasphemes *pativrata* by casting off her *thali* (her symbol of marriage) and drapes it over the butt of Anthony's gun (an equally transparent symbol of physical and sexual power).[6] Confounding marriage and rape, she sees marriage as a prolonged sexual domination by the male, and rape as a momentary violent aberration, but both as compensated by, and entailing, the man's responsibility for the woman. The familiar and somewhat clichéd polemic against sexual double standards also involves her in a more complex judgement of the two men: 'The man who lived with me for six months cast me off in an instant. And here is this man who committed a moment's folly, and has cherished me ever since without any

67

expectation of return . . .!' As long as the identity of 'wife' allows her to maintain also the identity of 'Brahmin woman' and thus create a zone of safety, she holds on to it. But with Anthony's death she can repudiate this identity and become 'Anthony's widow', a woman without a man. Wife/widow, Brahmin/not-Brahmin, protection/autonomy are alternating and opposed states and identities that Bhagirathi adopts as circumstances warrant them, with the goal, at one level, of mere survival, but at another that of social interrogation and critique as well.

Bhagirathi's foregrounding and deployment of her caste and marital identities are not, however, built upon a transcendence or obliteration of Anthony's sexual violation of her. Instead Bhagirathi presents herself to Anthony *as* the woman he has raped:

> The woman who stood before him gazing so fiercely . . . was that a woman's gaze . . . how was it that he hadn't fallen before it earlier? . . . No woman he had raped had ever come to stand at his door like this before, with a gaze that pierced like a spear.

Within Ramanan's frame, the female victim of rape-narrative becomes the subject of a second narrative, scripted by her, that escapes past models offered by male narratives ('no woman . . . had ever . . .'). Bhagirathi never allows Anthony to forget that the defining act of their relationship is his rape. Her insistent thrusting of her fallen status upon Anthony results in that foregrounding of the 'sexual differential' that Gayatri Spivak has emphasized in her discussion of the raped woman, the eponymous protagonist of the story 'Draupadi': an act that turns her for her enemy into a 'powerful "subject"', 'a terrifying superobject'.[7]

The identity of a 'raped woman' that Bhagirathi embraces is not based, it must be emphasized, upon a conventional acceptance of the *loss* of chastity, and thereby the diminution of 'full' womanhood. Ramanan allows Bhagirathi to make an appropriative, revisionary reading of the religious texts of Hinduism to apply to her situation. When Raghupathy, the priest, returns home from the temple, he is murmuring the opening invocation from the *Upanishads*:

> Purnam adah, Purnam idam, purnat purnam udacyate
> Purnasya purnam adaya purnam evavasisyate.
>
> (That is full and this is full.
> Out of that eternal whole
> Springs forth this eternal whole
> And when the whole is taken from the whole,
> There still remains the complete whole.)[8]

This description of Godhead as a metaphysical plenitude is taken by Ramanan as a description of human, including female, selfhood; and she finds sanction in it to repudiate the metonymic social definition of chastity as a woman's precarious 'possession' that can be lost, or as a 'component' of sexual integrity.[9]

Though the identity that Bhagirathi retains/adopts after her rape – as superior caste-subject, as another man's wife, as raped woman – is achieved within the subject-constitutive boundaries of her religion and culture, there is room for her to grow, improvise and assert herself within the 'prison'. One instance of this is her daily act of placing flowers at the feet of Anthony's statue of the Virgin Mary – and whether this is construed as an act of worship, a gesture of female solidarity, or a dignified concession to and recognition of Anthony's god, it is a deliberate and freely performed action. Another space of development is her growth into the role of manager of his property. Though not by her own calculation – it is Anthony who delegates power to her – she comes to handle all the produce and sale of his land; and when he dies she inherits part of his wealth. This inheritance is ultimately what prevents Anthony's death from becoming a second abandonment. She is compensated for her loss of social and caste status by acquiring economic power – as, precisely, 'Anthony's widow'.

Anthony's role in the 'charade' is not played only in response to the rules set by her; his is an active reformation whose model comes from his own religion. A strong if sentimental sense of sin leads him to piety, penance and charity. His celibacy is dictated by his characteristic conversion of the woman he has raped into the sexless maternal figure, the type of the Virgin Mary. Bhagirathi's relationship to the Virgin is not, of course, one of identity. The Hindu models of female chastity available to her are, as pointed out earlier, not sexless figures but heroic and 'innocent' married women. The dialectic between two sets of religious values, Hindu and Christian, as mediated by their norms of female purity, is a complex one here. Anthony's Christianity, we must note, is also encoded by Ramanan in social, as opposed to merely religious, terms. Indian Christians, especially in rural South India, are for the most part converts from lower-caste Hindu groups. Ramanan tacitly reinforces the stereotype of the rapacity of their 'original' caste identity (as non-Brahmin men), even while she grants them the 'redeeming' values of their new religious identity (as Christian men).[10]

It is clear that the ideological structures that the story both operates within and strains against, in its construction of the raped woman as subject, are shaped by the realities of its social, religious and cultural limits: but included in these realities is a certain liberalizing, modernizing discourse of 'feminism'.

There is a danger, in both story and criticism, of idealizing Bhagirathi's feminist individualism.[11] Her choices cannot be *themselves* valorized as feminist: as a destitute woman, she seeks not independence but male protection; when she repudiates her identity as Raghupathy's wife it is only to take on the designation of 'Anthony's widow'; she enforces Anthony's chaste behaviour towards her only at the cost of laying waste her own sexual life;[12] above all, she succeeds in securing her safety and purity only by entering a 'prison', as Anthony ruefully points out.

Ramanan explores the concept of the 'prison' creatively. Sociologists have observed that Indian women experience social space 'in such binary oppositions as private/public, danger/safety, pure/polluted'.[13] Ramanan deconstructs these oppositions by blurring spatial designations. Bhagirathi is raped in a 'safe' place, her home – paradoxically no place is considered more safe than a house whose doors stay open – which Anthony enters 'as if he owned it'. Bhagirathi herself is caught napping, 'her head pillowed on the threshold', and it is at the threshold that Anthony 'looms'. The threshold is, of course, the open space that confounds the inside of the house with the outside. After her rape, Bhagirathi is, literally, errant, a homeless woman forced to spend the nights in the porch of her husband's locked house, or the temple courtyard – spaces which are both within and without enclosures, marking her own indeterminate subject-status. The people of the village pronounce her a vagrant, a woman 'of the streets', that terrifying, ejected, antisocial female element, a bogey for 'good' girls.

The discourse of crime and punishment invariably foregrounds the concept of the 'prison' as the incarceration of the individual wrongdoer in the interests of the larger social good. But Bhagirathi's entry into purdah does not fit into this moral scheme – her re-entry into the domestic sphere is performed as an act of violent intrusion, not one of discreet disappearance. Her occupation of the woman's space that is designated purdah, or the inner rooms, is a form of territorial conquest. Purdah, in certain western feminist analyses, has been equated with 'rape, forced prostitution, polygamy, genital mutilation, pornography, the beating of girls and women', as instances of 'violations of basic human rights'.[14] But in such analyses, as Chandra Mohanty has argued, 'the institution of purdah is ... denied any cultural and historical specificity, and contradictions and potentially subversive aspects of the institution are totally ruled out.'[15] In 'Prison' the experience of purdah is precisely rewritten in terms of its 'contradictions and ... subversive aspects'. Segregation works both ways: Bhagirathi's occupation of the inner rooms confines Anthony to the hall – for her only a passage of transit (just as her expulsion from her husband's house has meant also his disappearance into a perpetual diaspora). Bhagirathi's entry into Anthony's house is a parody of his entry into hers.

Further, Bhagirathi refuses literal imprisonment, risking public exposure every day by going to the river to fetch water. Here Ramanan plays the private/public opposition into narrative and subject-constitutive areas as well. Bhagirathi becomes a public figure in the small village community, is ironically referred to as Anthony's 'woman', and is made the subject of ribald speculation and rumour. What remains a private matter is the truth, the chaste relationship of the man and woman. In the modern female *Bildungsroman*, the development of an individualistic female selfhood – as the example of Hawthorne's Hester Prynne so dramatically represents – builds upon such a polarity of private integrity and public opprobrium.[16] When a woman's consciousness of individualistic identity is forced into existence through social isolation brought on by the stigma of sexual impropriety – as a Bhagirathi's or a Hester Prynne's is – it stands in contrast to the politics of feminism. Terry Eagleton has confidently asserted, for instance, that 'a modern Clarissa would not need to die' because of the access she would (presumably) have to the help that women's groups would extend to her.[17] Victimhood, in such an argument, also provides the female subject with access to a sense of collective gendered identity based upon a shared oppression. In the absence of such organized resistance – and I have pointed out how Ramanan rules out such a solution within the terms of the narrative's discourse (its setting in a small rural community, in an unspecified past time, makes this entirely 'natural') – a tenuous individualism shapes the female subject's resistance. Ideally, this selfhood constitutes for the female subject existential freedom, space for growth and change, a full 'inner life', and some access to power, even if it ends as a costly or self-defeating venture. Clearly, the exercise of choice cannot be a sufficient condition of a woman's freedom when her choices are both limited and severely determined.

I have therefore tried to show how the female protagonist of this Tamil short story must both deploy her 'superior' identity as Brahmin woman and foreground her abject destiny as raped woman; how she is complicitous in a politics of caste as well as isolated by the brute reality of rape; how she *chooses* her prison as well as chooses a *prison*. The claims of a certain 'realism' do not permit more than this even-handed distribution of gains and losses for the oppressed female subject within the short story's narrative mode. Nevertheless, the politics of the story – its irony towards and polemic against sexual morality, its overt purpose to *épater le bourgeoisie* – results, inevitably, in a valorization of Bhagirathi's individualistic, even antisocial, will to survive. A feminist critical enterprise is therefore obliged, even while it is constantly aware of the story's balance of forces, to strategically privilege its incipient utopian gesture towards the reclamation of the raped female subject.

III

In Samuel Richardson's *Clarissa* (1748), and E.M. Forster's Λ *Passage to India* (1924), as in 'Prison,' rape serves as the 'allegory' of other political encounters. In *Clarissa*, the main characters are also antagonists in a deadly class struggle; in *A Passage to India* they are racial opponents in the colonial conflict. The female protagonist becomes the victim of rape as much because of her membership of her caste/class/race as because of her sexual identity: we might even say that she is less the object of sexual desire than the scapegoat in a larger struggle of forces.

In the two novels, however, the complex identity that is constructed for the female subject undergoes a curious transformation at the point of rape. Clarissa's cry, 'I am but a cypher', expresses a raped woman's perception of a total annihilation of self following upon the physical subjugation, coercion of will and psychological humiliation that she has been subjected to. Questions of volition, choice and agency, so central to the constitution of the individualistic humanistic subject of the novel, are significantly in abeyance.[18]

Clarissa Harlowe's self-extinction is compensated by her spectacular absorption

71

into her author's sympathies after her rape – figured within the text by the solicitude of her lover's friend Belford, and replicated in critical practice by the partisanship of a host of critics. A heroine so totally taken over by authorial and critical sympathy has no scope, or need, to develop any self-assertive dimension.

In contrast to Richardson's takeover of Clarissa Harlowe there is Forster's fastidious repudiation of Adela Quested after she produces her account of the supposed attack on her. She drops out of the narrative after the event only to reappear much later as a reduced and disoriented witness for the prosecution. Forster's limited interest in Adela Quested is replicated by most critics of the book, in both continents.

For Forster, it is the female *sensibility* (here Mrs Moore's) which has the best chance of developing interpersonal relations in the colonial situation; but because of female *sexuality* (Adela Quested's) these relations can also be jeopardized. The split within femininity between sensibility and sexuality results, interestingly, in the surrogacy of Mrs Moore's function after the Marabar caves episode. Mrs Moore suffers a trauma in the caves very similar to Adela's, falls ill, develops a cynical misogyny, dies and is apotheosized in a series of developments more appropriate to the raped Adela.

The reification of female victimhood is a familiar procedure in the fiction of several male novelists (one has only to think of Hardy's *Tess of the d'Urbervilles*, or Galsworthy's Irene Forsythe in *The Man of Property*). All that is really left for the raped woman to do is to fade away: Adela, doing the 'decent thing', retracts and returns to England; Clarissa, transcending her body's humiliation, falls ill and dies.

Paradoxically, at the same time that she becomes an existential cypher the raped woman also turns into a symbolic cause. She becomes the representative of her social group, the very embodiment of its collective identity. The taking of embattled positions around a raped woman's cause often marks an identity crisis for a group, as historical examples amply prove.[19] The woman's newly recognized identity – which may be more properly described as her function in an economy of sexual propriety and property – becomes an emotional war-cry and the prelude to the virtual disappearance of the concerns of the woman herself. Though Clarissa has been alienated from her family for a long stretch of the novel, once she dies her cousin rushes to avenge her in defence of the family's honour. In *A Passage to India* Forster shows British officialdom and its wives gathering around Adela Quested in an upsurge of sentimental patriotism (which is trivially shifted to the more appropriately symbolic railway official's wife: 'This evening, with her abundant figure and masses of corn-gold hair, she symbolized all that is worth fighting and dying for').[20] Ironically, Adela's project *not* to be an Anglo-Indian results only in the confirmation of her colonial identity, sentimentally acclaimed by her fellow Anglo-Indians and savagely asserted by Forster.

I intend these observations on the subjectification of the raped woman in the two novels to serve as a contrast to the consolidation of the female self in

'Prison'. The successive assumption, deployment and repudiation of superior castehood by Bhagirathi herself, her thrusting of her raped condition upon her rapist, and her determined self-fashioning, indicate the birth and development of feminist individualism in circumstances of necessity and survival.

Though Bhagirathi seeks her solution in terms of what I have called, for convenience, 'feminist individualism', this 'liberation' bears no resemblance, historically, to the individualism of the humanist subject who is at the centre of such western literary genres as tragedy or the novel (cf. King Lear, Hardy's Michael Henchard). We observe how this subject-position, when offered to female protagonists in the novel like Clarissa Harlowe or Adela Quested, breaks down under the assault of rape. Bhagirathi's 'selfhood' is, instead, a 'palimpsest of identities', both constituted and erased by history, so that in the gendered subject, religious, caste, class and sexual attributes are foregrounded in succession according to the exigencies of the situation.[21] Choice and necessity become indistinguishable in such identities-in-flux.

A feminist 'thematics of liberation', as Teresa de Lauretis has cautioned us, is insufficient to counter the force of masculine desire that invests all narrative.[22] This is why feminist texts of rape must also engage in textual strategies to counter narrative determinism. Such negotiations are achieved by and result in alternative structures of narrative.

One means to this end is the structural location of the rape incident at the beginning of a woman's story. Narrative beginnings differentiate closures. In 'Prison' the position of the rape scene at the beginning pre-empts expectation of its late(r) occurrence. Not only is the scene of rape diminished by this positioning but it is also granted a more purely functional purpose in the narrative economy, and narrative interest becomes displaced upon what follows. Ramanan is not alone in designating a narrative function to rape as the initiating moment of women's 'knowledge'. In both Alice Walker's *The Color Purple* and Maya Angelou's *I Know why the Caged Bird Sings*, the development of the female subjects' 'self' begins after the rape and occupies the entire length of the narrative.

Further, 'Prison' is marked by a laconic narrative mode through which Ramanan abbreviates an account of thirty years into a few pages, alternating between a terse past-tense narrative of representative, quotidian, routine events and a present-tense account of only four actual exchanges between different pairs of characters. The brevity of the story is itself based upon, and subverts, the recognition that desire is built upon the prolongation of suspense and the postponement of climax. *The Color Purple* is similarly innovative in its narrative devices: it creates generic instability by mixing history with utopian romance through its dependence on both causality and wish fulfilment in its story-telling. As a result, Celie's story, which begins with her rape by her 'father', ends with the restoration of her family, her economic independence and her creation of a community of equals. These endings, as Christine Froula points out, are 'all the more powerful in that they emerge from Celie's seemingly hopeless beginnings': 'Celie's beginning could have been a silent end'; but instead 'her ending continues the proliferating beginnings that the novel captures in its epistolary form, its characters' histories, and the daily revelations that Shug names "God".' A similar liberation is achieved in Angelou's *I Know why the Caged Bird Sings* by means of the framing of a narrative within narrative: the fantasy of the raped child is enclosed within, and her silence 'rescued' by the memoir of the adult writer.[23]

Clarissa, in contrast to 'Prison', develops a relatively short period of time – a matter of a few weeks – into the longest novel in the language, through an excruciatingly realistic transcription of events. In *Clarissa*, as in *A Passage to India*, the moment of rape is made the centre, virtually the exact structural centre, of the narratives, so that the plots describe a graph of climax and anticlimax around that point.[24] Having made the scene of rape central to their structures, the novels cannot altogether avoid on the one hand a certain tension, not unlike sexual titillation, and on the other a certain relaxation of tension, resembling post-coital boredom, around that point. The additional implication of a narrative structure which finds its centre in the representation of rape is that it must then seek a further (post-coital) erotic goal: this, as we shall see, is offered in the 'trials' – the death or disappearance – of the raped woman.

But at the centres of these narratives there is, of course, only absence. Neither novel actually represents the scene of rape, and this only partially for reasons of delicacy or sexual prudery. In his essay on *Clarissa*, Terry Eagleton has argued that rape itself is unrepresentable because 'the "real" of the woman's body' marks 'the outer limit of all language'.[25] This, it appears to me, is part of the male mystique built around rape (as around childbirth). Such narrative theory fetishizes rape as a limit of narrative, to be tested over and over. Eagleton implicitly opposes woman as 'real', or 'nature', to man and language. Richardson offers an ostensibly simpler explanation: neither actor in his epistolary drama, Lovelace or Clarissa, wishes to record the event of rape which – in terms of the psychological verisimilitude the novel is committed to – is natural enough. Wishing to guarantee female purity and absolve male responsibility, Richardson represents Clarissa as drugged, and Lovelace in a frenzy, 'not himself', when the act is perpetrated. It is for these 'reasons' that the act is 'unrepresentable' in this particular text. But so suggestive is this mimetic absence that ingenious critics have even asked whether Clarissa Harlowe was actually raped.[26]

In *A Passage to India*, the authorial reticence about the rape is part of the indeterminacy of meaning, the blur of events by means of which Forster hopes to convey the 'mystery' and 'muddle' of India. So while he accompanies Aziz on his itinerary to the caves closely enough to provide him with an alibi, Adela is left to wander the caves alone. At the end of the 'Caves' section, Fielding makes a weak attempt to ascertain the 'truth', only to be met with Adela's indifferent: 'Let us call it the guide. ... It will never be known. It's as if I ran my finger along that polished wall in the dark, and cannot get further.'[27] The omniscient author so much in evidence elsewhere in the novel to explain matters and settle issues never tells us what 'really' happened. *A Passage to India* pronounces that, virtually and legally at least, no rape was attempted on Adela Quested.

What are the implications of this silence at the heart of the text? *Clarissa* is a great proto-feminist novel, and *A Passage to India* is a major testament of liberal humanism: both, therefore, are works which might be expected to be unequivocal about an act of male sexual aggression against a woman. But their reliance upon, and doubts about, the woman's 'unsupported word' about her ordeal are the symptoms of a deep underlying male fear that rape could be a female lie, or fiction. How a 'normative narrative' may subvert even a feminist 'thematics of liberation'[28] is illustrated by the implications present in Jonathan Kaplan's film, *The Accused*, based upon the true life story of Sarah Tobias's attempt to indict her rapists legally. In an attempt to replicate the court's search to know whether the rape 'really' happened, the film succumbs to the device of the flashback, a device available *only to narrative* (and never to any court of law, however sedulously it may try to recreate the scene of crime). By replaying the scene of rape, it once again makes it central to the narrative, the 'climax' of the graph of its linear structure. If the absence of the scene of rape at the heart of a narrative (as in *Clarissa* or *A Passage to India*) serves to mystify its actual occurrence, the brutal naturalism of its cinematic representation in *The Accused* provides a confirmation that enforces the same conclusion: the 'unsupported word' of a raped woman cannot represent rape.

Rape is often treated as a female fiction or fabrication in another sense as well, one that suggests the complicity of the woman, particularly in social and cultural situations that permit 'free' man–woman relationships based on 'romantic' love. Historically, *Clarissa* reflects a period both marked and supported by changes in familial structures, where marriage based upon the partners' choice was beginning to prevail. *A Passage to India* is the product of a post-war period which witnessed the first major movement in women's sexual liberation and the emergence of the 'emancipated' woman (of whom Adela Quested is the type). Additionally, Clarissa and Adela are involved with men outside their social spheres; the situations are fraught with possibilities of misknowing, mixed signals, wrong timing, false interpretations, and projections of desire. In such changing and historical phases of sexual relationships, sexual consummation may convincingly be represented as the event that is premature and skewed, rather than gratuitous – and, therefore, not 'really' rape.

Female choice itself by association is debased in hypocritical confusion about involuntary desire. Clarissa's self-blame is also based upon the construction of an immutable 'male' nature (the 'brute'), and a 'female' nature (the 'lady'): so that when a woman is raped '... who was most to blame, I pray? The brute, or the lady? The lady, surely! for what she did was out of nature [i.e. she showed fondness for the brute], out of character, at least: what it did was in its own nature.'[29] We are not surprised, either, to find that in *A Passage to India* – in which Aziz indisputably did not rape Adela – Adela should feel an obscure guilt, endorsed by Forster, for a certain sexual laxness on her part towards Aziz, based on no more than her preoccupation with her impending marriage with Ronny, holding hands with Aziz while climbing the rocks, a tactless question to him regarding the number of his wives, and a passing mental admiration of his physical beauty!

In contrast, 'Prison', set in contemporary India, still records a society where marriages are arranged, and where all extramarital relationships between the sexes are inhibited if not entirely prohibited. Anthony's rape of Bhagirathi is a routine exercise of *droit de seigneur*, not the index of a relationship gone awry. Bhagirathi's 'responsibility' lies in allowing herself to have been seen by Anthony, in making a 'spectacle' of herself: 'Foolish Bhagirathi on the first two days had walked to the river four times to fetch water where Anthony was sitting alone on his porch.' The victims of familial rape in *The Color Purple* and *I Know why the Caged Bird Sings* are children, initiated into sexual knowledge by these early encounters, and though they internalize guilt in a complex way they are unequivocally 'innocent'. In both these novels, as in 'Prison', the fact of rape – even if not its graphic representation – is acknowledged in stark, brute terms, as the very premise upon which the narrative is built.

Literary representations of rape have difficulty in avoiding the replication of the act in the very movement of narrative. The fact that the enactment of rape takes place in private and secret places requires the author to conduct his readers into the innermost recesses of physical space. Richardson leads us into the bedchamber of Clarissa Harlowe, Forster into the dark and claustrophobic caves of Marabar. Or as readers we may be located in the space of the 'truth'-seeking spectators in a courtroom, as in *A Passage to India*. The counter-movement of novelistic narrative is precisely this emergence into public light. Having probed the private, the narrative then seeks to make public, to broadcast the privileged knowledge gained by the incursion. The female subject is caught up in this trajectory. It is her transgressive wandering (her 'error' in both senses of the word) that led in the first place to her confinement/imprisonment, the necessary condition of rape. The incarceration is followed by her re-emergence into the public sphere. Richardson narrates the long and elaborate public spectacle of Clarissa's dying, and Forster the public trial of Aziz, which is equally, of course, the trial of Adela. The succession of private ordeal by public display could not be more pronounced and – as raped women have again and again testified – more traumatic. These too are ordeals, trials like those of Ahalya and Sita, that appear to be necessary to absolve the raped subject of 'guilt', and thereby mark her fitness for re-entry into the social or moral domain.

The structuring of private and public fictional spaces; the intrusive, voyeuristic aspect of novel-reading; the pleasure of mastery and possession over the 'passive' text in reading;[30] narrative's very trajectory, its movement towards closure which traverses the feminine as object, obstacle, or space:[31] it is these inscriptions of desire/guilt in narrativity itself which are negotiated in a feminist reconstitution of the female subject of rape. Feminist texts of rape counter narrative determinism, as I have tried to show, in a number of ways: by representing the raped woman as one who becomes a subject *through* rape rather than merely one subjected to its violation; by structuring a post-rape narrative that traces her strategies of survival instead of a rape-centred narrative that privileges chastity and leads inexorably to 'trials' to establish it; by locating the raped woman in structures of oppression other than heterosexual 'romantic' relationships; by literalizing instead of mystifying the representation of rape; and, finally, by counting the cost of rape for its victims in terms more complex than the extinction of female selfhood in death or silence. While I agree that a feminist 'thematics of liberation' may not be a sufficient condition for rewriting the female subject/female reader of narrative, it may nevertheless generate the tensions and contradictions that allow the decentering of male desire and, with it, the sexual thematics that structures much narrative. Therefore the structural motors of narrativity are interrupted and significantly deflected by the forms of feminist individualism dictated by a text's history, ideology and cultural modes.

IV

While rape has been, and continues to be, a central issue in feminism, it is now possible to trace a clear opposition of theoretical positions and politics gathered around it. Literally, rape as the forcible penetration of the female body by the male sexual organ is the expression of male sexual domination and hence of patriarchy itself. Opposition to rape viewed thus – as an irreducible and universal fact of women's oppression – has served as one of the planks of a global feminist movement.

Other feminists have located the issue of rape within a more complex politics, based on the recognition that patriarchy is not the only structure of oppression in society, and that privileges and handicaps are heterogeneous, distributed unevenly among categories of both men and women. Rape figures, as metaphor, as the feared and fantasized possibility in the scenarios of all struggles. Women's sexual vulnerability is heightened by their identity as class/racial subjects. Rape as an act of male sexual violence may be viewed either as the paradigm of all heterosexual relations[32] or as the manifestation of aggression, the index of social lawlessness.[33]

When represented in narrative, these opposed positions, as I have argued, invest rape with different meanings for the female subject. Rape has its own structural figuration *as* narrative when it is read as the culmination of a sequence of events based on heterosexual 'romance', and therefore as the consummation of male sexual *desire*. But viewed as the gratuitous but systematic exercise of male sexual *power*, rape is stripped of the logic of narrative and becomes an isolated and arbitrary act of violence.

These different emphases must be located within different historical and sociological contexts. American feminist politics have grown out of and con-tributed to several significant aspects of social crisis in the west: the questioning of marriage as an institution, the emergence of gay liberation movements, the resistance to the harassment of women in the workplace, the phenomenon of independent single women, and the revelation of widespread child molestation, especially incest. Such radical feminism has naturally tended to call into question the entire issue of 'compulsory heterosexuality'. Typically, while implicating rape within a politics of heterosexuality, American feminism focuses on (the rapist's) individual pathology, and the violation of (the victim's) individual rights.

In India, on the other hand, most cases of reported rapes are instances of what we might call institutional rape, rape perpetrated by members of repressive state forces like the police or the army, or groups like landlords, upon helpless women of the oppressed classes, often when the women are in custody in police cells or bound by contracts of bonded labour. While the women's movement has achieved important gains in reform of rape laws, in this area it has generally followed upon, or worked in alliance with, civil liberties groups and democratic rights organizations.[34] The situation explored in 'Prison' is an imaginative reversal of the most commonly reported type of rape situation in India, the rape of *Harijan* (lower-caste) women by upper-caste landlords. Therefore rape as a phenomenon in contemporary India is more properly understood as the expression of (male) violence – sanctioned by various modes of social power – rather than of sexual desire.

Feminist texts of rape, accordingly, find their emphases differently in these different contexts. If the effect of Ramanan's story was highly cathartic, it was in large part due to the unusual frankness with which she represents female sexuality. For women to 'speak' rape is itself a measure of liberation, a shift from serving as the object of voyeuristic discourse to the occupation of a subject-position as 'master' of narrative.[35]

But sexual liberation is not encoded in the story in the radical and utopian terms offered by, say, *The Color Purple*: as women's relearning of desire and speech through the creation of female community. Instead, we must place 'Prison' in the context of its reception, marked by the popular outcry against its perceived anti-Brahminism, and the threat of state censorship against representing 'sex'.[36] Anything like Warner's absolute distinction between 'real' rape and the 'representation' of rape – persuasively advanced in the context of *Clarissa* and certain other western master-texts, as well as 'popular' genres like romance – breaks down in a historical situation where the literary text and feminist politics are engaged *upon* the same terrain and engage *with* each other through the dialectics of 'representation' and the 'real'.[37]

The critic who brings her own 'native' text, not available within the canon, or even in translation, to a comparative critical enterprise is seemingly a 'native informant' contributing to the 'master discourse'. She runs the danger of exoticizing her wares, or implicitly privileging them as more 'authentic' or more 'real' in content, or idealizing them as an alternative to western cultural aporias, or offering them as a textual 'enigma' that challenges western critical theory or even, broadly, its cognitive structures. I have tried to sidestep some of these dangers by my choice of a popular contemporary magazine story rather than a literary 'classic' as my representative text. My exploration of the text's con-tradictions – its invocation of 'universal' concepts, themes and structures (narrative, rape, feminism), as well as its simultaneous implication in the specific historical conditions of production (contemporary caste-politics, the women's movement in India, religious ideologies) – should lead to its being viewed simply as a demystified cultural *product*. The comparative method must not seek to relativize difference at the expense of denying a commonality of politics and cognitive structures.[38] The 'extreme relativist position', Satya Mohanty has argued, 'is in no way a feasible theoretical basis of politically motivated criticism.' If on the one hand I have relativized the different 'contexts of production of cultural ideas' through the comparative method, I have also sought to promote a 'genuine dialogue' among the feminist positions on the theories of rape and narrative that these different contexts throw up, thus hoping to retain the force of a 'political' criticism.[39]

NOTES

This chapter was originally presented as a paper at a special session on Comparative Feminist Criticism: History and Theory (convened by Margaret Higonnet and Joan Templeton), at the MLA Convention in New Orleans in 1988; and also at the University of California, Santa Cruz. It was subsequently also presented at the Gender Studies forum at Jawaharlal Nehru University, New Delhi. My grateful thanks to participants in all the seminars for their comments. The essay in substantially its present form also appears in a volume of comparative feminist criticism edited by Margaret Higonnet, *Borderwork: Feminist Engagements with Comparative Literature* (Ithaca, Cornell University Press, 1993).

This chapter has been, in some ways, a family affair. My grateful thanks to my mother for bringing 'Prison' to my notice, to my father for locating the book in which it appeared, and to both of them and my husband for information on many aspects of Tamil language, culture and society. I am especially indebted to Anuradha Ramanan for the hours she spent with me. Finally, my gratitude to Margaret Higonnet, friend, mentor and editor, for her support, her example, and more specifically, to the contribution she has made to this essay.

1 Ramanan revealed to me in personal conversation that her purpose in the story was reformist, and that she hoped to establish the need for the rehabilitation of 'fallen' women.

2 Two political parties, the Dravida Munnetra Kazhagam (DMK) and the All India Anna Dravida Munnetra Kazhagam (AIADMK), have emerged from this movement. The anti-Brahmin movement has made its consequence felt largely in the related spheres of education and employment, where massive reservation of places for 'backward' classes and tribes by the Dravidian parties in power has kept Brahmins out of state-run educational institutions, bureaucratic jobs and political appointments. A significant diaspora of Brahmins has occurred with the migration of the community to other states in the country as well as to countries in the west. A Brahmin Association has recently been formed to fight the issue of reservation. Since education and administration have been the traditional, and virtually monopolistic, preserves of the Brahmin community, there is now a severe diminution in its social role and functioning. At the same time Brahmin priesthood is no longer attended with divine

sanction or political influence; Brahmin priests are now only poorly paid performers of temple rituals and private worship in a few households. There is a significant decrease in the numbers of Brahmin men who opt for the priesthood, and consequently in the numbers of traditional Sanskrit institutions for the teaching of the 'vedas', or religious texts.

3 'Sanskritization' is the process of change among caste-groups towards the adoption of upper-caste customs, in areas such as dowry, religious ritual, temple worship, etc.

4 This argument is reinforced by a popular and controversial Tamil film, *Vedam Puthidu* (The New Veda), which articulately and intelligently attacks the caste system. But here too Brahmin values – vegetarianism, ritual purity, Sanskrit learning, non-violence – are valorized, and shown to exert ideological influence. Here the embodiment of such values is the Brahmin (male) child.

5 Ahalya, wife of the sage Gautama, is raped by the god Indra who comes to her in the night in the form of her husband. Turned to stone by her husband's curse, she is restored to human form only years later when the god Rama steps upon the stone. In the epic *Ramayana*, Sita, the wife of Rama, is abducted by the evil king Ravana, and held captive until Rama rescues her. But before she can continue to live with him, public opinion must be satisfied, and she undergoes an ordeal by fire to prove that she has remained chaste.

6 Ramanan's story, and the film based on it, created a great uproar. The Brahmin Association (see n. 2) launched a protest, both at the 'dishonour' of a Brahmin woman being raped, as well as the notion of her repudiating the *thali*. The *thali* is invested with a profound mystique.

7 Gayatri Spivak, 'Draupadi', in Elizabeth Abel, ed., *Writing and Sexual Difference*, Sussex, Harvester, 1982, p. 387.

8 *The Upanishads*, trans. Chitrita Devi, New Delhi, S. Chand & Co., 1973.

9 Ramanan in conversation with me.

10 I am grateful to Ania Loomba (Jawaharlal Nehru University, New Delhi) for pointing this out to me.

11 Some recent feminist essays on texts by cultural 'others' seem to me to idealize feminist individualism as a 'solution' to women's predicament. See, for instance, King-Kok Cheung, '"Don't Tell": Imposed Silences in *The Color Purple* and *The Woman Warrior*', *PMLA* 103, 2 1988, pp. 162–74.

12 Bhagirathi's nature is a passionate one, as Ramanan emphasizes: the cool porcelain figure of the Virgin's statue and the candle that burns dimly before it are contrasts to Bhagirathi's turbulence as she stands before the mirror putting on her *kumkum* (the dot on her forehead): 'the sweet memories ... of her married life ... dissolve in her heart like syrup'.

13 Rashmi Bhatnagar, 'Genre and Gender: A Reading of Tagore's *The Broken Nest* and R.K. Narayan's *The Dark Room*', in Lola Chatterjee, ed., *Woman/Image/Text: Feminist Readings of Literary Texts*, New Delhi, Trianka Publications, 1986, p. 173.

14 Fran Hosken, 'Female Genital Mutilation and Human Rights', *Feminist Issues* 1, 1981, p. 15. Hosken's position is discussed in Chandra Talpade Mohanty, 'Under Western Eyes: Feminist Scholarship and Colonial Discourse', *Boundary* 2, 3, 1984, pp. 333–58.

15 Mohanty, 'Under Western Eyes', p. 347.

16 See *The Scarlet Letter* by Nathaniel Hawthorne. I am grateful to Joan Templeton for bringing this analogy to my attention.

17 Terry Eagleton, *The Rape of Clarissa: Writing, Sexuality and Class Struggle in Samuel Richardson*, Oxford, Blackwell, 1982, p. 94.

18 Though critics have argued that Clarissa's illness, religiosity and death are acts of choice, strategy and covert power, such acts represent, ultimately, as Terry Eagleton

conccdcs, only 'a tragic option for self-extinction'. See ibid., p. 87.

19 See, for instance, the connections traced by Hazel Carby between 'lynching, empire and sexuality', in '"On the Threshold of Women's Era": Lynching, Empire and Sexuality in Black Feminist Theory', *Critical Inquiry* 12, 1985, pp. 262–77.

20 E.M. Forster, *A Passage to India*, New York, Harcourt, 1924, p. 181.

21 For an elaboration of this notion of female subjectivity, see Zakia Pathak and Rajeswari Sunder Rajan, 'Shahbano', in *Signs: Journal of Women in Culture and Society* 14, 3 (Spring 1989), pp. 558–82, esp. p. 573. Reprinted in Micheline R. Malson *et al.*, eds, *Feminist Theory in Practice and Process*, Chicago, University of Chicago Press, 1989, pp. 249–74, and Judith Butler and Joan Scott, eds, *Feminists Theorize the Political*, London and New York, Routledge, 1992, pp. 257–79.

22 See Teresa de Lauretis, *Alice Doesn't: Feminism, Semiotics, Cinema*, Bloomington, Indiana University Press, 1982, pp. 103–57. De Lauretis endorses Barthes's position that narrative is 'international, transhistorical, transcultural', but specifies that 'subjectivity is engaged in the cogs of narrative, meaning, and desire'; and, further, that 'the relation of narrative and desire must be sought in the specificity of a textual practice' (p. 106).

23 Christine Froula, 'The Daughter's Seduction: Sexual Violence and Literary History', in *Feminist Theory in Practice and Process*, pp. 139–62, esp. pp. 156, 161, 155.

24 Note the similar structural location of the retrospective narration of the rape scene in court in that great American classic of the 1960s, *To Kill a Mocking-Bird*.

25 Eagleton, *The Rape of Clarissa*, p. 61.

26 See Judith Wilt, 'He Could Go No Farther: A Modest Proposal about Lovelace and Clarissa', *PMLA* 92, January 1977, cited in Eagleton, *The Rape of Clarissa*, p. 61.

27 Forster, *A Passage to India*, p. 263. Margaret Higonnet has suggested to me that the 'guide' is a metaleptic figure. The 'guilt' of the omniscient author – our narrative guide – would explain his textual silence. In 'Forster's "Wobblings": The Manuscripts of *A Passage to India*', Oliver Stallybrass states that in Forster's early drafts and working notes on the novel there was, in fact, an assault. See Oliver Stallybrass, ed., *Aspects of E.M. Forster*, London, Edward Arnold, 1969, pp. 153–4.

28 The phrases are de Lauretis's, *Alice Doesn't*, p. 156.

29 *Clarissa*, London, 1962, Everyman's Library, 1968, 3 vols, vol. 3, p. 206.

30 The self-confessed experience of the (male) reader/critic, as articulated by William Beatty Warner, is one of pleasure and guilt: 'The "rape of Clarissa" as an imagined event which is cruel and uncalled for drifts toward, and becomes entangled with, "the rape of Clarissa" that we enjoy in reading, and repeat in our interpretations.' Here Warner equates rape and reading: since reading *Clarissa* is an entry into private correspondence, it involves, like rape, both the guilt and pleasure of 'violating a taboo'. In both activities there is 'guilt at using others for our pleasure'. See 'Reading Rape: Marxist-Feminist Figurations of the Literal', *Diacritics* 13, 4, Winter 1983, pp. 12–32, esp. pp. 31–2. But even in *Clarissa* – where it may be conceded that the subject-position offered to the reader is that of Lovelace, the secret reader/rapist – there is also an overt alignment between author and female protagonist that intrudes *pain* as an element in the passive process of *being* read and *being* raped that might conceivably dilute the aggressive pleasures of reading/raping.

31 De Lauretis, *Alice Doesn't*, p. 143.

32 This position is argued by Adrienne Rich in 'Contemporary Heterosexuality and Lesbian Existence', in Elizabeth Abel and Emily K. Abel, eds, *The Signs Reader: Women, Gender and Scholarship*, Chicago, University of Chicago Press, 1983, pp. 139–68. See also Catherine A. MacKinnon, *Sexual Harassment of Working Women: A Case of Sex Discrimination*, New Haven, CT, Yale University Press, 1979, and 'Feminism, Marxism, Method and the State: Towards Feminist Jurisprudence', in *Signs: Journal of Women in*

Culture and Society 4, 1983, pp. 635–58; and Monique Plaza, 'Our Damages and Their Compensation; Rape: The Will not to Know of Michel Foucault', *Feminist Issues* 1.3, 1981, pp. 33–4.

33 See Susan Brownmiller, *Against Our Will: Men, Women and Rape*, New York, Simon & Schuster, 1976; Julia R. and Herman Schwendinger, *Rape and Inequality*, London, Sage, 1983; and Germaine Greer, 'Why Men Fear Rape more than Women Do', *The Hindustan Times Sunday Magazine*, 13 September 1987.

34 See Madhu Kishwar and Ruth Vanita, eds, *In Search of Answers: Indian Women's Voices from Manushi*, London, Zed, 1984, p. 34

35 A rape scene is almost mandatory in all Indian movies; the film version of 'Prison' represents Bhagirathi's rape in the same stereotyped way. It is therefore only in Ramanan's fictional narrative that the contours of Bhagirathi's subjectivity take shape differently.

36 Censorship could be enforced by the application of the Indecent Representation of Women (Prohibition) Act of 1988, a legislation which divided Indian feminists. American feminism is similarly divided on the issue of pornography versus freedom of expression.

37 Where the relationship between representation (pornography) and the real (rape) is traced by American feminists in terms of cause and effect, the Indian woman writer must simultaneously forge a discourse of women within this ambit. It is this endeavour that Madhu Kishwar and Ruth Vanita, feminist activist journalists, fear is threatened by the success of the anti-pornography lobby: 'The only way for any writer to be sure of avoiding prosecution under this act would be never to mention women at all. Women could thus become the unmentionables of Indian society.' See 'Axed', *The Illustrated Weekly of India*, 7–13 August 1988.

38 In the words of Aijaz Ahmed, 'many of the questions that one would ask about the "third world" text may turn out to be rather similar to the questions one has asked previously about English/American texts' ('Jameson's Rhetoric of Otherness and the "National Allegory"', *Social Text* 17, 1986, pp. 3–25, esp. p. 9).

39 Satya Mohanty, 'Us and Them: On the Political Bases of Political Criticism', *The Yale Journal of Criticism* 2, 2, Spring 1989, pp. 1–31, esp. p. 15.

Since I wrote this chapter I have seen the following works that have provided welcome reinforcement and elaboration of several of my arguments: Brenda R. Silver, 'Periphrasis, Power, and Rape in *A Passage to India*', *Novel* 22, Fall 1988, pp. 86–105; Elliot Butler-Evans, 'Beyond Essentialism: Rethinking Afro-American Cultural Theory', *Inscriptions* 5, 1988, pp. 121–34, which discusses Alice Walker's story about interracial rape, 'Advancing Luna – and Ida B. Wells'; Sharon Marcus, 'Fighting Bodies, Fighting Words: A Theory and Politics of Rape Prevention', in Judith Butler and Joan W. Scott, eds, *Feminists Theorize the Political*, London and New York, Routledge, 1992.

4

THE NAME OF THE HUSBAND
Testimony and taboo in the wife's discourse

I

When the Hindu wife is killed or driven to suicide by her husband and his family she becomes a victim of 'dowry death', as such occurrences are popularly described. Because of the nature of the crime – almost always a death by burning that is made to resemble a domestic accident – the central and often the sole source of information about the circumstances of the death is the victim herself. Therefore her testimony – its content, its form, its credibility – is crucial if an indictment of her killers is to take place. The fact that convictions have taken place in only 3 per cent of all reported cases is an indication of the problematic status of the occurrence and nature of such testimony. In the first place there are legal obstacles to the admissibility of a burnt woman's 'dying declaration' as evidence, only recently overcome as a result of the intervention of women's groups.[1] But more often the dying women themselves maintain silence over their killing, in this observing an extension of the prohibition enjoined upon the good Hindu wife on uttering the name of the husband, a taboo founded upon the belief that with each such utterance his life is shortened by a day.[2]

Why, even when her accusation carries weight legally, does the dying wife more often than not acquit her husband and his family of the crime of killing her or driving her to suicide? Social pressures – fear, habit, consideration for her children or 'family honour', or a final access of charity or forgiveness – allow her to speak only to save him.[3] Her testimony is still conditioned by the ideology that will not 'name' the husband. Speech and silence – testimony and taboo – work towards the same end, the protection of the husband.

Wife-murder as a widespread social phenomenon in India expresses the socially sanctioned violence against women that reinforces and is reinforced by the ideology of husband-worship (*pativrata*). This chapter is an exploration of women's silence and testimony in this context – why and how the prohibition upon their speech is imposed and maintained, what the implications are of both silence and its obverse, speech, for the construction and understanding of

83

women's subjectivities, and how the social uneasiness wrought under the 'weight of [women's] long silence'[4] is nevertheless negotiated and resolved within the ideological resources of a culture that sanctions their killing under different circumstances and in many guises – as foetuses, as new-born babies, as young wives, as widows.

But I also argue that the counter to silence in the politics of representing subaltern resistance cannot, or cannot only, be speech. Because of the limits and ambiguities that surround both silence and speech in the project of subject-constitution, my argument goes on to propose that the category of 'action' be recognized as a significant alternative image in the textual representations produced by the cultural unconscious and, consequently, as an exploitable political resource.

The understanding of women's silences and speech has grown to be an area of crucial theoretical as well as political consequence for contemporary feminism. The retrieval of women's speech from neglected areas, literary and historical, is a major enterprise of feminist scholars committed to the project of redressing the imbalances of mainstream historiography and 'national' literary traditions.[5] Equally, feminist legal activism has had to engage with the status of women's speech in courts of law since women's testimony, especially when that testimony involves their indictment of a male aggressor, is often treated as problematic evidence.[6] The conversion of women's speech and silence into the categories of testimony and taboo is a specific attribute of feminist politics.

Since speech is identified as self-expression, and silence as self-extinction, they are closely tied into the project of subject-constitution. In a further move, since speech is regarded as a right, and the suppression of speech as a denial of that right in a democratic polity, the access to speech has defined social hegemony, just as its lack has defined subalternity in unequal social structures and situations. It is these procedures that I wish to problematize in this chapter – but not only by reiterating the truisms that silence and speech are never absolutely distinct categories, that speech is never transparent, and that silence is not always an imposition. Such assumptions do not any longer simple-mindedly ground theoretical arguments about subject-constitution. Rather I wish to explore the limits of subject-constitutive endeavours that remain moored within this problematic even as they question it, and to discover what alternative images are activated in the cultural unconscious outside this problematic, or in extension of it, particularly as they define women's resistance.

It is here that I invoke the category of 'action', viewed in complex relationship to silence and speech. Since speech and silence are related and identified in terms of the presence and lack of language, respectively, they are imbricated within the space of sameness and difference. 'Action', then, as a non-verbal category, exceeds and escapes this problematic. But it also operates within its structure by serving as the shadowy binary opposite to speech, in symmetrical correspondence to, and on the opposite pole from, silence. Speech thereby derives a contradictory status in liberatory discourses: in opposition to silence it is viewed positively as expressiveness, liberation, 'truth',[7] power; in opposition to action, it stands in danger of being dismissed as 'mere words'.

That these categories are in a perpetual state of shifting relations must be acknowledged. Either they are placed within a structure of strict and binary opposition to each other, or they are susceptible to a process of insidious permeation that dissolves their distinctive characteristics. This strategic shifting is well illustrated in Hannah Arendt's definition of 'human identity' in terms of speech and action which I shall be drawing upon in the course of my later argument. My focus, more specifically, will be on the question of how, in seeking to understand the contemporary social phenomenon of wife-murder in India, conceptions of silence, speech and action formulate the subjectivity of the female subject of this violence.

In the concluding section of this chapter, therefore, I examine the implications of the *wife*'s murder of the *husband*, as represented in a popular Hindi film, *Khoon Bhari Maang* (Forehead Smeared with Blood). That a possibility as preposterous as husband-murder could be conceived at all within the pervasive culture of *pativrata*, and then be developed into a popular, or 'formula', film, and as a next step pass the censors, and finally succeed in becoming a box-office success, i.e. find mass acceptance, argues the existence of a certain notion of the 'unconscious' which will conditionally accept such an 'action' – here, when it is shaped in the perfect and rigid symmetry of revenge – as the return of the repressed. Jennifer Wicke has argued, in the context of colonial subjection, that it is difficult for the oppressor simultaneously to 'sustain the fiction' that the oppressed are ' "other" ', and 'to continue to believe that they are without the potential to object to their abasement'.[8] It is the possibilities of the transference of this argument to the particular situation of systematic female killing in India that I wish to speculate upon in the concluding section of this chapter.

II

Though silence is not always a signifier of subalternity, the subaltern condition is invariably characterized and often successfully represented (especially in film) by silence. Taboos similar to those that interdict the wife's naming of the husband are often imposed upon inferior castes and classes in the interests of preserving the mystique and power of elite groups, as Ranajit Guha, for instance, has argued in his analysis of peasant insurgency. 'The class of signs ... least noticed in studies of [subaltern] insurgency', he points out, 'is what constitutes, according to Bourdieu, an "official" language.' '[V]erbal deference in colonial India', he states, upheld

> semi-feudal relationships between old and young, male and female, high
> caste and low caste. ... The ban was even more severe when applied to
> a woman. Particularly excluded were the names of her husband and some
> of his relatives. Transgression in the former respect could lead to her

being put out of caste at least for some time, as was the custom among the Dhanwar of Madhya Pradesh even until a few decades ago.

'Linguistic discrimination among castes' was similarly 'entrenched in some of the most ancient Sanskrit texts.'[9]

Contemporary theories of language (especially the Lacanian) themselves function to marginalize and exclude 'others' (animals, barbarians) by marking the link between human subjectivity and language as a 'natural' one[10]. Feminist theorists have complained that the Lacanian model excludes not merely the non-human or the problematically human, but also the feminine. 'In order to inhabit the "I" position in language i.e. the position of agentive declaration or agentive action, you have to exclude the feminine and image the "I" in the image of the phallus,' Susie Tharu points out.[11] The deprivation of speech, or the impoverishment of the modes of speech, of a group or individual implicitly becomes an index of social, even of species, inferiority.

If women and peasants are defined and marked as subaltern by the condition of silence, then by an extension of this argument into circularity they would not be subaltern if they could speak. This is Gayatri Spivak's categorical assertion, based upon her examination of the colonial archives of widow-immolation in the nineteenth century.[12] But she would distinguish between Foucault's description of the silence and non-existence that repression produces within the normative discourse of sexuality (in the west), and the 'violent aporia between subject- and object-status' that marks the 'woman-in-imperialism', the sati.[13]

In other words, where the content of silence cannot signify – being only silence – its space, its temporality and its facticity give form to its existence. It is this formalism that permits its representation in texts as a presence rather than as unrepresentable non-being. The Indian 'new wave' film, in particular, has made powerful use of silence in its narratives of feudal oppression, precisely on account of its ability to display the shuttle betweeen subject- and object-status that Spivak has marked in the colonial discourse of the gendered subaltern.[14] Further, since suffering may be effectively conveyed in visual terms alone, the absence of verbal expressiveness in the protagonists does not handicap film's portrayal of the subaltern as subject. Film's enormous potential for political and affective statement is, on the contrary, enhanced by the scope of such representation.

In two recent Indian films, *Daasi* (Bondmaid) and *Sati*, the almost total silence enforced upon the eponymous female protagonists (in *Sati* the heroine is literally mute) marks their total abjectness.[15] *Daasi* ends with the woman, a bonded servant in a feudal household, giving birth to the child she has conceived as a result of her rape by her employer, the zamindar; she must smother her labour cries from fear and under prohibition of speech. In *Sati*, a poor orphaned Brahmin girl born under an evil star, is symbolically married off to a peepul tree. She and the tree are then found struck dead together by lightning. Awe-struck villagers and members of her family see her as a sati. The subaltern's silence in such representations can signify only her abject condition – and perhaps, as well, enforce the irony of her silence being socially interpreted as docility, and sentimentally valorized (at least by viewers) as stoicism.

This mode of representation – the mimetic replication of silence as silence – does not, obviously, always serve as the expressive signification of the oppressed condition. Authorial silence about the silence observed by the fictional protagonist is also an aspect of the highly privileged mode of high bourgeois gendered individualism, as Kumkum Sangari has argued in the context of the 'open' ending of Henry James's *Portrait of a Lady*. As readers we are not privileged insiders to what Isabel Archer decides as to her future course of action (beyond the book) – or why. The respect author and reader accord to her privacy acknowledges the integrity of the 'sensitive' individual.[16] In another context I have speculated upon the crucial withdrawal of authorial omniscience about female 'consciousness' from the narrative as having other kinds of resonances. In the three literary and film texts I examine there – Tagore's story 'Saved', Gautam Ghosh's film *Antarjali Jatra*, and Anuradha Ramanan's Tamil short story 'The Embrace' – the joint deaths of husband and wife mime the performance of sati; and the mystery about what 'actually' motivates the wife at the moment of death allows the authors to decentre consciousness as the ground of subjectivity, as I suggested in chapter 1.[17] At the same time, as I want to suggest in addition here, though the texts question conjugal love, this move also allows them to stop short of attributing the death of the husband to any act (either of omission or of commission) of the wife's. The refusal to name the possibility of the wife's responsibility for the husband's death is an ideological manoeuvre that is made in response to a major cultural taboo.

Silence, by the same token that regards speech as the expression of the self, may become a barrier to a knowledge of the self, to its penetration by a perceiver. When this happens, the operation of silence becomes an operation of power rather than powerlessness. It has moved from being an involuntary or enforced ban on speech, to a freely chosen refusal to speak. Silence as withheld communication produces mystery and enigma; it expresses displeasure; it retains secrets; it demonstrates self-discipline or resistance (compare fasting; Gandhi's periodic vows of silence, or *mowna vritha*, served the same function as the fast); it is an index of heroism when maintained under torture. Silence as 'significant absence', in Barthes's term, is that 'zero degree of utterance' that 'testifies to the power held by any system of signs of creating meaning "out of nothing"'.[18] The conversion of socially imposed silence into a deliberate and voluntary statement, and the subversive 'reading' of silence as meaningful communication, motivates feminist theorists and practitioners of writing and film to exploit it as a form of political resistance.[19] The danger here is of romanticizing and thereby acknowledging alterity as the female condition. The expressiveness of silence cannot be invariantly resistant, just as its muteness is not inexorably negative. In the feminist theory and practice of 'reading' silence, our caution must be neither to pronounce definitionally that 'the subaltern cannot speak' nor to romanticize silence as the subaltern's refusal to speak. As feminist theorists who are not ourselves subaltern we are then led to speak 'for' the subaltern, or to provide them access to the social forums of speech, or to enforce the social receptivity to their verbal articulations. The politics of such intervention, as well as the consideration of subaltern gendered speech as an aspect of subjectivity, serves as the next stage of my argument.

III

The right to speech as the entitlement of every individual and group is not at issue since its political importance is the very premise of democratic society. But the right to speech as political imperative must be recognized as being of a different order of theorizing linguistic use from the grounding of human subjectivity in language. But even if we grant the theoretical premise that language is the *site* of human subjectivity – an assumption that implicitly grounds much western theory[20] – we must be wary of collapsing this into the position that speech, i.e. verbal expressiveness, is also its sole manifestation.[21] Hence, as I shall be arguing later, the periodic gesturing towards non-verbal behaviour that we perceive in social and political constructions of human 'nature'.[22]

Since I have argued that silence is not the definitional condition of the subaltern, and have also questioned speech as its 'corrective' condition, I propose to look at the contexts and conditions of the subaltern's and, specifically, women's access to speech in support of the latter problematization. Women's speech, in the first place, is often confined to to the space of the home; their denial of and exclusion from public spaces – platforms, pulpits, courts of law, educational institutions, parliaments – limits the reach and scope of their words. But when women *are* allowed access to public forums, the very exceptionality of this entry may produce various kinds of linguistic excess: confession, curse, polemic, diatribe, profession of faith, revelation and prophecy proliferate notoriously in existing accounts of, for instance, women's court trials. Though such 'speaking' does signify 'truth', as lies, fantasies, desire and distortion do by other means than referentiality, they stand discredited when judged by the standards of strict veracity – and as a consequence the speakers often invite retribution by being subjected to containment, punishment and backlash.

Negative social representations of women's speech serve to buttress the valorization of silence as a desired 'feminine' attribute; censorship, therefore, is not effected only through the explicit prohibition of actual utterance. Women's speech fails as statement, testimony or communication chiefly as the result of the successful operation of two kinds of strategies: one, by being pre-empted, i.e. invalidated in advance; and two, by being discredited, i.e. rebutted after the event. By describing women's speech as, or ascribing it to, lies, hysteria, comic volubility, empty gossip, or ignorance, patriarchy effectively deflects a great deal of its significance and force.[23] Other subtle and pervasive social mechanisms operate to subvert the subversion that the subaltern's speech may on occasion aim at. There is, for instance, the well-known prophylactic permission granted by the ruling classes to the 'lower orders' to transgress linguistic laws on specified occasions like carnivals, harvest festivals, mourning, etc. Social control and 'linguistic etiquette' is thus effectively maintained by hegemonic groups precisely by permitting, and creating occasions for, subaltern speech.[24]

Silence cannot, of course, be the literal and perpetual condition of human beings, however oppressed. Therefore inferior groups, and here I shall again confine myself to the specific instance of women, are users of language who are both excluded from and trapped within a sign-system that is not of their making. Under such circumstances they become prey to a very pervasive kind of 'false consciousness', manifested most banally, but also most dramatically, in the lie. Thus the dying wife's declaration acquitting her husband of killing her must be counted both as the power of language ceded to her and as a trap. Other instances of women being permitted, or using, speech only to buttress prevailing ideologies are ubiquitous. For instance, in the face of feminist historians' desperate search for the sati's 'voice-consciousness', in a context where her death is insistently projected as a voluntary act, little verbal evidence of her 'will' is available.[25] But ironically, in modern Rajasthan at least, numerous rumours circulate about her stated decision to die, as if to counter the negative connotations that her silence would otherwise produce. The powerful force of her utterances in favour of dying is conveyed through stories of her curse upon those trying to prevent her from burning (the 'sati *shrap*'). According to one such story, Roop Kanwar, the 18-year-old girl who was immolated in Deorala (Rajasthan), in 1987, pronounced the name of her husband for the first time in the context of declaring her intention to die. This transgression, the naming of the husband, was received, we are told, 'with exaltation rather than censure', as evidence of a 'supranatural impulse worthy of wonder'.[26]

Clearly the historian's response to such stories cannot be simple belief or disbelief; it can only be an alertness to the context in which the subject's exceptional access to speech was made possible, and to the use to which she really or ostensibly put this opportunity. Even such caution, however, does not provide the methodological route to the recovery of her subjectivity.[27] Speech is a 'contaminated' area for research into women's subjectivities, an insufficient as well as distorting expression of 'motive'. But I do not suggest that it is for that reason politically invalid. No critic or historian, after all, would treat speech as a transparent medium of the self even when she is obliged to credit such testimony as 'authentic'. Critical strategies of interpretation are crucially called into play in negotiating the complexities of subaltern speech.

All interpretations are contests of meaning, and hence must be viewed as struggles for power. Such contests are not enacted between the text's author (its 'originator') and the critic – this relationship is, on the contrary, traditionally not an agonistic one, but is structured hierarchically to place the critic in the secondary position of exegetist to the work in question. Struggles rather take place within the arena of differing interpretations freighted with different political agendas. Feminist interpretation of cultural texts makes its political investments transparent. Reading women's texts, as Susie Tharu and K. Lalitha have argued in the introduction to a major anthology of Indian women's writings spanning twenty-five centuries, is an attempt to read resistant narratives against the grain of the constrained and conventional forms in which such writings are invariably produced.[28] But an acknowledged will to power and desire invest these enterprises. Making subaltern voices heard requires in the subalternist, first, the operative premise that such voices exist; second and following upon this, the undertaking of arduous researches, i.e. the search for the voices, both archival and anthropological; and finally, their retrieval, transcription, translation, documentation, editorial labour, dissemination, critical revaluation and fight for admission into the 'canon'.[29] This radical enterprise is fraught with dangers, subject as it is to falsification, romanticization, failure of tact, the exorbitation of the critic and the consequent (re)inferiorization of the subaltern.[30] It is a task as fatal as it is necessary when the subaltern 'voice' is sought to be politically privileged. The subaltern's speech can never be univocal, singular and 'authorized'; but the appropriation of her voice, as I have tried to argue, is at least an equivocal strategy in political practice.

My discussion, above, about the limits of speech as a measure of subjectivity, argued through the problematization of the theoretical equation of human subjectivity with language use; the identification of the success of patriarchal strategies to pre-empt and discredit women's speech; the recognition of 'false consciousness' as endemic to subaltern belief-structures; the need for a problematic and interventionary speaking 'for' the subaltern by the writer/critic, is strikingly exemplified in a story by the Malayalam writer Lalithambika Antenjanam, 'Praticaradevata' (1938) (which appears in English translation as 'The Goddess of Revenge' in Susie Tharu and K. Lalitha's anthology *Women Writing in India*).[31]

In 'Praticaradevata', the narrator, a woman writer, is visited by a ghost as she sits at work late in the night. The ghost is that of Kuriyedathu Tatri, a Namboodiri woman who in 1905 had undergone the *smarta vicharna* or trial customarily held to try adulterous women and to excommunicate them from the elite Brahmin community of the Malayali Namboodiris. In her outpouring to the writer Tatri describes the condition of Namboodiri women poignantly. The Namboodiri Brahmin was often profligate, was allowed to marry several wives, and was free to abandon them when he chose. The women were confined to the inner rooms, and subjected to other severe restrictions. Tatri's husband, after a brief period of tempestuous passion with her, brings home a prostitute one day, and ejects Tatri, after mockingly advising her to become a prostitute herelf. Tatri returns to her parental home, only to find herself unwanted there too. Finding that her beauty attracts male glances, and deciding to exploit the sexual expertise she has gained in marriage, she does take to prostitution, becoming in course of time a rich and famous courtesan. Eventually her own husband returns to her as a client not knowing who she is. When he discovers her identity he flees in shock. Tatri is brought to trial, an opportunity she uses to name the Namboodiri men – rich, famous and influential men – who had slept with her. She is prevented from going on with her confession, consisting as it does solely of these disclosures, after she has named sixty-five men.

Tatri desperately wishes the writer to understand the reasons why she took to prostitution: she was denied any other options, she had been taught to exploit her beauty and sexuality, she needed to take revenge upon her husband. But above all she was motivated to act on behalf of all Namboodiri women 'caught in the meshes of evil customs ... tortured and made to suffer agonies' (p. 499).

Tatri seeks the writer's sympathy and her endorsement of her action. The first the writer freely offers; but she disagrees about the strategic effectiveness of her action for revenge. 'Consider now, what good did it do to society, that hurricane you set in motion? ... An affair that certainly created a turmoil, but did not succeed in pointing the way to anything positive. The end cannot justify the means, Sister' (p. 500). The ghost recedes, bemoaning her sinfulness and her wasted effort on behalf of her sisters.

But the writer does acknowledge Tatri's great achievement. 'From the heart of a great silence, you managed to throw out an explosive, brightly burning spark,' she assures her (p. 500). The editors of the anthology in their critical note similarly remark upon Lalithambika's own achievement: 'No Namboodiri woman dared speak about Tatri, and Lalithambika was breaking this silence when she wrote.' But both Lalithambika, and her persona, the writer-narrator within the story, ultimately judge Tatri's testimony to be politically ineffective – without, however, trivializing its unique individual heroism. I place their critique within the terms of my own argument, since the story traverses the spaces of history, law and writing that I have earlier identified as the three chief areas of feminist endeavours on behalf of women's speech.

In the first place, Lalithambika occludes Tatri's historical/material identity by representing her as a ghost, and by deliberately pushing back an event that had actually happened in 1905 to a time described vaguely as 'more than a hundred years ago'. Establishing the ontological identity of the supernatural visitor becomes a precondition for the writer's transaction with her, and hence for her belief in her story. 'But how can I have anything to do with you unless I know who you are?' she asks. Tatri, however, refuses human identity: 'I never want to be called a human being again, and particularly not a woman. To be human, how deceitful it is, how cruel, what an experience of agony' (p. 492). The question of the historical actuality of her narrative therefore remains a suspended one given the non-resolution of her human status. Women's voices from the past come to us only through ghostly visitations, not with the materiality of 'evidence'.

Then there is the question of the means and effectiveness of communication when women's narratives are at issue. Tatri's story has been so absolutely censored that no Namboodiri may mention her name. Tharu and Lalitha report that all the documents relating to the trial have been destroyed by the family.

91

Only Lalithambika's imaginative re-creation of Tatri's story – and that too in a hypothetical, unsettling vein – and her valuation of Tatri's defiance as feminist gesture has restored it to 'history', even as this history has been problematized as fantastical fiction. Tharu and Lalitha as editors have then resurrected, translated and historically and critically 'placed' Lalithambika's story of 1938 for contemporary readers. This mode of dissemination of gendered speech – through a relay of women bonded in 'sisterhood' – is poignantly imaged in the story itself by the formal device of the story within the story. In the writer's need to 'correct' Tatri's politics in the dialogic tailpiece we see the power, authority and irreducible necessity of interpretation in reading the subaltern's text.

There are, finally, the ways in which Tatri's testimony in the legal trial (the *smarta vicharna*), is censured, silenced, subverted, punished and contained, which the writer sympathetically reports. At her trial Tatri is allowed to name only sixty-five men when she claims she could have 'made it possible to excommunicate . . . sixty thousand men' (p. 499). Her motives in naming these men (including her husband), are easily trivialized: 'In the eyes of the world her sacrifice is remembered only as a legal affair involving a prostitute' (p. 500). Her very name is proscribed. Then there is the backlash: 'Men began to torture Namboodiri women all the more, using that incident as a weapon. We are close now to bowing our heads once again under the same yoke' (p. 500). The very men she named have female relatives whose 'agony' continues (p. 500). Tatri's action – she had seduced 60,000 Namboodiri men – fixes her reputation in history: her testimony – she had named sixty-five of them – is obliterated.

Lalithambika marks the moral explicitly in her story: female individualism is futile when the need is for a collective feminism. The writer asks: 'why did you not try to inspire all the other weak and slavish Namboodiri women? Why did you shoulder the burden of revenge all alone? In matters of this kind, Sister, individuals cannot triumph' (p. 500). But what the story equally demonstrates is the futility of (individual) speech and the need for (collective) action when wrongs have to be righted or revenge exacted by the resisting subaltern (woman). It is action as the resistant/revenge subaltern mode that I critique in the film that provides my text in the following section.

IV

In reading this film text, I speculate chiefly upon the anxieties, as well as the attempts at their assuagement, that in my view underlie the startling representation of a woman's murder of her husband. The popular Hindi film is not a genre known for attempting radical or heterodox ideological solutions to social problems, or, for that matter, even taking cognizance of such problems.[32] *Khoon Bhari Maang* (crudely translated as A Forehead Smeared with Blood)[33] presents the wife's killing of her husband as a response to his attempted murder of her. She retaliates not through recourse to legal (hence what would be primarily verbal) testimony against him, but through the violent and deliberate action of killing him herself.

The phenomenon of contemporary wife-murder ('dowry deaths') in India requires a brief exposition here. Wife-murders have been on the rise in many parts of India in the past two decades. In 1990, dowry deaths totalled 4,386 (up from 2,209 recorded in 1988).[34] The ostensible cause of the death of the victim is the demand for additional dowry made by the woman's husband and his family.[35] After suffering months or years of torture and cruelty, the woman is driven to kill herself, or is actually killed by the family, thereby making way for the husband to marry again (and thus bring in another dowry!). Her death is almost always given out as an accident, and since it is often caused by fire, it is not hard to give it the appearance of a kitchen mishap. Where the accident explanation fails, the husband's family will offer suicide as a cause.[36] Actual murder is almost impossible to prove in a court of law, given the circumstances of death in a domestic place and situation.

Feminists have recently begun to demand the replacement of representations of women as subjects of fear by emphasizing instead their 'will, agency, and capacity for violence'. Arguing in the specific context of rape, Sharon Marcus asserts that 'directed physical action is as significant a criterion of humanity in our culture as words are, and we [i.e. women] must develop our capacities for violence in order to disrupt the rape script'.[37] The 'rape script' does indeed seem to call forth such 'feminist solutions', even in the formula Hindi film, which shows the avenging raped woman triumphantly castrating her rapist.[38] But husband-murder cannot be classed as revenge within the same mould, if only because of the enormous variation that prevails between the social valuation of the husband and of the rapist (even if, as often happens in the popular Indian film, the two are identified in the same person – the rapist who marries his victim becomes unproblematically elevated to the status of husband).

Therefore I discuss the wife's killing of her husband not as a desired actual alternative to the existing recourses available to Indian wives ill-treated for dowry, and certainly not as a counter-phenomenon perceived in social reality. It is, on the contrary, its mere conceptualization – given how bizarre and far-fetched its realization in 'real life' would be – that takes on significance in the discussion of *Khoon Bhari Maang*.

At the same time, the possibility that a wife may be driven to kill her husband does not lack its premonition in the culture, given how widespread and blatant the ill-treatment she receives is. The wife's responsibility for the death of the husband is a possibility that is already coded within the taboo upon her utterance of her husband's name: by speaking his name she will shorten his life. Ashis Nandy also explains the relation between the Savithri myth – the myth of the wife who had reclaimed her husband from the realm of death – and the opprobrium heaped upon the Hindu widow in terms of such a recognition, for her husband's death is attributed to her 'failures in propitiation', even to her 'homicidal wishes magically coming true'.[39] In his researches on the cultural

93

sanction for sati, Nandy turns up a shadowy story of 'origins': 'The earliest available myth about sati speaks of a Rajput wife who poisoned her husband. From this "crime", Diodorus Siculus said in 314 BC, the "institution took its rise".'[40] We enter a spiral of cause and effect, and the mythical 'original' cause of the immolation of the widow (and, by extension, of the wife of the living husband in the modern dowry death), is the wife's perfidy! The husband, it seems, must kill, or be killed.

The scenario produced by this tortuous logic is familiar to us from other studies of insurrection and control. Tyranny is frequently less likely to be the social response to actual, enacted rebellion than an anticipation of it. Such anticipation is given credence by the construction of imagined scenarios – or even the actual provocation – of subaltern insurrection. And thus when actual revolutions occur, they are often in the nature of self-fulfilling prophecies. In a technique that initially differs from but finally resembles the process of scapegoating, the victim is feared rather than blamed – but is in either case punished as a measure of social safety.[41] Imagining, and imaging, the wife's murder of her husband, as in the film I discuss, appears to me to serve as such a prophylactic strategy.

Khoon Bhari Maang is quickly summarized. Rekha is a plain, naive and rich widow with two young children. She attracts the notice of a charming and plausible fortune-hunter, Kabir Bedi. He and his mistress plot to have him marry her, then intend to kill her off and marry each other on the inheritance. Bedi woos her successfully, largely because of his appeal to her children, and pressure from her family retainer, her friends, etc. They marry, but do not consummate their marriage because he delicately respects her memories of her first husband. On their honeymoon (on which they are accompanied by the children, as well as by the mistress, now masquerading as Rekha's friend), Bedi takes his bride on a boat ride, pushes her into the water, and sees her snapped up by the crocodiles infesting the river. Rekha, however, unknown to him, manages to swim to safety. She is badly mauled, but a kindly priest heals her with herbs and other country medicines. Her face, none the less, is horribly disfigured. She vows revenge upon her husband. Planning carefully, she goes abroad (to the USA?), has her face repaired and reconstructed by a plastic surgeon, and returns as a glamorous model. She then sets out to seduce her unsuspecting husband-that-was, goes with him to her old holiday retreat, and there pushes him into the river to be devoured by the crocodiles. She is reunited with her children and her new lover. The title of the film plays on the image of the good Hindu wife who fills the parting of her hair with *sindoor* or *kumkum* (a red powder) as a sign of auspicious wifehood; here she fills it with blood as a sign of revenge satisfied.

Popular film, regarded as a text of the cultural unconscious – as Wicke does the rash of wolf-child sightings in colonial India – images the fantasies of both dominant and repressed groups, expressing both fear and desire. It gives pleasure in a diffuse and pervasive way, without interpolating viewers into any specific, or singular, subject-position. The Bombay Hindi film can be viewed neither sentimentally as a popular art form 'of the people' nor suspiciously as 'put over' by the commercial film-maker, the movie Moghul. Its ideology is not identifiably either dominant or resistant, but can be selectively read as either because of the strategic ways in which it plays off fantasy against social convention.

The formula film's strict obedience to cinematic conventions of a certain order is a precondition of its mass appeal. In the first place, as fantasy, it has to be founded on the paradox of representing a recognizable unreality, i.e. it must be a representation that has no apparent connection to any known or existing social situation. In this sense, therefore, Bedi's attempted killing of his wife has little to do with the contemporary phenomenon of dowry deaths. Similarly the luxurious life style of the chief characters imaged in it – consisting of swimming pools in the backyard, race horses, holiday resorts – is routinely evoked in Hindi films as a realm of desire. The *modus operandi* of the attempted murder – feeding a person to crocodiles – is a completely bizarre and unlikely form of death for an upper-class urban wife (unlike the typicality of death by fire). And yet popular film would not 'work' unless it did have a relationship, mediated and oblique, with social reality. Therefore Bedi's murderousness, according to the film's script, is motivated by greed – as dowry deaths are; and Rekha's crocodile-mauled face does uncannily resemble the disfigurement caused by fire.

Second, popular film cannot allow itself the play of irresponsible and subversive possibilities; on the contrary, its narrative is strictly controlled so as not to transgress the boundaries of the morally and socially acceptable. Thus its very subversion is subverted and returned to the normative. However daringly envisaged the wife's murder of the husband may be, it is here controlled by a number of modifications that qualify the act's transgressive effect: (a) the husband who is killed is a second husband, a usurper who has taken the place of the 'authentic' first husband; (b) the marriage is not consummated; since Rekha is not guilty of desire for her new husband and thereby retains her loyalty to her first husband, she renders the second marriage, in a sense, invalid; (c) finally, the woman who kills her husband is no longer the woman who married him: her identity is comprehensively overhauled, her very appearance transformed. In some sense, therefore, it is not 'really' a case of husband-murder at all, since both 'husband' and 'wife' remain mere and inauthentic designations for the man and woman who marry.

Third, the structure of the action of the film is cast in the strict symmetry of revenge, down to the form of death meted out to the would-be murderer. The woman's killing of her husband is therefore a form of justice, even a form of divine retribution (in one scene in the film the icon of Kali/Durga, the avenging goddess, is explicitly displayed; and in the last fight scene Rekha, with her hair loose, wearing men's clothing, carrying weapons and riding a horse, is evoked as the visual analogy of the goddess). The motive of revenge in *Khoon* derives most immediately from the genre of the vigilante film, a recent phenomenon in Indian cinema that reflects a growing popular belief that, the forces of justice and order having broken down in a basically lawless society, only the righteous (who is invariably single and male but may sometimes be a 'gang', and sometimes even be female) can punish the guilty.

Finally, there is the major requirement of popular film, the happy ending. Not only is the victim's revenge successful, it also enjoys immunity from the law. It *is*, after all, the law.

These 'conditions of success' of the popular film's formula can be quickly contrasted with the different modes of structuring subaltern resistance in some of the other texts I have alluded to earlier. The unusual method of killing in *Khoon*, for instance, is very different from the deliberately banal realism of Anuradha Ramanan's story, 'The Embrace', in which the burning woman embraces her husband, setting him alight. Both the commonplace nature of this happening, and its futility as an act of overt revenge, are ironically pointed up by the author in a tailpiece to the story, given in the form of a newspaper account that reports the event as an accident in which 'a man died while trying to save his wife from death'. Compare, too, Rekha's impeccable success in the film with the self-destructive 'revenge' that Tatri seeks through verbal incrimination of her husband in Lalithambika's 'Praticaradevata'. The wife's killing of her husband in *Khoon* must also be recognized as entirely different in motive and impulsion from the 'crime of passion', or the murder for profit, that the popular mystery story so often attributes to the wife. Nor does the kind of bitter misogyny that Hemingway reveals in his exposition of Mrs Macomber's gratuitous shooting of her husband ('The Short, Happy Life of Francis Macomber') provide the underlying ideology of the film.[42] *Khoon Bhari Maang* is significantly different even from the formula 'revenge' film alluded to earlier. Where most films of the genre have been unabashedly anarchic, the act of killing in *Khoon*, though represented as in the others as self-righteous revenge, is executed in an exact and measured dose.

Revenge presented as justice, I have tried to suggest, functions as a warning to privileged groups (patriarchy/the ruling classes/elite castes) against exceeding the limits of a tolerable oppression of the lower orders. At the same time, by contemplating and then projecting the scenario of insurrection, it also paves the way for further – and more oppressive – measures of control. *Khoon Bhari Maang* does precisely encode this double message. It also subserves contradictory ideologies: it suggests that victimized wives can and may kill their husbands; but also that they should not, in the first place, marry the 'wrong' (i.e. here, the second) husband. Nevertheless, the crux of the argument of the film, from my point of view, is that it envisages 'action' as an option available to the oppressed, that it views this action as violent and revengeful but just, that its agent is a married woman, and that her victim is her husband. In the next, and concluding, section of this chapter, I examine the subject-constitutive bounds and possibilities of subaltern 'action' framed as resistance.

V

In making the distinctions between silence, speech and action, I have marked the differences among them chiefly as convenient category divisions, while remaining aware of their fluidity and permeability. Thus I have taken account of the silence that speaks, and the speech that fails as communication, as significant 'supplements' to the self-definition of each.[43] But in opposing 'action' to both silence and speech as a non-verbal and performative aspect of human subjectivity, my insistence on retaining difference is, I am aware, more problematically defended. The theorization of the speech-act – the functioning of verbal utterance as deed – propounded chiefly by John Austin, undoes the strict opposition between the categories of speech and action. But even for Austin, as John Llewelyn points out, the 'performative' aspect of speech is only narrowly applicable to such 'operative' 'legal' instrumentality as that which 'effects a transaction, brings about a conveyance or a bequest or, more ceremonially, a marriage, a baptism or the opening of a new town hall, by using certain forms of words in certain appropriate circumstances'.[44] Such speech acts, in a given, actual, social situation are more likely to occur in privileged rather than oppressive social situations, or among collective rather than individual subjects. Hannah Arendt also refuses the strict separation of speech and action, arguing that it is only together that they define 'human identity'.[45] But this imbrication and complementarity of the two in human activity breaks down in Arendt's argument when she discusses the nature of 'politics', defined by her as the realm of the 'public' (as opposed to the private). In this argument action and speech become opposed and hierarchically positioned activities.[46] Action is associated with the prepolitical, with violence, with the 'private' realm of home and domestic life, i.e. the despotism of the household, or of Asian empires; whereas speech, separated from such crude action, implies the political, the discourse of persuasion, the public realm.[47] Ranajit Guha also connects action and speech in insurgency by showing how peasant uprisings are invariably accompanied by the desecration of language, 'either by direct abuse addressed to ... superiors or by adopting the latter's mode of speech'.[48] Guha points out that traditionally subaltern 'calumny, contemptuous talk or intimidation' was defined as 'action, or "sahasa", that is, a crime of violence'. But equally, such verbal defiance, presumably when unaccompanied by action, was quickly and efficiently checked.[49]

The point of my quick demonstration of the deconstructive possibilities inherent in the action/speech polarity is to concede the arguments of the theorists quoted above (linguist, political scientist, historian). Rigid distinctions between speech–silence on the one hand, and action on the other, admittedly cannot be maintained. But I wished also to disclose the hierarchization of speech over action that persists in these, as in most, analyses of human activity.

This hierarchization fits my own identification of action (without words: see Arendt, 'Only sheer violence is mute, and for this reason violence alone can never be great.')[50] with subaltern resistance, and of speech (including speech-acts) with elite control. The silence enforced upon the former is in the imagination (desire/fear) of both groups broken through the agency of action rather than speech.[51] In the actual control of subaltern insurgency as well, according to Guha, 'verbal violence [was] relatively unimportant for purposes of administrative or judicial intervention', since it is 'violence against person and property that dominates events of this kind'.[52]

When I began to work on this chapter it was with the conviction that *Khoon Bhari Maang* was – and only could be – a unique text, a rare figuring forth of the repressed. In the course of its writing I began to hear of other texts, films, television features, plays, documentaries, which also represented the wife's killing of the husband.[53] I turned up news items of such murders, though these invariably attributed the wife's motive to adulterous passion.[54] In a given 'overdetermined' period, such as prevails in India today, the value of women's lives is trivialized so comprehensively that such narratives are bound to gain currency.[55]

I do not celebrate these findings, or offer this prophecy in a spirit of social analysis. As I see it, they carry little significance for the phenomenon of wife-murder. As should be clear by now, I have treated the wife's retaliatory killing of her husband in the context of the 'dowry death' phenomenon merely as a conceptual possibility. I have not placed the category of 'action' outside discourse: and it is only within the discursive space of the name of the husband that silence, speech and the action of revenge are located and their relations explored.[56] The stifling dialectic of speech and silence is simply extended to accommodate a third term; and in view of the limited cognitive structures within which we theorize resistance, such expansion has, I believe, its uses.

NOTES

1 Geeta Luthra and Pinky Anand (advocates who argued the case of Ravinder Kaur, burnt to death in 1983) have also set forth the significance of two Supreme Court judgements, which state that in cases of suicide by married women circumstantial evidence may be admitted in place of direct evidence. See *Manushi* 54–5, September–December 1987, pp. 22–4.

2 The magical powers of language are affirmed in similar prohibitions traditionally imposed upon the wife's reading and writing which were also claimed to be fatal for the husband. Interestingly, the interdiction of the Name acts exactly like its opposite, the incantation (the 'japa' or repeated chanting of the Name of the Lord, an important aspect of Hindu religious worship). In both cases the signified is mystified and exalted.

3 Shalini Malhotra's death was a well-publicized case, and one that shows the difficulties of using the dying declaration as evidence in court. Shalini died on 21 April 1989. She gave out differing statements of what had caused her fatal burns.

The first one which she made immediately on arrival at the hospital was given under duress – her mother-in-law had allegedly threatened her sisters and parents with retribution if she told the truth. It was only later that Shalini went on record to say that she had given her first declaration under pressure and that she had actually been set on fire by her husband.

This article also relates the ambiguity surrounding the dying declaration(s) of Raisa Khatoon who died in January 1990. See Ranjna Mathur, 'Licence to Kill', *Illustrated Weekly of India*, 7–13 March 1992, pp. 7–9. Shalini's second confession, spoken from her hospital bed, was recorded live on national television. In spite of the publicity and the nature of the evidence, however, the trial against her husband and his family is still pending, and the accused are free on bail. See the news report, 'Justice still eludes Shalini', *The Times of India*, 15 July 1992.

4 The phrase appears in the epigraph to Shashi Deshpande's novel, *That Long Silence*, London, Virago, 1986, and is taken from a speech made by Elizabeth Robbins to the WWSL, in 1907.

5 Such seminal works as Joan Kelly's *Women, History, Theory*, Chicago, University of Chicago Press, 1984; Barbara Smith, ed., *Home Girls: A Black Feminist Anthology*, New York, Kitchen Table: Women of Color Press, 1983; Cherrie Moraga and Gloria Anzaldua, eds, *This Bridge Called My Back: Writings by Radical Women of Color*, New York, Kitchen Table: Women of Color Press, 1983; Sandra Gilbert and Susan Gubar, eds, *The Norton Anthology of Literature by Women: The Tradition in English*, New York, W.W. Norton, 1985; and Susie Tharu and K. Lalitha, eds, *Women Writing in India: 600 BC to the Present*, Delhi, Oxford University Press, 1991 are products of such an enterprise. The list, needless to say, is not intended to be comprehensive.

6 In Iran and Saudi Arabia women cannot give evidence in a court of law at all; in Pakistan the evidence of two women is equal to that of one man; rape laws in all countries notoriously give little credence to the woman's 'unsupported' word.

7 According to Plato *lexis* adheres more closely to truth than *praxis*. See Hannah Arendt, *The Human Condition*, Chicago, University of Chicago Press, 1958, p. 178, n. 4.

8 Jennifer Wicke, 'Koko's Necklace: The Wild Child as Subject', *Critical Quarterly* 30, 1, Spring 1988, pp. 113–27, esp. p. 117.

9 Ranajit Guha, *Elementary Aspects of Peasant Insurgency in Colonial India*, Delhi, Oxford University Press, 1983, pp. 40–1. Women and *sudras* are traditionally forbidden to hear or recite the Vedas. In *The Politics of Language 1791–1819*, Oxford, Clarendon, 1984, Olivia Smith also proposes that language reflected class division. 'At moments of political conflict, such as trials for sedition or the discussion of repressive legislation, these concepts were used to justify the denial of political and social rights to the vulgar.'

10 Wicke, 'Koko's Necklace', pp. 114–15.

11 Susie Tharu, 'Women Writing in India', *Journal of Arts and Ideas* 20–1, March 1991, pp. 49–66, esp. p. 52.

12 The phrase appears in Gayatri C. Spivak, 'Can the Subaltern Speak? Speculations on Widow-Sacrifice', *Wedge* 7/8, Winter/Spring, 1985, pp. 120–30, esp. p. 130.

13 Ibid., p. 120.

14 See Chapter 2, esp. p. 52, where I discuss in the film, *Antarjali Jatra*, the refusal of Jashobati, the woman condemned to die as a sati, to be treated as an object of sacrifice, or as a subject who must escape her death.

15 *Daasi* (in Telugu), dir. Dasari Narayana Rao, 1990; *Sati* (in Bengali), dir. Aparna Sen, 1990. In one of the earliest films in this genre, *Aakrosh* (in Hindi), dir. Govind Nihalani, 1980, the protagonist, a man who has killed his wife's rapists, stubbornly refuses to speak thereafter, even in his own defence.

16 Kumkum Sangari, 'Of Ladies, Gentlemen, and the "Short Cut"', in Lola Chatterjee, ed., *Woman/Image/Text: Feminist Readings of Literary Texts*, New Delhi, Trianka, 1986, pp. 99–100.

17 See Chapter 1, pp. 32–3.

18 Guha, *Elementary Aspects*, p. 46. Guha compares Barthes's zero sign with the Sanskrit grammarian Panini's notion of *lopa*. Guha quotes the commentary of Vasu: 'this grammatical zero has all the rights and liabilities of the thing which it replaces. This blank or *lopa* is in several places treated as having a real existence' (n. 81).

19 Many of the essays in a special issue of the journal *Discourse* 8, Fall–Winter, 1986–7, 'She: The Inappropriate(d) Other', discuss these processes. Trinh T. Minh-ha stipulates that 'silence can only be subversive when it frees itself from the male-defined context of Absence, Lack, and Fear (as Feminine Essence). When it becomes a language of its own' (see 'Introduction', pp. 3–8, esp. p. 8). This happens in the Sri Lankan film-maker Leslie Thornton's *Adynata* which is described by Linda Peckham as a 'not speaking with language/speaking with no language': 'Thornton uses [women's] position outside language, a lack of speech, as a response in itself, a form of signification that treats these representations [of women and the Orient] to both an emptying out and a redistribution of meaning' (see her 'Not Speaking with Language/ Speaking with No Language: Leslie Thornton's *Adynata*', *Discourse* 8, pp. 103–13, esp. p. 103).

20 Wicke, 'Koko's Necklace', pp. 113–16.

21 I am grateful to Rukmini Bhaya Nair for pointing out to me the distinction between 'site' and 'manifestation' in this context. She is not, of course, responsible for the clumsiness of my exposition!

22 See chapter V, 'Action', in Arendt's *Human Condition*. 'To act, in its most general sense, means to take an initiative, to begin ... to set something in motion' (p. 177).

23 Literary representations of women as ignorant, loquacious or incoherent have produced well-known comic figures like Fielding's Slipslop, Sheridan's Mrs Malaprop, Dickens's Flora Finching and Joyce's Molly Bloom. As Olivia Smith observes, 'If one's language is condemned, no means exist of refuting the charge' (p. 30). In rebuttal of such representations, Bell Hooks asserts the value of 'talking back', in particular, and of women's speech in general, especially in black communities. She concludes her essay by speaking movingly and powerfully of the political value of speech, especially

> for the oppressed, the colonized, the exploited, and those who stand and struggle side by side, a gesture of defiance that heals, that makes new life, and new growth possible. It is that act of speech, of "talking back" that is no mere gesture of empty words, that is the expression of moving from object to subject, that is the liberated voice.
>
> ('Talking Back', *Discourse* 8, pp. 123–8, esp. p. 128)

24 Guha, *Elementary Aspects*, p. 45.

25 For the feminist emphasis on 'voice-consciousness' in establishing the sati's 'will,' see Chapter 2, pp. 53–5.

26 Shakuntala Narasimhan, *Sati: A Study of Widow Burning in India*, New Delhi, Viking, 1991, p. 91.

27 Refer also to my chapters on sati in this book.

28 Tharu and Lalitha, *Women Writing in India*, 'Preface', p. xviii.

29 Ibid., pp. xvii–xxv; see also their comprehensive 'Introduction', pp. 1–37.

30 For a more detailed discussion of 'reading resistance' in women's narratives, see my review of *Women Writing* in *Book Review* XVI, 3, May–June 1992.

31 'Praticaradevata' appears on pp. 490–500. All page numbers for quotations from this story appear in parentheses within the text.

32 The division between popular and serious cinema in India is a well-known phenom-enon. 'On the whole, today's big popular cinema is conservative,' observes Chidananda Das Gupta, one of Indian cinema's leading critics. See his 'Indian

Cinema: Tradition and Change', in Pupul Jayakar *et al.*, eds, *India*, Bangkok, Media Transasia, 1985, pp. 84–9, esp. p. 85.

33 *Khoon Bhari Maang*, dir. Rakesh Roshan, 1988.

34 These figures were furnished at a national workshop on 'Women and Law', held in January 1991, and quoted in B.S. Padmanabhan, 'Gender Justice: Eyes still Closed', *The Hindu*, 7 December 1991. In the past eleven years the total number of married women killed was 13,630, according to the figures in Mathur.

35 Madhu Kishwar is among the chief Indian feminists who now argue that dowry is by no means the sole, or even the chief, cause for the killing of married women. See her 'The Real Murderers', *Express Magazine*, 9 April 1989.

36 Amendments to the Dowry Prohibition Act of 1961, carried out in 1984 and 1986, and changes in the Indian Penal Code, the Criminal Procedure Code and the Indian Evidence Act, were responses to the increase in dowry-related deaths. Section 498-A was introduced in the Indian Penal Code providing for the prosecution of those responsible for dowry deaths, which covered abetment to commit suicide; and according to a new section (113-A) of the Indian Evidence Act, 1872, the burden of proof of innocence is upon the accused when the death of a woman occurs under suspicious circumstances within seven years of marriage, and when cruelty against the woman is established. Nevertheless, charges under Section 498-A are very difficult to substantiate. See D.N. Gautam and B.V. Trivedi, *Unnatural Deaths of Married Women with Special Reference to Dowry Deaths*, New Delhi, Bureau of Police Research and Development, Ministry of Home Affairs, Government of India, 1986, pp. 4, 5, 10.

37 Sharon Marcus, 'Fighting Bodies, Fighting Words: A Theory and Politics of Rape Prevention', in Judith Butler and Joan W. Scott, eds, *Feminists Theorize the Political*, New York and London, Routledge, 1992, pp. 385–403, esp. p. 401.

38 For a review essay on the 'female vigilante' films, see Madhu Kishwar and Ruth Vanita, 'Male Fantasies of Female Revenge', *Manushi* 48, September–October 1988, pp. 43–4.

39 Ashis Nandy, *At the Edge of Psychology*, New Delhi, Oxford University Press, 1982, p. 9.

40 Ibid., p. 8.

41 Nineteenth-century novels, for example, vividly image the fear of class revolution; Dickens's numerous mob scenes are often explained in the light of this fear. See also Wicke, who points out that, 'ironically, but with a pithy logic, the rash of stories [about wild/wolf children] occurred after the Mutiny and generally were seized on by the Anglo-Indian community' (p. 117).

42 Ernest Hemingway, 'The Short Happy Life of Francis Macomber', in *The Essential Hemingway*, London, Jonathan Cape, 1947.

43 'Supplement' is used in the senses Derrida gives it, both as that which functions as a 'surplus, a plenitude', as well as that which 'supplements, [adding] only to replace'. See *Of Grammatology*, trans. Gayatri Chakravorty Spivak, Baltimore and London, Johns Hopkins University Press, 1974, pp. 144–5.

44 John Llewelyn, 'Responsibility with Indecidability', in David Wood, ed., *Derrida: A Critical Reader*, Oxford, Blackwell, 1992, pp. 72–96, esp. p. 78.

45 Arendt, *Human Condition*, pp. 177–9.

46 Ibid., pp. 26, 27.

47 Ibid. B. Honig has discussed at some length Arendt's 'reliance on [a] series of distinctions ... [between the] performative and the constative'. Treating these distinctions as binary oppositions, Arendt then 'maps them onto a (historically invidious) public/private distinction that lies at the (shifting) center of her work'. The distinctions are, nevertheless, constantly susceptible to 'permeation'. 'Action', in Arendt's argument, is given a domestic space, but it 'refuses' to stay there. This, says Honig, is 'the real risk of action – in this refusal. ... Action produces its actors;

episodically, temporarily, we are its agonistic achievement.' See B. Honig, 'Towards an Agonistic Feminism: Hannah Arendt and the Politics of Identity', in Butler and Scott, *Feminists Theorize the Political*, pp. 215–35, esp. pp. 223–4.

48 Guha, *Elementary Aspects*, p. 48.

49 Ibid., p. 45.

50 Arendt, *Human Condition*, p. 26.

51 Arendt's definition of the muteness of sheer violence, as well as the point I am making about the fear of violence going berserk in the absence of speech, is well borne out by an early 'new wave' Indian film, *Aakrosh*, referred to earlier. In *Aakrosh* a tribal woman, raped by a group of politicians, kills herself. The husband murders them in revenge; and then refuses to speak a single word in his own defence, even to his lawyer. The end of the film shows him run berserk and kill his sister. We can only guess that he does so to save her from a fate similar to his wife's.

52 Guha, *Elementary Aspects*, p. 48.

53 Of these, a 1990 production, *Haque*, dir. Mahesh Bhatt, most clearly indicts the husband as a man deserving to die. I am grateful to my colleague, Ratna Raman, for drawing my attention to this film. I also heard of a documentary film made by Gita Sehgal with the self-explanatory title, 'The Provoked Wife: A Film on Family, Power and Dramatic Violence'.

54 *The Times of India*, dated 3 November 1991, for instance, carried this news item prominently: 'Wife, lovers held for man's murder.' Another news item in the same newspaper, dated 2 February 1992, reports the murder of a rickshaw-puller Saran, and adds that 'the police suspect involvement of Saran's wife'. The recent case of Kiranjit Ahluwalia, an immigrant Indian woman in Britain, who murdered her husband after ten years of suffering from his ill-treatment of her, became a *cause célèbre*. Ahluwalia was acquitted on appeal. My examples are chosen at random.

55 I here adapt a phrase from Wicke, who speculates upon 'the increased sensitivity to the possible finding of wolf children' actually producing 'one or two actual examples' (p. 117).

56 To prevent 'discourse' from being trivialized I refer the reader to Teresa de Lauretis's essay 'The Violence of Rhetoric: Considerations on Representation and Gender', *Semiotica* 54, 1/2, 1985, pp. 11–31. It is within the discriminations that de Lauretis makes between concept, expression and actual violence in the Foucauldian notion of discourse (p. 18) that the action of husband-murder must be located: as a concept and expression whose entry into the discursive confers a tangible 'reality' upon it, but as a retaliation to domestic violence whose materiality lies largely outside the social.

5

GENDER, LEADERSHIP AND REPRESENTATION

The 'case' of Indira Gandhi

I INTRODUCTION

Indira Gandhi's[1] historical importance as a woman leader of a postcolonial democratic nation and as an influential third-world political figure has not yet been subjected to extended feminist enquiry. Feminist analyses of women political leaders have been for the most part insufficiently grounded in a feminist theory, chiefly because that theory has itself been deeply divided and ambivalent on questions of political power and authority and women's relation to these. Within such a cognitive structure an adequate gendered perspective on women leaders cannot be realized. Since feminist theory – admittedly by no means a single or homogeneous body of speculation and argument – is primarily and significantly shaped by and contributes to the needs of the women's movement, we might justifiably turn to the latter for a formulation of the issue of women and political power. But women activists too have failed to propose a significant 'mass collective fight for power', remaining content for the most part to bring pressure upon governments from outside, or to back sympathetic candidates, or at best to propose a 'women's party' independent of party affiliations. In the United States, for instance, the strategy followed by women's groups that seek political clout is primarily to form organized 'lobbies' in Congress to press for legislation on women's issues. But no radical rethinking on the issue of political power has emanated from women's movements even in the west in spite of the recognition of the need for such a formulation.[2]

My argument broadly views the problem in its two aspects, the conceptualization of subjectivity, and the issue of power. Feminist attitudes to the 'elite' female subject-in-power and to political power are strikingly marked by disagreement and debate, the terms of which I briefly rehearse here.

In the first place feminists' ambivalence towards political power has to do with their opposition to the intrinsic role of the state, and in particular with its repressive and coercive machinery, armed force and the ideology of dominance. Feminist/feminine values are as a consequence located in opposition to authority/command, in (non-authoritarian) caring, maternal and pacifist roles;

103

hence women are assigned a separate sphere of social activity, and envisage an alternative social order outside political structures.[3]

In opposition to this posture of radical separatism, other feminist political scientists have questioned whether 'the power relations that have always characterized politics and the organization of state power can be explained purely in terms of masculine value and instincts'. Further, to define women as alterity would seem to reintroduce, 'however unwittingly', 'exactly that distinction of natures and their connection to politics' which all the major western political philosophers have urged, and which feminism has been 'most at pains to deny or at least to reduce'.[4] Chantal Mouffe undertakes a comprehensive rebuttal of the feminist postulation that 'feminine values' should become the 'model for democratic politics'.[5]

The conception of power itself therefore has to be radically reconstituted if we wish to retain the critique of power without simultaneously embracing alterity. At one level this seems to involve no more than a semantic manoeuvre if we accept the broad distinction that feminist anthropologists have drawn between 'power' and 'authority'. The distinction is based on the nature of decision-making processes: those 'enacted through publicly recognized institutions' are derived from the exercise of authority; whereas 'the influence exerted through informal channels' is an aspect of power.[6] Authority requires 'cultural legitimation', since it encodes 'the right to make a particular decision and to command obedience'.[7] Women leaders (especially in monarchic systems) derive their authority through succession, divine sanction etc., or from attributes of race or class or caste; gender is therefore reduced to a minor consideration in our understanding of politics. In this division politics is viewed as a determinate style of functioning so that analysis cannot attach itself to the sexual identity of the figures of authority.

A specific 'feminine', if not feminist use of power is spelt out as a result of this distinction, in terms of strategies of persuasion, manipulation, bargaining, simple suggestion and other forms of influence which are non-coercive and non-threatening but effective in gaining ends.[8] But it is doubtful whether these strategies can be actually 'institutionalized' in place of traditional forms of political power, or whether the designation of the exercise of political power as 'authority' advances feminist thinking on the subject very greatly. Similarly the theory of power offered by Nancy Harstock, a theory 'grounded at the epistomological level of reproduction', does not specify precisely *how* this understanding will inform 'the political struggle necessary to develop areas of social life modeled on this activity'.[9]

The second area of disagreement among feminists is strategic: since political authority is subsumed within the larger social structure of patriarchy, some feminists would argue that change is effected less through political machinery than through socio-economic, cultural and attitudinal reforms. None of the women leaders in the South Asian countries where female leadership has strikingly predominated concerned herself in any overt way with women's issues, and even less with women's movements. Mainstream politics in these countries may well be regarded as having been less significantly influenced by the prominence of women leaders at the top than by the pressure of mass women's movements upon government policy and functioning.

Nevertheless, the experience of women's movements, especially in third world countries, has increasingly pointed to the need for more direct control of policy and praxis by women's interest groups. Though the success of women's movements in South Asian countries in recent decades, and especially the impact of the International Decade for Women (1975–85), has resulted in gains for women through better laws and increased opportunities, these have not significantly improved the basic indices of women's status (literacy, wealth, life expectancy, employment and physical safety). These indices have remained largely unchanged when they have not actually deteriorated. Women activists therefore have increasingly begun to perceive that it is only by gaining access to decision-making that women can influence issues. It is only 'what cuts deep in politics that cuts deep all around'. Women's participation in the political process cannot be confined to the right to vote (the first victory won by organized women's movements in the west seeking political equality), but must also include access to public office and the administration of laws.[10] Further, many feminists complain, 'patriarchy' as an analytical category has begun to lose its cutting edge; therefore more specific domains of power and resistance need to be identified – and that of politics emerges as a crucial one.

If the arguments I have briefly rehearsed above relate primarily to issues of power and politics, another area of contention centres upon the related issue of female subjectivity.

In general, historical women leaders have been regarded – rightly – as individual figures and isolated examples not sufficiently or significantly representative of the status of the women of their society and in their times. Given the existing structures of leadership, individual women who achieve positions of authority owe them either to birth and circumstances (class, caste, race, religion, family position), or to personal endeavour ('merit'). (Broadly speaking, the two 'types' are represented by Indira Gandhi and Margaret Thatcher respectively.) The role of gender may be largely negated in both instances.

The feminist opposition to individualism, specifically 'meritocratic' individualism, is understandable as an ideological position. Successful women who 'make it' do so as a result of internalizing male norms; and in turn are conferred honorary malehood largely in a gesture of tokenism. But we must not forget that, as Gayatri Spivak points out, in the 'historical moment of feminism in the west', 'female access to individualism' has occupied an important position.[11] There is another danger in repudiating individualism, one that Nancy Harstock has briefly touched upon: that of women's embracing a form of abjectness in reaction to dominance.[12]

My purpose in drawing this sketch of feminist positions on political power and the elite woman-as-leader is not primarily to argue the inadequacy of feminist thinking in this area, or to press for the reconciliation of the oppositions, or to advance a more consistent and unified feminist position. On the contrary, I grant the often equal correctness and validity of widely divergent positions on these issues. It is precisely this impasse – both theoretical and political – that makes it imperative to attempt an intervention that will reframe the problematic to take into account both: (a) the historical reality of political leaders in our time who are (or even simply happen to be) women, as well as (b) the possibly utopian feminist goal of reshaping the affairs of the world.

In considering Indira Gandhi as a representative contemporary woman leader, in the next section of this chapter, I offer a brief biographical and political/historical analysis; but while in explanatory terms this would cover the individual 'case', as method it would address the issue of gender only tangentially. Therefore I seek to identify (in the following section) the cognitive structures which organize social and cultural perceptions about female authority in a handful of Indian popular as well as high-cultural texts which represent the female subject as leader. The implications of these in relation to feminist views on power and subjectivity occupy the next section. I conclude with some free-wheeling speculations on questions of theory, politics and method, ranged around an alternative instance of women's political leadership which accords better with the politics of feminism and offers feminist theory a more suitable paradigm of female subjectivity in power. My attempt to re-situate the problematic – primarily of course a theoretical exercise, but typically one that is grounded in the historical instance – is, of necessity, a tentative one.

II INDIRA GANDHI

What explains Indira Gandhi's rise to power and her success as a leader? The answer must be sought both in the specificity of her individual case, as well as in the more general paradigm of the woman leader particularly as it is produced in contemporary South Asian countries.

Two opposed but not contradictory explanations, in biographical terms, for Indira's rise to power are often debated: one, most frequently advanced by Indira herself, is that she became a leader despite herself and against her own inclinations;[13] the other, that her drive for power was inherent, manifesting itself even in childhood, and finding support in circumstance, example and destiny. The first explanation is supported by the absence of any special precocity in her youth, her relative inconspicuousness in political affairs during the years of her father's prime ministership, her lack of charisma (she was a poor speaker, and was often nervous at public functions), and Nehru's own reticence in pushing her as his designated successor.[14] What supports the second are examples of her high-handedness and strong will in her childhood, epitomized in the story of her fantasies of herself as a Joan of Arc and her leadership of a children's Vanar Sena ('Monkey Brigade', a group of young freedom fighters);[15] her special and intense relationship with her father; his 'grooming' of her, in a sense, to inherit

106

his mantle: her early socialist sympathies and political shrewdness; her lifelong acquaintance with influential political figures including world leaders;[16] her qualities of independence, self-sufficiency and shyness which made her a lonely person who developed very few personal relationships; her undeniable love for her country and commitment to serving the people.[17] Some combination of choice and destiny, it would appear, propelled her to leadership.[18]

In her attitude to power Indira revealed conflicts and contradictions that are interesting to observe. While in general there is no evidence of megalomania in her personality, the deep conviction that only she could, and must, lead her country was extraordinarily strong. But the determination to hold on to power was occasionally weakened by expressions of weariness, and of a longing for the quiet, ordinary, private life, mountain retreats, family ties, the pursuit of civilized pleasures.[19] While there is little evidence of introspection about the ethics of power, and indeed a great deal of self-righteousness, neither was she insensitive to world opinion or history's verdict. During the Emergency, for instance, we learn that she felt panic-stricken, as if riding a tiger and not being able to get off it.[20] As she grew increasingly paranoid about her close associates, she became correspondingly more certain about her power over the masses. Though at first, like her father, a secularist and rationalist she came to develop religious superstitions later in life.[21] Examples of such conflicting views can be multiplied. Clearly, no explanation in psychological terms, single and simple, can account for the phenomenon of her exercise of power.

The question of gender irresistibly poses itself here, since its reality was undeniably negotiated at every juncture of her life: from being born against the expectation of a son in the family,[22] to the problems of married and family life, the prejudices of a sexist society,[23] and the chauvinistic rules of 'politics' in the narrow sense.[24] The larger field of gender and the woman leader must now be surveyed for the common features it may present.

As Raunaq Jahan has pointed out, it is in modern South Asian countries – India, Pakistan, Bangladesh, Sri Lanka (and we may perhaps include Burma and the Philippines) – that the largest number of women leaders have held power (or served in the opposition) for the longest periods of time.[25] Jahan's analysis, based on these instances, is a comprehensive one: all these women leaders (Indira Gandhi, Benazir Bhutto, Hasina Wajed, Khaleda Zia, Sirimavo Bandaranaike) succeeded male relatives (husbands, fathers); all of them were propelled to their positions by party support; therefore none of them was a grassroots politician; all belonged to affluent families and came from elite or ruling classes; and in all the countries 'weak institutionalization' allowed dynastic succession to prevail even under the democratic system of government.[26] Jahan adds that generally these women assumed leadership during periods of crisis. They were chosen by the party bosses at least initially because of their 'relative political inexperience', their perceived tractability, and their ability to appeal to the people's 'sympathy and support'. The masses were willing to accept female relatives as 'natural guardians of the dead leaders' political legacies', both personally incorruptible and unquestionably committed to the continuation of the male leaders' policies (pp. 851–2). In the case of some of the older women leaders we may add that they could claim some legitimacy in their own right through their background of nationalist activity in liberation struggles.

Certainly this broad profile fits the case of Indira Gandhi. Her succession to power was made possible by various factors, among them her background as a freedom fighter, her hereditary 'right to rule' and her membership of an elite (i.e. westernized, upper-class, dominant caste) ruling class. The woman leader in modern South Asian nations emerges as a 'type' produced under sharply specific historical conditions.

But the empirical/historical analysis, while central to any understanding of contemporary female leadership, does not finally produce, we notice, the crucial gendered explanation. The issue of women and power remains mystified – or is trivialized. Raunaq Jahan, for instance, at the end of her fine political analysis, concedes that it is the process by which women establish themselves and function as political leaders *after* being elected that is the crucial area for feminist investigation, but that this aspect has never been 'fully analysed' – or attempted in her own essay (p. 852). Other similar empirical studies of 'women and elites', like Epstein and Coser's collection, are useful in drawing the broad patterns of women's political participation in specific structures of government, but do not venture into an analysis of their actual exercises of authority.[27] The political scientist, Kanti Bajpai, draws a catalogue of illuminating parallels and differences between Margaret Thatcher and Indira Gandhi, but avoids what he calls the 'subterranean' explanation that is required to draw the conclusions from it: 'Quite what these (and other) similarities and differences add up to in any reckoning of successful political leadership of women in power I shall not be rash enough to attempt'.[28] Rhoda Reddock (of the Institute of Social Studies at The Hague), like many feminist anthropologists, does not believe that a gendered explanation of political authority is called for; she dismisses women leaders, especially in postcolonial nations, as incorrigibly and inevitably patriarchal in their attitudes:

> Many women achieve positions of leadership but by then have so imbibed the male-oriented values of the organization that little difference is visible between their approaches and those of men. ... They can be even more oppressive than the men to whom 'power' is not such a novel experience.[29]

Psychoanalytical models of explanation, like Carolyn Heilbrun's, that draw upon familial structures, the influence of the father, sibling rivalry etc. to locate the female leader within the paradigm of achieving women, while persuasive and useful, are not entirely cross-culturally valid.[30]

In the light of the limits of these analyses, women leaders' exercise of political power must be located, in addition, I believe, within the broader social and cultural paradigms that it shapes and is shaped by in order that we may perceive how 'female' authority is constructed and understood.

III REPRESENTING MOTHER INDIA

One kind of identity that Indira Gandhi sought and was accorded was identi-fication with the nation: India is Indira. In such an identification the female subject is no longer perceived in metonymic relationship to the nation, as its leader, but as an actual metaphor for it, its equal and its visible embodiment. This transposes a familiar equation of the nation with the mother, already a trope of nineteenth-century nationalist discourse ('Bharatmata'). Represented as the 'mother', the woman leader is well able to reconcile aspects of nurturing and service in opposition to the authority of the father, as well as to subsume both parental figures into a single complex authority figure.[31] This representation has received its most eloquent, large-scale celebration in the post-Independence Nehru era in Mehboob Khan's epic film melodrama, *Mother India* (1957), arguably the greatest classic of Indian cinema.

Mother India is not, however, based on Indira Gandhi – she was not yet at the time of its making a national leader, or even a prime minister in the wings. Radha, the eponymous heroine, is a subaltern figure, a peasant woman whose life is one long unending struggle; at the end of it, however, she has achieved the status of the village matriarch, a venerated quasi-leader figure. The opening of the film shows her being pressed by a political leader to inaugurate the new canal whose gushing water will bring prosperity to the village. She refuses the honour, and thinks back to her life up to this point – the long flashback is the film's narrative.

Mother India celebrates woman in the linked roles of daughter of the soil (soil = India), and mother of her sons. The former aspect reminds us of Pearl Buck's *Good Earth*. Radha is the strong, stoic, sacrificing toiler, the equal and partner of her husband. She struggles against the flinty soil, the elements, the village moneylender and the fate that successively destroys her cattle, her husband and two of her four sons. The film represents her in a succession of memorable images which are stark, static and iconic: when her bullock dies she lashes herself to the plough and we see her straining, animal-like, in the fields; at day's end she is silhouetted against the setting sun with the upraised plough on her shoulder; she is daubed in mud and slime as she labours in the fields. Singing stirringly of the earth as the mother, she keeps the villagers from fleeing to the city after drought and flood have successively ravaged the village. It is in this role that she becomes identified with India, epitomizing the Gandhian ideology that 'India lives in her villages'. Dominated by her larger-than-life suffering and heroism, the film merges earth, mother and nation to create 'Mother India'.

In her familial roles, Radha is the devoted daughter-in-law, the uncomplaining wife, and the protective mother. Her husband loses his arms in an accident, and after being rendered useless by this loss (his symbolic castration), he leaves the village never to return. Radha is therefore a grass widow; her progressive growth, isolation and independence are underlined by this abandonment. Her two sons are a study in contrast: the older is a 'good' boy, the younger an affectionate but rebellious wastrel. As mother, Radha is less tender and nurturant than stern and sacrificing. Birjoo, the younger son, chafing at the injustice of their lot and the machinations of the wicked moneylender, becomes a *dacoit* (an outlaw bandit), and attempts to carry off the moneylender's daughter. Then Radha, always an upholder of female honour and chastity, kills her own son rather than let him bring disgrace to the village. This is her ultimate sacrifice, her transcendence of motherhood to achieve the accolade the film's title bestows on her, Mother India.

Such a representation, with its mythic appeal and proportions, is readily accepted by the film's viewers. The apotheosis of motherhood, the elevation of it to its largest dimensions, results in a suprapatriotism. The acceptable face of leadership is service; it denies power, stresses sacrifice, and positions the hierarchy of public duty and private affections to give primacy to the first. There was no need for Indira Gandhi to draw conscious attention to the parallels – the mythic resources of such symbolic transformation already existed.[32] Subaltern peasant and elite leader are united by class-transcendent patriotism and motherhood.

In the familial/dynastic aspects of identity that many third-world women leaders have embraced, as daughters, wives/widows, or mothers, gender is an inevitable component. It is invested with considerable affect (especially in populist appeals to the masses). During the 1985 election campaign Rajiv Gandhi emotively reminded the Indian people of his mother's death: 'I am her son, she was my mother'. Sonia Gandhi's collection of the letters between Indira and Nehru is entitled *Freedom's Daughter* in a bestowal of symbolic meaning on the filial relationship. Indira herself used every opportunity to flaunt her (actual) Nehru identity as daughter, as well as her (symbolic) maternal concern for the people of the nation; and the two were not unrelated.[33] It was during the 1967 elections – when she was as yet only 50 – that Indira was first hailed as 'Mother India'. In a speech she said to her village audience, 'Your burdens are relatively light because your families are limited and viable. But my burden is manifold because crores of my family members are poverty-stricken and I have to look after them'.[34] Thus gendered family identities – especially motherhood – are culturally capable of sustaining metaphoric expansion to embrace dimensions of leadership. *Mother India* became the most memorable record of the possibilities of such transformation.

In contrast to the popular, even mythic, appeal of this early commercial film's representation of 'Mother India', there are the more specifically political critiques of Indira Gandhi's prime ministership in the post-Emergency period. I shall consider briefly here two fictional representations of this history. The first, O.V. Vijayan's 'The Foetus', is one of a group of stories that the author has described as 'allegories of power' which are explicitly concerned with 'power and terror, occasioned by India's brief experience of Emergency'.[35] The story begins with the curse visited on an unnamed village ruled over for many years by 'the Lady, widowed Sovereign', who remains immured and hidden in her fortress. Her foetus, 'immaculately conceived', sets out from her womb in the darkness to hunt, kill, rape and brutalize the villagers. Only the village Priest and the Astrologer are able to withstand its power. The Foetus commands a following of 'young scions of the gentry', and these are joined by other foetuses produced by the Foetus's rape of the village women. As the Foetus grows in power, successively subduing the Insurrectionist (a 'revolutionary materialist', now grown old, silly and feeble), the village school and rebellious fleeing peasants, the Priest and the Astrologer decide to invoke the love of the Devi (the Goddess) by chanting the prayer litany to her. The Foetus is then persuaded to return to the womb and be born as a child. But both mother and son die in the childbirth, and the village is finally delivered into freedom.

It is a strange, powerful and horrible tale. The focus is on the Foetus, immature and rapacious son, seemingly the product and instrument of the Lady's will, along with his following. But though her widowhood and the consequent legend of 'immaculate conception' are invoked to grant her an initial autonomy and status, these become eroded by the growth of the foetus and her progressive loss of control over it. She remains invisible in the text, as in the narrative – only her portrait is seen and worshipped (represented in 'the carnal fullness of middle age, pregnant, naked'), and her voice is heard, 'honeyed', promising the young men the growth of the Foetus into their future leader. She too is the product of her ancestors who have 'for many generations ... willed their power' over the village, and it is this power, the narrator explains, that 'manifests itself in this blob of slime'.

The use of allegory is a strategic device of disguise, in this case made necessary by the contemporary pressure of censorship. Contemporary readers would of course have had no difficulty in developing point-by-point correspondences between the story and the people and events of the Emergency. At the same time, allegory allows political positions to be confounded with the moral, so that tyranny may be represented as evil, and freedom as good; and the complexities of history and circumstance may be dissolved into the simplicities of metaphysical confrontation. In allegory the forces of despotism, rapacity, lust, reason, faith, revolution and love are merely embodied in individual figures without necessarily motivating or explaining human behaviour. Therefore the Sovereign, representing metaphysical evil and political (dynastic) power, though perceived in explicitly sexual terms, is not gendered in any other significant way. The antagonistic force that delivers the people from the Sovereign-Foetus is also a female power, now the 'goddess'. Since Vijayan casts the story as a fable of destiny, the 'goddess' can only 'stand for' the divine powers of grace. Since it was the historical collective will of the people that prevailed in the overthrow of Indira Gandhi in 1977, the prayer that invokes the goddess must represent the law, or the Constitution, through which means the Emergency was revoked. We might speculate upon the possible schizophrenic division of the figure of authority itself into a despotic (secular, actual, sexual) Sovereign, and a benign (divine, abstract, asexual) goddess, to account for the contours of this drama.

Another postmodernist fable, Salman Rushdie's *Midnight's Children* (1981), also makes the Emergency and the role of Sanjay Gandhi the defining aspect of the representation of Indira Gandhi. Rushdie's protagonist, Saleem Sinai, born at the stroke of midnight on 15 August 1947, India's day of Independence, is a child of history whose destiny is twinned with that of the nation. But he begins to perceive the obscure enmity and persecution of that other individual who views herself as India's destiny, Indira Gandhi.

> Was my lifelong belief in the equation between the State and myself transmuted, in 'the Madam's' mind, into that in-those-days famous phrase: India is Indira and Indira is India? Were we competitors for centrality – was she gripped by a lust for meaning as profound as my own – and was that, was that why...?[36]

Saleem has displaced upon her his own jealousy of her real powers to lead the nation – as against his mere fantasies of doing so (p. 395). With the help of astrologers, the Prime Minister tracks down the children of midnight so that she might combat 'the deep and widespread conspiracy' that justified the imposition of Emergency. The Emergency, the Prime Minister's 'child', is made analogous to Adam Sinai, Saleem-Shiva-Parvathi's son, who is born on the stroke of midnight of the very day of the declaration of Emergency, 25 June 1975.

She then unleashes Sanjay and his Youth Congress – 'men with the same curly hair and lips-like-women's labia' as himself – to destroy the city slums and sterilize the men. Saleem is imprisoned in a Widow's Hostel in Benares – 'the widow sucked me into the private heart of her terrible Empire' (p. 433) – and then tortured to reveal the whereabouts of the 578 other midnight's children, and finally castrated.

Rushdie presents a certain Indira Gandhi, historically the Prime Minister of India and in 1975 a widow for fifteen years, as 'the Widow', Saleem's nemesis and rival, and his literal castrator. Unlike the widows of Benares, bereaved women whose 'true lives ended with the death of their husbands', 'the Widow' seeks to be 'Devi, the mother-goddess in her most terrible aspect, possessor of the *shakti* of the gods, a multi-limbed divinity with a centre-parting and schizophrenic hair' (p. 438). The powerful negative connotations of Hindu widowhood, viewed in the popular imagination not merely as the misfortune of women but as their destruction of the male, are associated with a (widowed) Prime Minister whose defining act is the massive sterilization programme of the Emergency.

This 'Widow' is one of (but also 'above all') the scores of 'women who have made me; and also unmade ...' (p. 404). Saleem goes on to ruminate:

> How are we to understand my too many women? As the multiple faces of Bharata-mata? Or as even more ... as the dynamic aspect of maya, a cosmic energy, which is represented as the female organ? ... Maya-shakti mothers, but also 'muffles consciousness in the dream-web'. Too-many-women: are they all aspects of Devi, the goddess ...?

> (p. 406)

Thus the circuit is made between individual, historical figures – a Saleem Sinai, citizen – and Indira Gandhi, Prime Minister of India; between the male victim, and the female principle of energy; between a midnight's child and a woman leader sharing a common national destiny.

As in Vijayan's 'Foetus', the Sovereign/Widow does not make a physical appearance in the text but remains an invisible force. It is her agents – her son, Sanjay, and his cohorts; Shiva, the other midnight's child, Saleem's rival; Rukshana Sultana, the 'Widow's Hand' (who does the 'Widow's work') – it is these figures who execute the acts of vandalism and destruction. In both texts, widowhood is made a significant aspect of gendered identity, an indication of power-over-the-male and of female autonomy. This, however, is undercut by the role of another male figure, the son-as-agent, whose uncontrolled depredations are those of a Frankenstein's monster. Thus reproduction as an aspect of female sexuality is here not 'natural' motherhood but a bizarre perversion. The particular manifestation of despotism in forcible sterilization programmes made it possible to link it with the perversion of sexuality (castration, rape) as well as the preservation and promotion of dynasty (the power of the son). In addition there is the reference to Sanjay Gandhi's 'following' of lumpen youth represented as a kind of reproduction-by-cloning, a representation which further reduces the 'originating' powers of the sexual female. In compensation for her reduced powers of agency – i.e. the reduction of her powers of control (leadership), as well as of femininity (reproductive motherhood) – the Mother/Sovereign is now represented in terms of an abstract, metaphysical energy or evil, the feminine principle. Actual power is explained or replaced by symbolic power, the woman by Woman, the widow by the Widow, the individual by the type, the leader by the goddess, history by myth.

Between *Mother India*, product of post-Independence nationalism, and 'Foetus' and *Midnight's Children*, born of the Emergency trauma, stretches the history of Indira Gandhi's leadership. *Mother India*'s romanticized socialism and its endorsement of Hindu goddess-mother-worship allow the subaltern peasant woman to attain the status of village matriarch, and the conflict between actual motherhood and symbolic (nation's) motherhood to be resolved by the mother's unequivocal sacrifice of her son in the interests of the well-being of society. But the same paradigm of motherhood–nationalism that represents leadership as service also accommodates the representation of leadership as despotism by a simple reversal of the female leader's priorities. For the Indian intelligentsia the Emergency came to serve as an epitome rather than an aberration of Indira Gandhi's rule, occurring virtually in the nature of a self-fulfilling prophecy. The connection between Sanjay's participation in politics and the imposition of Emergency, by no means entirely coincidental, made it possible to view Indira's partiality as a mother as a weakness that harmed national interests.[37] There is therefore some historical justification for Rushdie's and Vijayan's representation of Indira-during-Emergency in terms of motherhood. But the hostility in their foregrounding of her widowhood must remain inexplicable except as a

culturally conditioned misogyny; and their recourse to supernatural explanations of 'feminine' power (the goddess) is a complete surrender of historical
analysis.

In all three texts the structure of narrative is allegorical, thus making possible
the continuity of private–public roles in the representation of the subject. The
embodiment of authority in a female figure is one of the ways in which power
is gendered female (as caricatures of the headmistress or nanny indicate). In
India the most facile investment of power in the female is through the concept
and embodiment of the goddess as 'Shakti', 'Durga', or 'Kali'. This meant that
the recourse to military force did not have to be occluded in Indira's projection
of her personality. Her declaration of a state of emergency in the country in
1975, marked by the repeal of democratic norms, and her military adventures –
the successful war against Pakistan, anti-terrorist curbs in the states – made
clear that the basis of political power is invariably armed force. Indira's
assassination foregrounded the inescapable violence that lies close to the surface
of any exercise of authoritarian power in the modern state – 'those who live by
the sword die by the sword' – even as it transcended that violence by turning
her into a martyr. The woman leader as martyr or sacrificial figure neatly fits
back into the maternal paradigm. Gender thus constructs the mode of female
authority, and motherhood/goddesshood provides a single metaphor for diverse
female roles.

The allegorical mode also reproduces a common perception about the lives
of the leading Indian nationalist leaders, whose personal lives were seen in terms
completely usurped by their political activity. Like them, Indira Gandhi may be
viewed as having had only a single dimension to her life, lived as it was so
entirely in the public gaze. Even the letters Nehru wrote to her from jail when
she was a girl were consciously pedagogic, and have been published and widely
read for decades. By and large, therefore, there was no sustained interest in
uncovering the 'personal' areas of her life. Ashis Nandy offers an explanation
for the seamless 'identity' of the woman leader in terms of an 'Indian consciousness' that conflates male and female sexual attributes. Therefore the reason
'some women in India reach the pinnacles of public power and recognition
while women in general have kept out of large areas of public life' is that women
in power are judged as 'castrating' and 'phallic', and men as 'effeminate'. He
goes on to explain that a woman leader's

> public success does not seem to detract from private womanliness. In
> other words, in such instances the Indian woman can more easily integrate
> within her feminine identity the participation in what by western standards
> are manly activities but in India are either not defined in terms of sex
> roles or are tinged with transsexual or bisexual connotations.[38]

Whatever may be the validity of such broadly 'culturalist' explanations, the
Indian public is undoubtedly less interested in disclosures of the private lives of

its political public figures than, say, the British (in their royal family), or the American (in, say, the Kennedys).[39]

The modern 'factual' genre of biography, in contrast to allegorical representations of the individual 'life', is predicated upon a dichotomization of the subject into a private 'self' and a public 'figure'. Contemporary media, in particular, direct their efforts to penetrating the façade – as it is perceived – of the public figure to get at the private, or real – as that is perceived – self. Inevitably, Indira became also the subject of biography. The spate of biographies, including memoirs, collections of letters, tributes, memorial volumes, even a dramatization of her early life, that have appeared, many of them following her death, and several published in the west, possess the interest of adding the dimension of the 'private' life to the available knowledge about her.[40] At the level of the merely popular, this interest is a matter of gossip about aspects of her sexual and family life.[41] At its best, the 'private' dimension is perceived as having explanatory potential for an understanding of her leadership.[42]

When such representations focus upon a female subject who is a 'public' figure, the dichotomy further intensifies: the private self (alone) is gendered female, and the public figure, whether mask, persona, or role is scrupulously represented in non-sexist 'neutral' terms. The two spheres are so absolutely separated that the female subject comes to be seen as a split or schizophrenic personality. Her 'private' traits may, however, be seen as irresistibly intruding upon public behaviour, and predictably, in these circumstances, it is the 'feminine' traits such as maternal fondness or irrationality that are made responsible for the weaknesses in official functioning. An early biography of the Indian leader is titled, significantly, *The Two Faces of Indira Gandhi.*

In representing the woman leader in terms of biography there is also the trivial popular interest in her 'femininity' which leads to her being viewed either as 'feminine' despite her authority, or as 'unfeminine' (desexed, 'masculine') because of it – in either case, a correlation between gender and authority is unproblematically assumed. Gendered attributes are read off from details of appearance, manner, dress, interests, relationships with both sexes, etc. An article by P.C. Alexander, Indira's Principal Secretary, is, for instance, typical. Entitled 'Behind the Iron Lady Image', it contains the following defence: 'Far from being an Iron Lady, Indira Gandhi always remained basically an Indian woman. ... She was feminine not only in her personal grace and charm but in her attitudes, reflexes and reactions'.[43] Indira's domestic interests and her commitment to 'soft' issues as a leader (child welfare, culture, environment, etc.) were similarly viewed as aspects of her 'femininity'. (This is an area where, it seems, male leaders may be equally represented in terms of their gender: in western societies possessing a strong male ethos, in terms of their machismo – sports skills, military exploits, etc. – and in cultures like India in more pronouncedly androgynous terms, as both Gandhi and Nehru were.)

While in the film and fictional texts I have cited the woman leader is transposed into more familiar gendered identities as mother, wife, or goddess, her authority, i.e. the active agency of leadership, is mystified precisely because of this transposition in one of several ways: by being benignly viewed as 'service'; or by being displaced upon male actors; or by being attributed to an abstract 'feminine' principle of energy. In the typical biographical representations of Indira Gandhi, the problem of reconciling gender and authority is resolved through the familiar dichotomizing of the subject into a private self and a public persona; and here it is the 'self' alone that is gendered female. But where such resolutions are not possible or acceptable, as in feminist thinking, alternative representational modes must be constructed that refuse this problematic. But the irreconcilability between gender and authority remains a crucial block to developing a theory and praxis of women's political power. The questions of power and subjectivity as feminism has posed them within the matrix of representation require further elaboration.

IV REPRESENTATION: CULTURE AND POLITICS

Representation in both the senses of the word – i.e. culturally as a construct shaping, and conditioned by, social/historical cognitive modes, and politically as a 'standing for and protecting the interests of a constituency' – is central to any discussion of leadership.[44] My discussion of the modes of subjectification of the female leader was intended to mark the strategies of representation that certain texts of the culture resort to in their attempt to reconcile femaleness and authority.

'Representation' in the second sense that democratic politics enforces – where the one stands for and protects the interests of the many in the nation's legislative and executive bodies – is also a concept that is rendered problematic in the case of women leaders. Often women leaders adopt a 'tough', even ruthless and authoritarian political style that effectively pre-empts any possible identification or partisanship on their part with women as a sex or as a group.[45] Women leaders' sharp disjunction from the collectivity of the women of their nation, in terms of both status and solidarity, highlights their unrepresentativeness. The divorce must be viewed, further, in the context of the overall inconspicuousness of women in political activity precisely in those countries that have been led by women. As a recent workshop on Women and Politics organized by UNESCO and UNIFEM (United Nations Fund for Women) reported:

> Neither the late Indira Gandhi nor Mrs Corazon Aquino's leadership roles have influenced women lower down the line. ... Women remain on the periphery of the spheres of power and influence and even in terms of awareness, party membership, contesting elections, voting or deliberate abstention from voting and decision-making, women's participation has been unimpressive.

The report also suggests that women voters do not necessarily cast a female vote at election time: instead 'votes are shaped by the factors of caste, class and ethnicity'.[46]

Given this failure of representation at all levels women leaders can be accommodated within feminist theoretical and political models only with difficulty. But the reasons why the mutual disowning of women leaders and feminism cannot be simply left at that, as a matter of separate and unrelated areas, need to be briefly discussed.

What I wish to develop here is an analogy between the woman leader and the woman writer, and explore the problematic of the one *via* the other as a means of illuminating the first − a relatively little considered issue in feminist thinking − through reference to the second, an area of considerable feminist theoretical investment. The historical, i.e. actual, woman leader, like the individual woman writer, admittedly does not radically unsettle the question of women's political power or of women's writing, as the case may be, simply by virtue of existing. But once we concede that women's access to political power/writing is important for a feminist politics then the recovery of the subjectivity of the leader/writer − from the *premise* that gender significantly constitutes it − can begin, simultaneously with the enquiry into the relevance of gender to the activity in question.

Jacqueline Rose's capsule history and perceptive analysis of feminism and literature in the essay 'The Institution of Feminism'[47] will serve as my guide through the territory. Rose locates the beginnings of the women's movement in the critique of representations of women in literature (Millett, Ellmann, etc.), a critique based upon the recognition that representation is a crucial area for women's oppression and liberation. There is a similar recognition, as I have tried to show, particularly in women's movements in third world countries, that *political* representation for women, i.e. their participation in political decision-making, is essential for the effective attainment of women's rights, which accompanies the recognition that most social and political structures repudiate women-in-power or view them negatively. Rose locates the next step of feminist literary critical endeavours in the 'focus on women writers as a counter-history to the dominant literary paradigms and preferences', which also meant 'opening up literature to the wider arena of sexual inequality'. Similarly, feminist political theory remarks upon the exclusion of women from the political process, especially from leadership, identifies women leaders and their modes of access to and exercise of authority, and calls into question the evaluative criteria by which leadership is judged. The dangers that Rose perceives in the second move, namely the co-optation of the woman writer within the literary institution and the consequent 'marginalization of the question of gender and sexuality', are implicit in political practice as well. Thus 'any affirmative discourse risks reinscribing itself back into the terms of the literary [political] as such'. The individual woman writer/leader may therefore be acclaimed both from a feminist as well as a mainstream perspective but for different and even opposed reasons.

Rose refuses to grant that the transition from the critique of male discourse to the attention to women's writing in feminist criticism is a progression, though it is certainly a logical next step. 'Affirmation' is a politically complex move for several reasons: the danger, already noted, of the co-optation of women's writing/leadership within the mainstream of the institution [literature, politics]; the frequently reactionary content of women's writing [leadership], the result of 'a regrettable internalisation of a patriarchal norm'; and finally feminism's uncertainty over whether participation in the literary as such or in political power can be claimed by women when it is simultaneously criticized from a feminist perspective as a politically suspect – i.e. hegemonic or dominant – activity/institution. The simple valorization of women writers/leaders, or women's writing/leadership, is not – as it cannot be – the central preoccupation of feminist theory.

But affirmation as a political project that considers 'a difference of political voice' to be at stake leads to the idea of a 'female aesthetic'. This aesthetic can take the form either of the 'assertion of a liberal conception of selfhood', or of 'the undoing, disintegration or negation of sexual and linguistic identity as such'. There are similar and equivalent processes to be observed in a political theory that privileges women's leadership as a 'difference of political voice', where the first position corresponds to the celebration of the achievement of power and rank by women, and the second to the radical conceptual revisions of power and the embrace of a specifically 'feminine' mode of power that deconstructs the 'dominant paradigm of sexual difference'. Rose warns of the possibility of the rarefication of this position (its becoming 'another version of the aesthetic of modernist high prose'), as earlier I noted the danger of feminists embracing radical alterity in a posture that might become ultimately politically disempowering.

The difficult negotiations that feminism must enter into with the literary make possible its major interventionary thrusts into the situation of women. These are identified by Rose as first, 'that wider redefinition of the literary which brings it into connection with other cultural forms as well as with other modes of historical and political critique' relating to race, class and sexual differences; and second, the articulation between subjectivity, language and institution which feminist criticism brings to bear upon the 'domain of fantasy and the vicissitudes of psycho-sexual life'. It should be similarly possible for a feminist political theory to broaden the scope of its enquiry to include the historical, cultural and social dimensions of the structures and institutions of political power. Just as the problem of women's exclusion from writing (or speech) is not a problem that can be resolved by 'simply encouraging more women to speak', the problem of women's exclusion from political power is also not one that is resolved by encouraging more women to vote. The question of representation in both cases 'exceeds the liberal notion of equal access to rights'. Rather the problem requires a return to a form of critique but this time to the examination of the 'forms of libidinal investment and mastery through which individual and collective identifications are secured and upon which they come to rely for holding representational images in place'. We would ask: 'What are the points of connection between a sexual imaginary and the accredited forms of collective discourse and speech?' Rose argues that it is the 'intractability of these unspoken scenarios which makes other forms of transformation often so difficult to bring about'. My long section on representations of women-in-power in the texts of contemporary Indian culture was an attempt to identify such a 'collective discourse and speech' on female authority, though without having recourse to the specific psychoanalytical procedures that Rose advocates.

Rose rounds off her discussion – fortuitously, for my purpose – with an investigation into the 'psychic investment in the image of the woman' impelled by the re-election of Margaret Thatcher for a third term at the time of her writing of the essay: 'It is another instance where the importance of the image, whose particular force feminism has always recognized, leads outside the literary and educational institutional, passing this time into the general reaches of public fantasy life'.

The question of representation, then, straddles feminism's address to both the literary and the political. But I have no wish to subsume the one into the other. Clearly the question of political power is morally and politically more vexed for feminism than that of writing is. And even when feminism acknowledges the necessity of women's access to political power, the woman leader is less easily recuperable for a feminist politics than the woman writer because of her more problematic, and different, 'representation' of the collectivity. The typical transaction that takes place in the project of feminism cannot be consummated when the party of the first part is the elite woman. The 'agency' of leadership allows only a single subject-position for the leader – even where the function of leadership as domination is replaced by service, this position is marked by isolation, difference and individualism. In my discussion of Indira Gandhi I have tried to invoke gender as the 'lived' experience of the woman leader in order to fracture her monolithic (non-gendered) dominant identity – to find that as method this yields only biographical anecdote or analytical impasse. The exploration of the limits of cultural attitudes and cognitive structures also reveals the occlusion of gender in the representation of the woman leader. The elite female subject brings both the category of the subaltern as well as the solidarity of feminism to crisis.

The typical female subject of feminism has been the subaltern woman, or specifically the woman-as-victim, whose subjectivity post-structuralism has helped conceptualize as discontinuous, heterogeneous, changing and contingent[48] – or, as we may say, less than one. The fractured identity of this subject may enter into alliances with groups, which then makes possible a feminist politics.[49] The collectivity represents her from the premise of a shared, universal experience of oppression and handicap, i.e. powerlessness. Though this premise has been radically questioned by women of colour, working-class women, third-world women – subaltern women themselves – feminist theory has recently begun to answer the challenge from a variety of positions.[50] Thus feminism builds upon

119

a solidarity that either disguises or legitimizes difference and hierarchy.

If we see synecdoche as the non-representational figure for feminism − a figure where the more comprehensive term is used for the less comprehensive, or vice versa − then we can understand why the singular, individual, hegemonic female subject complicates the equation by being both more (i.e. hegemonic) and less (i.e. singular) than the collectivity. This makes it imperative then to conceptualize 'female leadership' in different terms − in terms that will explore the ontology of the *collective* subject.

The subjectivity of the collective may be described as 'greater than one' in contrast to the 'less-than-one' subaltern subject. It is a subjectivity that is formed under the pressure of solidarity − a 'value', as Terry Eagleton maintains, 'without which no significant social change is ever conceivable'. Much postmodern thought − Eagleton designates 'deconstruction' specifically − is 'either silent or negative about the notion of solidarity ... conflat[ing] it in Nietzschean fashion with a craven conformity to the law'. Eagleton defends 'unity or identity' by invoking the dialectical thought of Adorno:

> The given social order is not only a matter of oppressive self-identities; it is also a structure of antagonism, to which a certain notion of identity may be critically opposed. It is because so much post-structuralist thought mistakes a conflictive social system for a monolithic one that it can conceive a consensus or collectivity only as oppressive.[51]

Fredric Jameson, from a similar perspective, shifts the terms of the discussion (of the Marxian 'realm of freedom') from the individual subject generally conceptualized only as the autonomous subject, or as the decentred subject, to take into account a 'reinvention of genuine collective life, in which, if one likes, the subject is therapeutically "decentered" by other people, but which amounts to a whole new mode of being on which people can live'. The ontology, as Jameson terms it, of this collective life requires an exploration of the 'genuine transformation of *being* which takes place when the individual subject shifts from purely individual relations to that very different dynamic which is that of groups, collectives and communities'.[52] Jameson later identifies the 'new form of group being' in feminism whose 'political force' derives largely from 'its collective dimension, its status as the culture and the ideology of a genuine social group'.[53]

Clearly, however, the celebration of collective life is not free of utopian or wish-fulfilment desire. The implication in Jameson's praise of the feminist movement, that a collective identity follows naturally from the mode of collective struggle, cannot always be sustained, because as we saw, the identity of 'women' in the movement has had to take into account differences among them. The opposition to the forms of collective life comes also from other political and theoretical feminist positions. Chantal Mouffe, for instance, warns that a 'communitarian type of politics' is 'incompatible with the pluralism that is constitutive of modern democracy', and conflicts also with democracy's 'notion of rights'.[54] Nancy Harstock, while sympathetic to the notion of power vesting in the community, fears 'the submersion of the identity of the individual in the community', and of women thereby falling into a 'form of the female pathology of loss of self, a fluidity that may submerge individual identity'.[55]

In the theoretical work of most Marxist and feminist thinkers, collective praxis is still primarily conceived of as an aspect of struggle and resistance, not of power and leadership. Undoubtedly the move from the one to the other envisages a progression or leap from the stage of political struggle to the attainment of its goal, a move that at this historical moment is utopian because it is premature. What I have in mind is less such a radical social and political resolution than the more modest identification of structures of collective government where they *already* exist, and their adaptation/co-optation to the purposes of political power for women.[56] In India local governments, specifically village *panchayats*, provide an (infra)structure with(in) which women's groups might function with such a sense of collective identity while exercising leadership, since at this level of administration the Indian government also permits 30 per cent reservation for women. 'Positive intervention' (i.e. quotas, socialization, social controls), as Cynthia Epstein maintains, is needed to create access for women.[57] The path to political power for women, as she envisages it in her conclusion, is by 'all the routes that men take', as well as by 'some new routes of their own in concert with all women'.[58]

I end therefore with the story of Vitner, a small village in Maharashtra.

In Vitner a women's panel was elected to the *panchayat* (village governing body) in January 1990, and 125 women were given a share in their husbands' property. Vitner was consequently honoured as a Jyotiba village (after Jyotiba Phule, the great social reformer), for establishing women's rights in these areas. These major steps came after several years of planning and action by the *Samagra Mahila Aghadi*, a women's organization backed by the *Shetkari Sanghatana* (Peasants' Group).

In spite of the shortage of women experienced in mainstream politics, the 30 per cent quota for women is now being filled by women who have been active in women's groups. But it was only in 1986 that the *Shetkari Mahila Aghadi* pioneered the idea of 'a mass collective fight for power' and proposed all-women's panels at village, municipal and district local bodies. In elections in 1989 five villages in Maharashtra elected all-woman *panchayats* with its support.

Gail Omvedt points out that, contrary to the predictions even of sceptical feminist activists, *dalits* and leftists that the women leaders would only be 'puppets' of the men in their families, and would belong predominantly to the dominant castes, the elected women who have come to 'local political power as part of a collective fight' are from the lower classes and castes, and resist not only male political power but also the 'forces of communalism'. Though they face problems in political activity and especially in fighting elections, they have been successful in bringing about much needed improvements in the village. The success of this handful of all-women *panchayats* is leading to the increasing participation of women in local politics and pointing to the strategies by which this may be achieved.[59]

Vitner is, of course, no more than an indication of a future trend of women's political participation. A certain historical conjuncture of the women's movement, peasant movements and political party realignments has made this mode of political power possible. It may well be that the traditional hierarchy of decision-making, within the pyramidal structure that places leadership at the apex, will be powerfully determining in most political situations. The problems of collective leadership at the actual, pragmatic level have undoubtedly to be negotiated at every stage. The case of Vitner's *panchayat* also makes clear that women's access to political power must be accompanied by access to economic independence as well so that subalternity may be meaningfully overcome.[60] It is not the case that the existential reality of gender – as social role, biological destiny, or historical limit – is transcended here any more than in the instance of the Indian woman leader.[61]

But where in the latter the reality of gender is repressed in practice and mystified in representational modes, in the other it crucially and centrally determines the group's political decision-making as well as makes transparent its 'interest group' priorities. Thus among the women *panchayat*'s first enterprises was the provision of drinking water in Vitner. The men of Vitner village admitted that no earlier (men's) *panchayat* had thought of investing money to solve the problem of fetching water since it was 'women's work'.[62] A subaltern female collectivity, occupying the seat of political power, at one stroke alters the priorities of government and the model of women 'at the top'.

NOTES

1 Indira was born in 1917 into a family already steeped in nationalist politics. Her father, Jawaharlal Nehru, later free India's first Prime Minister (from 1947 to 1964), and her grandfather, Motilal Nehru, were closely allied with the Nationalist Congress party and were soon to come under the sway of Mohandas Gandhi.

After a turbulent childhood and a chequered education, she married Feroze Gandhi in 1942. Her sons, Rajiv and Sanjay, were born in 1944 and 1946. In these years she was also active in the freedom struggle, spending nine months in jail at one time. When Nehru was chosen Prime Minister of newly independent India in 1947, Indira gradually took over as her father's hostess in the Prime Minister's residence in New Delhi, and the inevitable estrangement with her husband took place over the years. Feroze Gandhi died in 1960 of a heart attack. Indira's political role during her father's lifetime was a low-key one, though she served as president of the Congress party in 1959, and in this capacity clashed with Feroze, whose political sympathies were markedly left-wing and oppositional.

The question of a successor to Nehru had exercised political observers for years before his death. Indira was always perceived as a possible successor though her stature as a political figure was insignificant. When Nehru died in 1964 it was Lal Bahadur Shastri who succeeded as Prime Minister, but Indira was made Minister for Information and Broadcasting in his cabinet. Out of her father's shadow she quickly revealed her political skills and ambition and, when Shastri died after only two years in office, she was elected Prime Minister, due to a combination of her family name, her acceptability to the Party bosses, and the mass following she was able to command. She led her party to resounding success in the next elections in 1967. In 1971 she conducted a successful war against Pakistan which led to the liberation of East Pakistan (now Bangladesh).

But the years that followed were filled with turmoil and unrest, which the opposition parties were quick to exploit. Indira had followed her father's liberal, secular, socialist and non-aligned policies in domestic and foreign affairs. But her political style of suppressing dissent from her cabinet, colleagues and party members, her demagoguery, the unchecked corruption in government, the increasing upper-caste atrocities against the lower-caste *Harijans*, widespread communalism, and, above all, the growing and as yet unofficial power of her younger son, Sanjay, soon snowballed into a massive national disenchantment with her rule. In June 1975, she took the unprecedented step of announcing a state of emergency, suspended all civil liberties, imposed restrictions on the press, and arrested all opposition political leaders. This was the closest the leader of a democracy could come to exercising the powers of a dictator.

The Emergency became notorious for Sanjay's programmes of mass sterilization and destruction of urban slums. Indira removed the Emergency restrictions and called for fresh elections in 1977. Her party was routed and she herself lost. The opposition parties, brought together in a loose coalition called the Janata party, came to power with Morarji Desai as Prime Minister. Indira and Sanjay were prosecuted for their Emergency excesses through elaborate trials and courts of inquiry. But by the time these could be concluded the Janata party had broken up through internal dissension, and elections were held again in 1980. Indira had used her spell in the political wilderness to ingratiate herself once more with the masses, and with the slogan 'Garibi Hatao' (Remove poverty), she swept back to power.

Sanjay Gandhi was given the official position of General Secretary of the Congress party, and was increasingly perceived as a successor to Indira Gandhi. In 1980, however, he died in a plane crash. Rajiv, the older son, gave up his job as an airline pilot to become his mother's trusted aide and a General Secretary of the Congress party. Indira was facing, apart from the endemic problems of poverty, corruption and communalism, secessionist movements in Punjab, and continuing unrest in Assam and Kashmir. Terrorism in Punjab under the leadership of Bhindranwale, whom Indira Gandhi had in a sense earlier recognized as a Sikh leader, reached such proportions that she was finally obliged to send the army into the Golden Temple in Amritsar to flush out the terrorists hidden there. This sacrilege, as it was perceived, and the cost in human lives and damage to the temple, earned her the hostility of the Sikh community.

The Congress was still the only significant political party in the country and it is likely that Indira would have won elections in the following year despite her decreasing popularity. But in October 1984 she was assassinated by her own personal bodyguards, Sikhs who were avenging 'Operation Bluestar' (the temple entry).

2 Gail Omvedt discusses the Indian context in 'Women, Zilla Parishads and Panchayat Raj: From Chandwad to Vitner', *Economic and Political Weekly*, 4 August 1990, pp. 1687–90, esp. p. 1687. I provide here a short bibliography of works on women in politics in the USA and Europe since I do not refer further to these contexts at any length in the rest of this essay. Linda Carstarphen Gugin, 'The Political Roles of American Women', in Mary Anne Baker *et al.*, eds, *Women Today: A Multidisciplinary Approach to Women's Studies*, Monterey, CA, Brooks/Cole, 1980; Jean Kirkpatrick, *Political Woman*, New York, Basic Books, 1974; and *The New Presidential Elite: Men and Women in National Politics*, New York, Russell Sage Foundation and the Twentieth-Century Fund, 1976; J. Jacquette, ed., *Women in Politics*, New York, Wiley, 1974;

123

M. Githens and J. Prestage, eds, *A Portrait of Marginality: The Political Behavior of the American Woman*, New York, McKay, 1977; S. Tolchin and M. Tolchin, *Clout: Womanpower and Politics*, New York, Coward, McCann & Geoghegan, 1974; Cynthia Fuchs Epstein and Rose Lamb Coser, eds, *Access to Power: Cross-National Studies of Women and Elites*, London, George Allen & Unwin, 1981.

Gugin's essay points out that most women's lobbies extend support to women's issues, not to women, to functional feminism, not ideological feminism (p. 255).

3 See, for instance, Isaac Balbus, 'Disciplining Women: Michel Foucault and the Power of Feminist Discourse', in Seyla Benhabib and Drucilla Cornell, eds, *Feminism as Critique: Essays on the Politics of Gender in Late-Capitalist Societies*, Cambridge, Polity, 1987. Balbus argues that Foucault overlooks the 'disproportionately male ... orientation' towards power, 'and obliterates in the process the distinctively female power of nurturance in the context of which masculine power is formed and against which it reacts' (p. 120). See also Sara Ruddick, *Maternal Thinking*, London, Verso, 1989, and Jean Bethke Ehshtain, *Public Man, Private Woman*, Princeton, Princeton University Press, 1981, discussed by Chantal Mouffe, 'Feminism, Citizenship and Radical Democratic Politics', in Judith Butler and Joan W. Scott, eds, *Feminists Theorize the Political*, New York and London, Routledge, 1992, p. 374.

4 Ellen Kennedy and Susan Mendus, 'Introduction', in Kennedy and Mendus, eds, *Women in Western Political Philosophy*, Brighton, Wheatsheaf Books, 1987, p. 18.

5 Mouffe, 'Feminism', pp. 373–6.

6 See Eleanor Leacock, 'Women, Power and Authority', in Leela Dube, Eleanor Leacock and Shirley Ardner, eds, *Visibility and Power: Essays on Women in Society and Development*, Delhi, Oxford University Press, 1986, p. 109.

7 Simi Aforja, 'Women, Power and Authority in Traditional Yoruba Society', in Dube *et al.*, *Visibility and Power*.

8 Ibid., p. 137.

9 Nancy Harstock, *Money, Sex and Power*, Boston, Northeastern University Press, 1983, p. 255. In this context Nancy Harstock refers to Hannah Arendt's praise of Rosa Luxemburg, who was 'not concerned with herself but with a collectivity', in this displaying a 'feminine' notion of politics (p. 253).

10 This and the foregoing discussion are based on the proceedings of a seminar reported in the *Indian Express* (30 September 1990), 'Women's Role Nominal in Policy-making'.

11 Gayatri Chakravorty Spivak, 'Three Women's Texts and a Critique of Imperialism', *Critical Inquiry* 12, 1, Autumn 1985, pp. 243–61, esp. p. 246. Spivak is here referring to Elizabeth Fox-Genovese's argument in *New Left Review* 133, May–June 1982, pp. 5–29.

12 Harstock, *Money, Sex and Power*, p. 253.

13 Inder Malhotra, *Indira Gandhi: A Personal and Political Biography*, London, Hodder & Stoughton, 1989, p. 37. Malhotra reports her comment to a friend, upon becoming Prime Minister, that she felt exactly like the man who did not want to be king in Robert Frost's famous poem. But in a letter to her son, Rajiv, she had earlier quoted some other lines from the same poem: 'To be king is within the situation / and within me' (pp. 87–8).

14 Indira wrote that Harold Laski had advised her not to 'tag along' with her father, but that she did not mind. She was responding to the 'loneliness' she felt in him. See Dorothy Norman, *Indira Gandhi: Letters to a Friend 1950–1984*, London, Weidenfeld & Nicolson, 1984, p. 8.

15 Indira's Joan of Arc fantasy is described in her aunt Krishna Hutheesingh's autobiography *Dear to Behold*, London, Macmillan, 1969, p. 44, and alluded to by Nehru also in a letter to Indira in 1936 (see Sonia Gandhi, ed., *Freedom's Daughter: Letters between Indira Gandhi and Jawaharlal Nehru 1922–39*, London, Hodder & Stoughton, 1989, p. 269).

16 Gandhi was a powerful influence on Indira. See Norman, p. 19.

17 Her will, written shortly before her death, movingly expresses this:

> No hate is dark enough to overshadow the extent of my love for my country; no force is strong enough to divert me from my purpose and my endeavour to take this country forward ... I cannot understand how anyone can be an Indian and not be proud.
>
> (Text at Indira Gandhi Memorial Trust, New Delhi. Quoted in Malhotra, *Indira Gandhi*, pp. 307–8.)

18 For a discussion of the implications of choice and destiny in female leadership, see my 'The Feminist Plot and the Nationalist Allegory: Home and World in Two Indian Women's Novels in English', forthcoming.

19 See, for instance, the interview she gave to Fredda Brilliant, *Women in Power*, New Delhi, Lancer International, 1986, pp. 413ff.

20 See Malhotra, *Indira Gandhi*, p. 193, for an account of her distress at the implications of Emergency. The comment about 'riding a tiger' was made by Indira to J. Krishnamurthy, the philosopher.

21 The major influence on her was a yogi, Dhirendra Brahmachari, who from yoga teacher became one of her closest confidants and advisers.

22 In Hindu society a son is considered an asset and a daughter a liability. As the wealthy Motilal Nehru's only son, Jawaharlal was also expected to produce a male heir. Motilal's wife expressed her disappointment at Indira's birth: 'It should have been a son'. But Motilal declared: 'This daughter ... may prove better than a thousand sons' (ibid., p. 26).

23 There was widespread prejudice about Indira's being a widow since widowhood is considered an inauspicious state. In matters of dress, and behaviour towards the opposite sex, the Prime Minister was required to be circumspect. There was protest, for instance, against her shaking hands with 'foreign men' (ibid., p. 109).

24 In her early years of prime ministership she was nicknamed 'dumb doll' (ibid., p. 93). One of her opponents suggested that the Congress in 1966 throw out 'this pretty woman' so that she did not have to 'suffer pain and trouble beyond her endurance' (ibid., p. 103). General Yahya Khan, President of Pakistan, had referred to her at a public function as 'that woman'. These are only a few examples of sexism in public life.

   Indira was capable of being wryly humorous about the anomalies of being a woman in power. In response to President Johnson's hesitation about how she should be addressed, she is reported to have said: 'You can tell him that some of my cabinet ministers call me "sir". He can do so, too, if he likes'. After her death, Helmut Schmidt, former Chancellor of West Germany, described her as 'Zoon politikon' (political animal without gender). Malhotra calls this the 'most remarkable comment on Indira, in the context of women and power' (p. 191).

25 Raunaq Jahan, 'Women in South Asian Politics', *Third World Quarterly* 9.3, July 1987, pp. 848–70. All further references to this essay are indicated by page numbers given within parentheses in the text.

26 The political scientist, Bhikhu Parckh, propounds a 'distinctly Indian version of the dynastic principle', which enabled Indians to assimilate dynastic succession 'into the Hindu theory of rebirth'. Therefore, though Nehru and Indira did not overtly nominate their offspring as their successors, Indians felt sure that they alone would ensure 'ideological continuity' of rule. See 'How Indian is the First Family of India?' *The Times of India*, 28 August 1989. For the view that the dynastic theory of succession does not apply to India, see Subrata K. Mitra, 'India: Dynastic Rule or the Democratization of Power?' *Third World Quarterly* 10.1, January 1988, pp. 129–59. Mitra argues that in India the two requisites of this form of succession, nomination

of a successor by a ruler, and *a priori* acceptance of this by the ruled, have been lacking.

27 See Epstein and Coser, *Access to Power*.
28 Kanti Bajpai, 'The Making of Maggie', *Express Magazine*, 2 September 1990.
29 Rhoda Reddock, 'Women's Liberation and National Liberation', in Reddock, ed., *National Liberation and Women's Liberation*, The Hague, Institute of Social Studies, 1982, p. 15.
30 Carolyn Heilbrun, *Reinventing Womanhood*, New York, W.W. Norton & Co., 1979.
31 For an extended discussion of 'The Ideology of Motherhood' in Indian culture see the special issue (Review of Women Studies) in *Economic and Political Weekly*, 20 October 1990.
32 I do not want to develop the similarities too assiduously, but the coincidence of Indira's being a widow, and having two sons (one 'good' and one 'difficult'), like Radha, is certainly remarkable.
33 During the 1977 elections, for instance, she declared: 'We the Nehrus have a long history of sacrifice. ... We want to serve the country even when some people are against us. Our family will continue to do so in future'. Quoted in Kuldip Nayar, *The Judgement*, New Delhi, Vikas, 1977, pp. 172–3. Nayantara Sahgal, her cousin, observes trenchantly that though Indira repeated this insistently, there was not much evidence of sacrifice on her part. See *Indira Gandhi: Her Road to Power*, London and Sydney, Macdonald & Co., 1978, p. 13.
34 Malhotra, *Indira Gandhi*, p. 104. However, the view also prevailed, among political analysts, that Indira never quite fitted the role. Bhikhu Parekh writes: 'Something of an older sister and stern headmistress, her cold cynicism and partisanship, as also an early death, prevented her accolade of rashtramata (mother of the nation)' ('How Indian is the First Family of India?'). The press reacted to news of Indira's squabbling with Sanjay's wife, Maneka, with disillusionment: 'the Prime Minister and her household are the subject of bazaar gossip; the great mother image nudged by the stereotype mother-in-law image. ... The image of the only leader we have bruised; another illusion gone'. See Arun Shourie, *Mrs Gandhi's Second Reign*, New Delhi, Vikas, 1983, pp. 26–7.
35 'Foetus' is included in *After the Hanging and Other Stories*, translated from Malayalam by the author (New Delhi, Penguin, 1989). The other stories in this group, 'The Wart', 'Oil', 'The Examination', are similarly filled with images of disease, abnormal growth, decay – a mix of *Macbeth* and Kafka.
36 Salman Rushdie, *Midnight's Children*, London, Picador, 1982, p. 420. All references are to this edition, and page numbers have been indicated within parentheses in the text.
37 Inder Malhotra concludes his biography of Indira thus: 'Some say that both India and Indira would have been better off if she had loved it a little more and her sons, especially Sanjay, a little less' (p. 308). Ashis Nandy expresses the view that Indira's reliance on her son was not a weakness on her part – we must not forget 'the instrumental use Indira Gandhi made of her son in seeking his loyalty'. He compares her with other third-world leaders who similarly 'fall back on their relatives to create a second tier of political leadership'. See 'Indira Gandhi and the Culture of Indian Politics', in *At the Edge of Psychology*, Delhi, Oxford University Press, 1982, pp. 126–7. For Sanjay's actual role in India's political life, and especially during the Emergency, see Kuldip Nayar's *The Judgement*.
38 Nandy, 'Woman versus Womanliness in India', *At the Edge of Psychology*, p. 42.
39 Bhagwan Josh, a historian, describes the widespread protest in India at the depiction of the Rani of Jhansi's alleged affair with a British officer in a play by a British playwright, Phillip Cox, written in the 1930s. He concludes that 'a defeminised image

of the Rani forms an inseparable part of the cultural mythology of Hindu Nationalism' (Letters to the Editor, *The Times of India*, 18 July 1992). This 'cultural mythology' might offer another reason for the relative sanctity of the private life of the woman leader.

40 A few of these are: K.A. Abbas, *Indira Gandhi, Return of the Red Rose*, Delhi, Hind Pocket Books, 1966; Uma Vasudev, *Indira Gandhi: Revolution in Restraint*, Delhi, Vikas, 1974 and *Two Faces of Indira Gandhi*, Delhi, Vikas, 1977; Mary Carras, *Indira Gandhi: In the Crucible of Leadership*, Boston, Beacon Press, 1978; Dom Moraes, *Mrs Gandhi*, Delhi, Vikas, 1980; Pupul Jayakar and Raghu Rai, *Indira Gandhi*, Delhi, 1985; G. Parthasarathy and N.Y. Sharada Prasad, eds, *Indira Gandhi: Statesmen, Scholars, Scientists and Friends Remember*, New Delhi, Indira Gandhi Memorial Trust and Vikas, 1985. Malhotra's and Sahgal's biographies and Sonia Gandhi's and Dorothy Norman's collections of letters have been referred to already. A recent account of the Emergency period, Raj Thapar's *All These Years: A Memoir*, Delhi, Seminar Publications, 1991, discusses Indira Gandhi's personality and politics at length.

41 See Malhotra's brief recounting and dismissal of these in chapter 11 of *Indira Gandhi*, 'The Matriarch at Home'.

42 The blurb to Norman's volume of letters says: 'To all those who have judged Indira Gandhi on the strength of her public image this book will give an added dimension, the key to a true assessment of one of history's most important figures'. The introduction similarly professes that the letters will 'illuminate and reveal the private individual behind the public image' (p. xiii).

43 P.C. Alexander, 'My Years with Indira Gandhi – 2', *Economic Times*, 30 August 1990.

44 For the two senses of representation see Vicki Kirby, 'Corporeographies', *Inscriptions* 5, 1989, pp. 103–19, esp. p. 112.

45 Margaret Thatcher was equally indifferent to the women's movement: 'What's it Ever Done for Me?' (*New Statesman*, 7 October 1977), cited in Donna S. Sanzone, 'Women in Politics: A Study of Political Leadership in the United Kingdom, France and the Federal Republic of Germany', in Epstein and Coser, *Access to Power*, p. 44.

46 For a report on the workshop on Women and Politics in seven south-east Asian countries organized by UNESCO and UNIFEM (United Nations Fund for Women), in June 1990, see *The Times of India*, 'Women are still Political Outsiders', 19 June 1990. A report on the 1991 elections in Bangladesh comments on the irony of there being fewer than ten women contesting the 300 parliamentary seats in spite of the two main contending parties being led by women. These women, Sheik Hasina Wajed (AL) and Begum Khaleda Zia (BNP), only played the 'respective roles of dutiful daughter and devoted wife'. Women's issues have been given low priority on political agendas. See Rajashri Das Gupta, 'Women without Power', *Express Magazine*, 24 February 1990. Though in Pakistan and Bangladesh women have a separate quota in Parliament, their presence in local government bodies, in the bureaucracy and in the armed forces is insignificant. See Jahan, 'Women in South Asian Politics', pp. 857–64. Govind Kelkar provides figures for India: a maximum of only 6.77 per cent of members of state legislatures and 7.1 per cent of members of Parliament have been women, while in local decision-making bodies women may be as few as 1 to 2 per cent of the total number of members. In the 1977 elections only 30 per cent of the seats were contested by women. See 'Women in Post-Liberation Societies: A Comparative Analysis of Indian and Chinese Experiences', in *National Liberation and Women's Liberation*, p. 33. The number of women elected to the Lok Sabha (lower house of Parliament) reached a record high of 44 in 1984, but has dropped to 28 in the last elections, in 1991. While some parties reserve 30 per cent of all seats for women candidates this applies only at the *panchayat* (village bodies) level, not at the national level. A male candidate is perceived by the party as 'less of a risk', according

to Mamta Banerjee, a woman minister. See Kankana Das, 'Woman Power', *Sunday*, 8–14 March 1992.

47 Jacqueline Rose, 'The State of the Subject (II): The Institution of Feminism', *Critical Quarterly* 29, 4, Winter 1987, pp. 9–15. All quotations are from this essay; I have not indicated page numbers because of the brevity of the piece.
48 See for an illustration Zakia Pathak and Rajeswari Sunder Rajan, 'Shahbano', *Signs: Journal of Women in Culture and Society* 14, 3, Spring 1989.
49 Ibid.
50 These are well exemplified in a recent collection of essays edited by Judith Butler and Joan W. Scott, eds, *Feminists Theorize the Political*, London and New York, Routledge, 1992.
51 Terry Eagleton, *The Significance of Theory*, Oxford, Blackwell, 1990, pp. 55–6.
52 Fredric Jameson, 'Interview', *Diacritics* 12, Fall 1982, pp. 72–91, esp. p. 82.
53 Ibid., p. 90.
54 Mouffe, 'Feminism', p. 378.
55 Harstock, *Money, Sex and Power*, p. 253.
56 Terry Eagleton has spoken of the ways of desiring utopia 'feasibly', rather than 'uselessly': one must 'attend to those fault lines within the present that, developed or prised open in particular ways, might induce that condition to surpass itself into a future'. See 'Nationalism: Irony and Commitment', in Eagleton, Fredric Jameson and Edward W. Said, *Nationalism, Colonialism, and Literature*, Minneapolis, University of Minnesota Press, 1990, p. 25.
57 Epstein, 'Women and Elites: A Cross-national Perspective', in Epstein and Coser, *Access to Power*, p. 6.
58 Epstein, 'Women and Power: The Roles of Women in Politics in the United States', in Epstein and Coser, op. cit., p. 141.
59 All quotations in the foregoing paragraph are from Omvedt, 'Women, Zilla Parishads and Panchayat Raj', pp. 1689 and 1690.
60 Chetna Gala emphasizes the importance of – and the difficulties encountered in – getting women a share in their husbands' property in Vitner. See her 'Trying to Give Women their Due: The Story of Vitner Village', *Manushi* 59, July–August 1990, pp. 29–32.
61 Chetna Gala interviewed women *panchayat* members about the difference the election had made in their lives. One said: 'What difference can it make to our daily lives? We still do the same work. Even the *sarpanch* (village leader) goes to fetch firewood. Labour is written in our fate. Do you think a male *sarpanch* would work in the fields? We have to work both in the fields and at our home'. But the women ultimately agreed that they now earned more respect in the village (ibid., p. 31).
62 Ibid., p. 31.

6

REAL AND IMAGINED WOMEN
Politics and/of representation

I INTRODUCTION

The construction of women in terms of recognizable roles, images, models, and labels occurs in discourse in response to specific social imperatives even where it may be offered in terms of the universal and abstract rhetoric of 'Woman' or 'women' (or the 'Indian woman', as the case may be). As Kumkum Sangari and Sudesh Vaid have pointed out in the introduction to a collection of essays that explores the project of 'recasting women' in colonial India, 'womanhood is often part of an asserted or desired, not an actual, cultural continuity'.[1] Elsewhere Sangari has argued that

> female-ness is not an essential quality. It is constantly made, and redistributed; one has to be able to see the formation of female-ness in each and every form at a given moment or in later interpretations, and see what it is composed of, what its social correlates are, what its ideological potentials are, what its freedoms may be.[2]

If we acknowledge (a) that femaleness is constructed, (b) that the terms of such construction are to be sought in the dominant modes of ideology (patriarchy, colonialism, capitalism), and (c) that therefore what is at stake is the investments of desire and the politics of control that representation both signifies and serves, then the task of the feminist critic becomes what Jacqueline Rose describes as 'the critique of male discourse' born of 'a radical distrust of representation which allies itself with a semiotic critique of the sign'.[3] What is required here is an alertness to the political process by which such representation becomes naturalized and ultimately coercive in structuring women's self-representation. In the first two parts of this chapter I undertake this essentially analytical task of ideological critique, pointing to the emergence of a 'new Indian woman' in media and official discourse in India today, a construction which serves not only to reconcile in her subjectivity the conflicts between tradition and modernity in Indian society, but works also to deny the actual conflict that women existentially register as an aspect of their lives.

129

But if we are to avoid the cultural determinism that follows from the argument from construction, we must also locate the liberatory space for resistance that it allows (from the premise that what is 'made' can be 'unmade' or made differently). But neither can resistance be simply a matter of feminist assertion, or the product of a politically desirable feminist invention. Rather the 'ideological', as Susie Tharu suggests, must itself and *inherently* be viewed as the 'articulation of complex, sometimes contradictory and unevenly determining practices' so that 'a theory of struggle *within the ideological*' becomes possible (emphasis in original).[4] As I see it, there are two constraints that are usefully identified here as limits to the project of reading resistance: one is to view resistance as inescapably structured by the terms of the dominant though not ultimately reducible to it; and the second, to beg the question of the extent and effect of resistance. In the context of feminist literary criticism Rose locates feminism's 'counter-history' of women's writing as the logical second step in the critique of male discourse which, though susceptible to this form of recuperation, must nevertheless be risked as an aspect of any radical discourse.[5]

In the last section of this chapter I therefore offer a quick sampling of such a 'radical' discourse of women whose political value rests in the fact, simply, that it exists – however tenuously and ambivalently – and which to ignore is to avoid the larger historical and institutional enquiry into the conditions of its possibility. That further enquiry lies outside the scope of this chapter, but my description of feminist self-representation in the contemporary Indian discourse of women tries to push towards the recognition of a larger social dynamic and movement that frames it.

II A NEW BRAND OF WOMAN

In the contemporary discourse of women in India a significant mode of interpellation and projection can be perceived in the construction of a 'new' 'Indian' woman. She is 'new' in the senses both of having evolved and arrived in response to the times, as well as of being intrinsically 'modern' and 'liberated'. (Ipshita Chanda points out that the adjectives new/liberated/modern are taken to be 'metonymous – saying one is to imply all the others by the logic of this sign-system that groups itself around the figure of woman'.)[6] She is 'Indian' in the sense of possessing a pan-Indian identity that escapes regional, communal, or linguistic specificities, but does not thereby become 'westernized'. The primary site of this construction is commercial advertisements in the media, both in print and on television.

The image of the 'new Indian woman' is of course derived primarily from the urban educated middle-class career woman. Advertisements for consumer products – chiefly food, clothes, cleaning products, contraceptives, beauty products, household gadgets – are addressed to this class of women, who command an independent income and/or (at least) exercise control over spending it.[7] They are therefore a response to the actual reality of the existence of a small but growing and significant female population in Indian cities. The woman portrayed in these advertisements is attractive, educated, hardworking, and socially aware. The last attribute is indicated by her having a family of the right size and constitution (two children, invariably one boy and one girl), providing the right nutrition for her family, being excessively hygienic, and exercising conscious and deliberate choice as a consumer. In interpellating the users of these products as 'new' women, the advertisements not only provide an attractive and desired self-image for women in general, but also provide a normative model of citizenship that is, significantly, now gendered female. The power and success of the representation derive not from fantasy but from an embellishment of reality and from the 'liberal' idiom in which it is couched.

Such an analysis is neither new nor particularly rewarding since it informs, and is overtly acknowledged in, the formulations of image-makers themselves. For instance, an article in the advertising section of the financial daily, *The Economic Times*, entitled 'Cashing in on Woman Power', identifies the purchasing power of career women, the new roles that they play in society,[8] and their high viewership of television[9] as the reasons for the construction and targetting of a 'new Indian woman' in advertising.[10] It is more productive to discern the ideological manoeuvres, more subtle and coercive, that underlie the explicit and strategic uses of the image to sell products. One purpose of such procedures, as Ipshita Chanda has astutely noted, is 'to obliterate the political project of feminisms and appropriate certain aspects of the women's movement's agenda into the construction of a new sign system which revolves round the subject position "woman" '.[11] The liberation of women is separated from the con- temporary women's movement: by making liberation a matter of individual women's achievement and choice, the development of the new woman is made to appear as a 'natural' outcome of benevolent capitalist socio-economic forces.[12] The 'modernization' of the Indian woman can then be valorized as a painless, non-conflictual, even harmonious, process, in contrast to the discomforts produced by political feminism.[13]

The new Indian woman's liberation is rendered safe in a number of other ways that assuage social fears.[14] A longer and more nuanced analysis of the whole range of commercial advertisements than I can undertake here would show, for instance, that there is a sharp polarization between representations of younger and older women. The young woman, or more accurately, the teenager, may enact actual rebellion, or even project sexual desire;[15] whereas the older woman, invariably married, exercises her autonomy – her education, her earnings – on behalf of the family's well-being (or, at a pinch, conjugal sex). Both rebellion/sexuality in the one case, and financial autonomy on the other, are controlled and made acceptable by a certain 'femininity' that is encoded as physical charm.[16] The polarization, in any case, subtly deconstructs itself into continuity: the young woman's freedom, because it precedes marriage and domesticity and will therefore be 'naturally' tamed by them in due course, makes her youth a sanctioned space for a last fling of rebellion. The 'new woman' does not, in either case, jeopardize the notion of a tradition which is preserved intact in the idealized conjugal and domestic sphere.

Advertising's co-optation of precisely those areas of women's liberation that the women's movement has marked out for itself – sexuality, work, marriage and family – for defining its images of womanhood, works as all co-optation does: as simultaneously a form of sharing in the spoils and as a displacement. Thus at one level it is not in conflict with the goals of feminism;[17] at another, as we have seen, it undercuts them by offering a similar desired image of the liberated woman arrived at by a different trajectory. More strikingly, advertising targets the most frequent sites of women's oppression – sexual harassment, domestic work, dowry demands, marriage rituals, the joint family – and re-defines them in glamorized or, alternatively, trivialized terms as the sites of remaking female identity. Thus the woman who attracts stares from a male crowd on a street, bus or in any other public place – a harrowing experience of everyday sexist harassment for women – is imaged as the ideal of the attractive and sexually desirable woman. Elaborate scenes of decking and beauty rituals at weddings as well as sentimental leave-taking scenes between mother and daughter idealize marriage in soft-focus, sepia-tinted photography. Among the most clichéd and successful ideas for cleaning products, for instance, is the image of the insouciant and elegant housewife who uses the advertised product to clean tubfuls of clothes or toilets without a trace of distaste or drudgery.[18] An advertisement for a popular *supari* (betel nut), *Pan Parag*, even defuses a dowry-taking scene. In a meeting between the parents of the prospective bride and bridegroom, the bride's parents are relieved and happy to learn that the only demand made by the groom's parents (preceded by a reassuring: ' Do not fear!') is for the provision of *Pan Parag* for the occasion. In other words, it is not only women (as the new users and buyers of commodities) who are recast in this project; their social contexts are also transformed in order to provide more benign accommodation to the new mode of social being that is now offered to them. If such a major social reorganization can seemingly take place so effortlessly around the figure of the new woman, what need for a revolution?

The construction of the new Indian woman must attend to her national identity as well as her modernity; she is Indian as well as new. The Indian identity is largely a function of the nation-wide reach of commercial adver-tisements. Though Indian manufacturers and advertising agencies periodically acknowledge the need to have more region-specific advertising – especially in the context of marketing in rural areas – they have tended to develop and project a homogenized message across the country (except for dubbing or translating the verbal medium). It is primarily the class provenance of the upwardly mobile Indian whom the advertisements interpellate that most effec-tively irons out regional differences; within the cultures of the urban professional middle class in all parts of the country a certain uniformity already prevails, which then lends itself to a further homogenization. The status of Hindi and English as the country's official languages has given the cultures spawned by them (or an amalgam of them) the force of a (dubious) pan-Indian identity.[19] (Where the 'regional' retains its uses in identifying a product's 'origins', it is now coded as the more fashionable 'ethnic'.)[20] The development of an 'Indianness' free of chauvinistic regional markers among its citizenry is, of course, one of the declared aspirations of the Indian State. But its achievement in commercial advertising, ironically, can only be represented through 'westernizing' the Indian consumer. This, however, calls forth its own rationalization in terms of the new world order. Gurcharan Das, Chairman of Proctor and Gamble in India, explains in an article on 'The Modern Indian' why, though 'the modern Indian is less confident with the thought that he is not very "Indian"', he can nevertheless 'justify himself by thinking that he is a citizen of the new global village in which capitalism, democracy are a global inheritance just like the English language'. Das endorses the word 'modern' ('it is a positive word'), and endows the modern Indian with energy, pragmatism, national competitiveness; he is a conscious internationalist who 'like his western counterpart tries to cope with the anxiety of separation by losing himself in the zealous pursuit of consumer goods. They help him to forget that he is uprooted, atomised, and part of a faceless, lonely mass society'.[21] The modern Indian joins the postmodern club!

In this context it is the Indian *woman*, perennially and transcendentally wife, mother and homemaker, who saves the project of modernization-without-westernization. 'Good' modernity, as Tejaswini Niranjana calls it, must be only skin-deep.[22] It is only the female subject who can be shown as successfully achieving the balance between (deep) tradition and (surface) modernity, through strategies of representation that I discuss at greater length in the following section.

III A WOMAN FOR ALL SEASONS

If commercial advertising foregrounds the 'modernity' of the contemporary woman at the same time as it carefully respects her connections with 'tradition' (chiefly symbolized by the family and the values it supports), then state television (Doordarshan) celebrates the traditional but refurbishes its image to make its values 'up to date'. The contemporary discourse of women may thus be seen as negotiating a strategic resolution of the contradictions that women experience in their lives as a result of the contrary pulls of the ideological categories of 'tradition' and 'modernity': primarily by conflating them so that there is no longer any essential conflict between the values they represent.[23]

As the 'matter' of television programmes women are highly visible: in addition to their appearance in the films, public information shorts and commercials which are relayed by the medium, there is a predominance of women-centred serials and documentaries on women's issues produced by Doordarshan itself. For an explanation of how Indian television's scope and functioning create an influential 'official' discourse, I draw upon Arvind Rajagopal's perceptive analysis of the contradictions inherent in a situation in which a progressive diminution of the autonomy of Doordarshan accompanies a progressive increase in its regulatory function:

> As a state apparatus [Indian television] is held to represent the universal interest in its promise of progress. Every expansion and innovation in the system is done in the name of education and development. Its development becomes a means of expanding the presence of state in society: television becomes an expression of state interests. While the infrastructural expansion for television was accomplished swiftly and successfully, the state could not generate the innovative capacity necessary to attract viewing audiences. From a completely state-dominated medium, then, television became a carrier of commercially-sponsored privately produced programs, though the state retained veto power over them. ... While commercial forces enter as an influence on Doordarshan programming, at the same time their influence outside television is reduced. Advertising gets diverted to television, as do audiences. 'Talent' from the film industry increasingly seek television as an outlet. Thus the state becomes the ringmaster of a larger portion of the public sphere. More and more media culture passes through the sieve of state inspection and supervision.[24]

State television's hegemonic influence as an ideological apparatus, as Rajagopal goes on to demonstrate, may be perceived most spectacularly in its representations of women and religion.

The conceptual and political space occupied by women in the television medium is identical to that of religion, and hence representations of women and religion frequently coincide. The relationship between the two is not only homologous, but also metonymic – hence the significance of the two television serials of the epics, the *Ramayana*, followed by the *Mahabharata*, whose central female figures became symbols of 'our' 'national' culture.[25] State-sponsored television, with its dual obligations in its representation of women and religion – on the one hand to acknowledging the state's constitutional commitment to equal rights (in the case of women) and to secularism (in the case of religion), and on the other hand to developing a new idiom of 'nationalism', equated with a valorization of the traditional (which is preserved, precisely, in and by women and religion) – redefines the two terms flexibly. The traditional is represented as the timeless, and hence inclusive of the modern, while the modern is viewed merely as a transitional phase which disguises the permanent 'essence' of timeless tradition. Thus female figures from history, myth and religion in many television programmes are invested with status and autonomy and serve as the mouthpiece of liberated sentiments. The Draupadi of the gambling scene in the *Mahabharata* is, of course, the most memorable example of such a representational strategy; but see also the more recent example of the eponymous heroine of *Mriganayini*, the sixteenth-century commoner queen of the king of Pomar.[26] Consider also the brief rendition of Laxmibai, the Rani of Jhansi as evoked in one of a series of television 'shorts' celebrating the Indian nationalist movement which the Congress government issued in 1989, in the months before the general election. Ania Loomba describes the affective elements of the film perceptively:

> Within the nationalist tradition she [Laxmibai] has been vigorously cel-
> ebrated as a model of female – as opposed to feminist – valour; she is the
> exceptional, mardani or masculine woman, the honorary man who is one
> of the models for Indian womanhood. The film continues this tradition of
> glamorizing her. We see the Rani stripping her womanly weaknesses along
> with her jewelled bracelets, and donning militant masculinity by picking
> a sword and plunging it into a sheath at her waist. She is next seen on
> her horse, riding in seductive slow motion over a rolling landscape to the
> words of a film song. ... Then a low-pitched male voice recites lines of a
> popular poem celebrating the Rani's ability to fight 'like a man'.[27]

The seemingly 'revisionary' readings of the texts of the past undertaken in these serials do not so much lead to real change as legitimize the texts as universal and timeless documents.

More suggestively, by arguing that exceptional women of learning, or achieve-ment, or military prowess were by no means absent in the valorized Indian past, they undercut the contemporary need for an organized women's movement for achieving women's equality. The occluding of representations of 'ordinary' women from a selective reading of the past was an influential strategy of colonial orientalists and nationalists for reclaiming a 'golden Vedic age', as Uma Chakravarti has shown;[28] in the present context it is a strategy that seeks to pose that 'high' tradition – in response to the questions of feminists, among others – as one always already sensitive to the issues of feminism.

By the same token, contemporary liberated female figures, elite, westernized, educated, professional – as represented, for example, in such popular serials as *Rajani* or *Udaan* – simultaneously and effortlessly hold on to the traditional values of husband-worship, family nurturance, self-sacrifice and sexual chastity. Their exemplary virtue – as well as virtuosity – is a saga of an individualism that functions for the social good rather than at odds with it. The media critic Iqbal Masood analyses the 'feminism' of *Udaan*, a serial about Kalyani, a woman police officer. Kalyani does not even dream of 'collective action on behalf of her sex or class' – instead she wants power for herself and her family through the restoration of her father's lost feudal position, a form of social mobility which is possible in the contemporary social context only by securing a position in the country's elite bureaucracy.[29] In the representations of both kinds of women – women in history and myth who are 'modern', as well as contemporary women who are 'traditional' – women (and religion) are made to serve as harmonious symbols of historical continuity rather than as conflictual subjects and sites of conflict.

Nevertheless, the state is forced to recognize that outside the harmonious world it presents on the broadcasting medium, women's groups and religious

135

groups do exist as such conflictual subjects and sites of conflict – if only because they quickly reveal themselves as watchdogs of their interests in the medium. The protests against negative representations (of women, or religious/communal/regional groups) range all the way from the initiative of individual cranks, to the more programmatic campaigns of fundamentalist groups, opposition political parties, civil rights groups and women's groups; and their politics would vary largely from the extreme reactionary to the progressive and radical. The form of such protests – outcries in the press, public rallies, court injunctions for stoppage of a serial – inevitably calls for as it calls forth the state's censorship machinery.[30] The actual politics of such an opposition has been analysed forcefully by Madhu Kishwar elsewhere and I shall not rehearse this debate here.[31] But it is significant that the state views censorship, i.e. the excision of offensive representations, as a sufficient and efficient part of its strategy of representing progressive images of women and religion in the broadcasting medium. Its responsiveness to demands from interest groups for the banning of negative representations is invariably prompt, partly because of the ease with which such a move can be made, and at least partly because of the benevolence it can thereby display towards these embattled groups.

Of greater significance is the fact that the demand for banning 'sex' scenes, particularly in the films relayed by Doordarshan, a demand originating most often from women's groups, is made on behalf of preserving 'family values'.[32] Television is a family medium by its very nature; and the family, as Indian feminists have argued, is an institution that the state supports fervently.[33] The state's support is expressed not only through the operation of strict codes of censorship in television programmes, but also in the ways the latter negotiate representations of the conflict between women and the family. Women's issues – dowry, discrimination against girl children, reproduction, health, work – are subsumed within the framework of the 'larger' good of family and society. One public information shot issued by the Directorate of Family Planning, for instance, shows a happy family consisting of a couple with their two children, both girls. The couple announce their decision to have no more children though they have not produced a son; the affection and happiness in the expressions of the two children are caught frequently in close-up, in an obvious attempt to show that their parents do not slight them on account of their sex. But it is not the rights of girl-children – to live, most fundamentally – that *is* stressed in this short, but the norm of the small family. By thus aligning women's rights and the family's well-being as directed towards the same goal, the medium defuses the conflicts between women and the family which is such a crucial feature of contemporary Indian society.

There is also the danger of unforeseen alliances springing up between women's groups and reactionary social forces, a phenomenon feminism must guard against as the authors of a recent book on the contemporary women's movement in India warn. Thus women's fight against pornography is sympathetically viewed by the moral right; their demand for a ban on abortion following sex-determination tests is supported by right-to-lifers; their campaign against the government's family planning programmes dovetails with a liberal notion of individual rights; and their demand for a uniform civil code for the nation is endorsed, for communal reasons, by fundamentalist Hindu groups.[34] In such a context many specifically *gendered* issues can be deflected on to other areas in official discourses and representations.

The combined hegemony of global consumer capitalism and national state broadcasting is undoubtedly a powerful one in the interpellation and construction of women in contemporary India. But even as we are alert to the ways in which the 'new Indian woman' is brought into being in response to specific social, economic and political imperatives, equally we perceive how the unresolved contradictions between gender and culture are foregrounded in other arenas of representation. The 'public' space is not a vacuum simply filled by 'professional advice, marketing strategies, government programs, electoral choices, and advertisers' images of happiness', as Richard Fox and T.J. Jackson Lears describe the work of 'intellectuals' in capitalism.[35] Other symbols and images already exist which contest those produced by the audiovisual media.[36] Chief of these in India is the print medium of newspapers.

Newspapers' regular coverage of atrocities against women, and their reports and features on other women's issues, is undeniably marked by a commitment primarily to 'news value' rather than by concern for the rights of women. A recent letter circulated to women activists by the national newspaper *The Statesman*, announcing a special weekly page for women, carries this appeal: 'What we wish to achieve through our special page is (1) create greater awareness of and (2) provoke public debates on the discrimination against women inherent in our social attitudes, stereotyped concepts, customs, values, laws etc'. But even this programmatically liberal document feels bound to go on to distinguish between and privilege 'objective exposés' over 'didactic discourses', as an aspect of the discourse of women in print journalism.[37] Nevertheless, even given this emphasis, as well as the superficiality, distortions and sensationalism of much press reporting,[38] the visibility of women in public life has significantly increased as a result of their representation in news stories. By being made visible as part of and as participating in the recognizable public world – the workplace, the street, other public forums – they become 'public' figures themselves, drawn out of the privacy and invisibility of the home. This is a measure of their 'reality'. The controversies around women in India in the past decade, as around religion (the most famous instance being the Shahbano case), have arisen out of the conflict between communal/familial values on the one hand and the concept of rights as an individual, legal entitlement on the other. To a large extent it is the print medium (supported by other forums like university campuses, public rallies, law courts, and parliament) that has mediated the shift for women from invisibility in the private sphere to representation in the public sphere.

But because women are represented in news stories in one of broadly two ways – (a) as victims of physical violence (rape, assault, abduction, domestic torture, murder), or of legal injustice (sexual harassment at work, discriminatory wages, inheritance and other matters covered by personal law), or (b) as protestors against social injustice (such as price rises, dowry deaths, communal riots, environmental hazards) – their relationship to the social structure is marked as external and adversarial rather than as integral and ambivalent. As Judith Butler has pointed out, the traditional view of 'agency' seems to require that we think about persons 'as instrumental actors who confront an external political field'.[39] In the Indian context the implicit dichotomy between tradition and modernity once again structures the discourse of women as a conflict between indigenous social practice and 'modern' legal rights, leading to an insidious and threatening attack upon the latter on behalf of the former in certain portions of the popular press and the reactionary right. An article in the weekly English journal *Sunday* ('Woman Power') pronounces definitively that 'feminism is no longer a politically correct term in India'. It disapprovingly contrasts 'feminists' with members of voluntary organizations and international and government agencies who work for 'women's uplift'. If the 'new woman' in India is assertive about her rights – as she is perceived to be – it is not because of the women's movement but because of 'the precepts her mother taught her'.[40] Thus the women's movement is rendered alien and irrelevant to the Indian social and political context. Similarly, a Shahbano or a Rupam Deol who seeks the recourse of the law to establish her rights is easily reduced in the normative discourse to a puppet of her male relatives, of political or religious groups, or of women's groups; or else regarded as a victim of inauthentic 'western' values.

The feminist project therefore becomes one of exploring conceptual alternatives for representing women's autonomy within viable social structures that refuse this framing, an exploration I undertake in the next section.

IV REAL WOMEN

In the handful of texts I cite in this section – picked at random from a survey of contemporary culture – the representation of the relative freedom of women is encoded neither as an absence of conflict (as in commercial advertisements), nor as the resolution of conflict (as in television images), but as the product of a specific conjuncture of social and historical circumstances. Thus Saoli Mitra's one-woman dance-drama about Draupadi, *Nathabati-Anathabat* (lit. 'Having Husbands but like a Widow', i.e. 'The Married Woman Bereft of Protection'); Sheba Chachi's portfolio of photographs of women, *Feminist Portraits*; the eighteenth-century Telugu woman-poet Mudupalani's 'Radhika Santwanam' ('The Appeasement of Radha') which the nineteenth-century courtesan and scholar Nagaratnamma revived and reprinted, and which Susie Tharu and K. Lalitha translate and present in their anthology *Women Writing in India*; Ketan Mehta's *Mirch Masala* and Aruna Raje's *Rihayee*, two films about rural women's communities in western India; *We Were Making History*, Stree Shakthi Sanghatana's record of the oral histories of women in the Telengana peasant movement of the late 1940s[41] – the common features and concerns of these texts are meaningful for an exploration of alternative structures of representation. A feminist consciousness that is historically 'modern' informs the subjectivity of the women represented in these texts; and/or an actual or incipient female solidarity (the condition of collectivization) is set in motion; thematically, issues of tradition and modernity are engaged with strenuously; and formal innovativeness marks their textual modes. I do not set this out as a list of preconditions or sufficient conditions for the 'correct' representation of women, but only as an attempt at a succinct description of a disparate and randomly chosen collection of contemporary texts. What follows is a brief and necessarily inadequate description of each of these texts.

Saoli Mitra produced her one-woman prize-winning show, *Nathabati Anathabat*, in New Delhi in December, 1991. She bases her script on the story of Draupadi in the *Mahabharata*, as interpreted by the historian Iravati Karve,[42] narrating it through song, dance and dramatic forms that are adapted from a number of traditional and folk forms. The formal innovativeness and strenuousness of her production are remarkable. Draupadi is the princess of Videha who is obliged to marry all the five Pandava princes though it is Arjuna whom she has chosen. Insulted by the Kauravas after her husbands' defeat at the gambling-table, she is saved by Krishna's intervention; and the great battle of Kurukshetra between the two clans is fought by the Pandavas at least partly to avenge the insult offered to her. Draupadi is read by Karve as a woman who suffers, endures, rebels and asserts herself, a 'true daughter of the earth', unlike the Sita of the *Ramayana*. It is this version of Draupadi that Mitra presents, using her as a voice and her story as a means to indict oppression, war and the structures of male power.

Sheba Chachi's photographs were part of an exhibition of the work of a group of Indian and Asian photographers. Chachi describes her attempt at developing portraits of her 'friends, sisters' in the women's movement in Delhi as 'incomplete, not representational'; they interrogate dominant stereotypical representations even as they try to sidestep the stereotypes of militancy, 'angry eyes, raised fist, shouting mouth'. Chachi therefore composes her portraits by placing her subjects among settings, objects, symbols chosen by themselves, forming a 'mosaic' of 'multiple images'. She wishes to convey

> not the single essence, but a pattern of visual nodes.
> Pegs to pin a web, weave a story.
> For that is what I hope to do; tell you these stories
> as I have heard, fine or faulty.[43]

My only access to Mudupalani's poem, 'Radhika Santwanam', is through the few extracts published in English translation in the recent anthology *Women Writing in India* (1991). The editors, however, provide a detailed description of the poem and its reception. 'Radhika Santwanam' is a *sringaraprabandham*, a genre of erotic poetry that is used for narrating the story of the divine lovers,

Krishna and Radha. Mudupalani's originality consisted of shifting the focus of the poem to Radha, and making her 'sensuality' and her 'initiative', her 'satisfaction or pleasure' inform the poetic resolution. One of the extracts ('If I ask her not to kiss me') illustrates the aggressive eroticism of the woman through the lover's admiring and indulgent description of her love-making:

> If I ask her not to kiss me,
> stroking on my cheeks
> she presses my lips hard against hers.
> ... fondles me, talks on, making love again and again.
> How could I stay away
> from her company?

In addition to Mudupalani's scholarship and her technical expertise in verse-forms, her 'radical' assertion of the centrality of women's pleasure marks her poetic greatness and explains her importance for a project of the retrieval of women's voices from the past.[44]

Ketan Mehta's film *Mirch Masala* (Red Chilli Spice) (1989), is set in rural Gujerat, and tells the story of the oppression of the labouring classes, especially the women, by the local landlords. A group of women employed in the spice factory decide to resist their oppressors, and accordingly barricade themselves in the factory and hold their attackers off with ammunition consisting of the red chilli powder they make in the factory. *Rihayee* (1990) is less uncompromisingly militant and more problematic as a feminist statement. In a village in rural Rajasthan whose men migrate in large numbers to the city in search of work, the women are susceptible to the sexual advances of a persuasive Gulf-returned seducer, a 'native son' returning to the village for a holiday. One of the village women, Takkoo Bai (the film's protagonist), becomes pregnant by him, but refuses to abort the child partly because she has hopes, based on an astrologer's prediction, that it will be a son (she already has three daughters), and partly because of her opposition to abortion. At the village *panchayat* she is indicted by the old (male) members for her immorality. But the village matriarch rises to her defence and supports her rights over her own body. At this all the other women unexpectedly take Takkoo's side and threaten to leave the village if she is expelled. The husband who returns is also shown as someone who understands her sexual needs and supports her decision. The film's resolution may not be entirely realistic, but it poses the problems of rural society, the dilemmas of the men who migrate and the loneliness of the women who are left behind, the question of the double standard, the proposition that women must exercise their rights over their own bodies, in terms both of desire and of reproduction, and the possibility of a female solidarity based on shared oppression and sympathy, in an idiom that is forthright and powerful.

Finally, I cite *We Were Making History* (life stories of women in the Telengana people's struggle) by members of Stree Shakti Sanghatana in Hyderabad. These stories constitute an invaluable oral history; they are the spoken reminiscences of about twenty women who had been part of the peasant struggle against feudal oppression – bonded labour, exploitation, rape – in rural Andhra Pradesh in the 1940s. The editors and other members of the women's organization, Stree Shakti Sanghatana, who perform this task of recording, collecting, editing and publishing these stories, also speak of the problems and dangers of reading them as transparent accounts of events and feelings: 'As anyone actually engaged in recording life histories finds out, neither memory nor experience is exempt from ideological processing. ... hidden conventions and models shape the "fiction" through which we grasp and project our lives'.[45] Nevertheless, the overwhelming impression the book creates is one of liberation, a new optimism and a sense of participation in the stirring larger events of history that for women cannot but be emancipatory in the widest sense.

Several of these texts (*We Were Making History*, *Mirch Masala* and *Rihayee*, as well as Raja Rao's 1937 novel, *Kanthapura*[46]) describe the period of women's collective struggle as a 'magic time'. These periods are not fortuitous conjunctures of 'the (wo)man and the moment' but contingent events grounded in specific historical and social circumstances. K. Lalitha and Vasantha Kannabiran offer the analysis that 'it is only in ... periods of social dysfunction [war or revolution], with the breakdown of constant surveillance and the mechanisms of discipline that normally objectify them, that women rush forth to grasp the opportunities for response and growth that become possible'.[47] Though the women who participated in the Telengana movement talk with 'nostalgia and warmth' of 'the best period of their lives', the contradictions of their experience are sharply drawn not only in terms of its inherent strains and conflicts but of its temporal limits. As in the nationalist movement, when the struggle is called off, the women return to their previous traditional lives. Thus gains are made seemingly only to be lost. But often the women claim that some residual progress remains. The narrative of women's 'progress' is read as three steps forward and two steps backward, a slow and imperceptible advance.

In the other texts I invoke – Mudupalani's resurrected poem, Chachi's photographs, Mitra's performance – it is individual, not collective, women who are represented. But the powerfully forged relations between the 'authors' and the subjects of their representations produces the appropriative gesture – across time and distance – that marks the establishment of solidarity. In a further appropriative move the contemporary critic may claim these texts as politically meaningful in the context of our own times.

Thus for Tharu and Lalitha, Nagaratnamma, the poem's original publisher (1887), is a figure who 'anticipates' their own 'critical initiative', and the story of Mudupalani's life, her writing and the misadventures of 'Radhika Santwanam' serve as an 'allegory of the enterprise of women's writing and the scope of feminist criticism in India'. For these critics the poem raises the critical questions of contexts, politics and resistances that frame women's writing and therefore engage them most deeply in their own work.[48]

Responding to Sheba Chachi's photographs, the poet Vishwapriya Iyengar identifies closely with the artist's vision which allows her 'an emotional entry into her frame-of-reference': 'It is a quest for identities for me as much as it is for the photographer'. In the newspaper feature that she writes, her responses take the form of brief idiosyncratic poetic interjections that accompany the texts.[49]

The critic Shuddhabrata Sengupta is similarly led into a politically fraught search for 'what makes for the modern' through a critical engagement with his text, Saoli Mitra's re-enactment of the Draupadi story. His validation of her work in these terms is particularly significant at a time when 'a resurgent Hindu fundamentalism' puts tradition to politically dubious use. 'The kind of theatre that *Nathabati-Anathabat* represents', in contrast to this use in the television serial, for instance, is centred 'neither ... round an invitation, nor an evasion or a reverence for tradition. It is centred rather on a self-conscious relation to it'. He goes on to analyse Mitra's script and performance in ways that usefully begin to formulate the project of 'modernity' in India today:

> Hers is an assault by the profane on the sacred, and one cannot but be delighted with the ease and the anarchic wit with which she dismembers sacrility. Several canons are violated in this process, heroes become human, gods disappear or are pushed to the margin, desire not duty is celebrated as an ethical imperative – and that is refreshing, and being a woman she takes upon herself the freedom not to be willowy and graceful, but to be grotesque and comic and serious by turns. Of this, perhaps unconscious, rejection of femininity is born a healthy and skeptical androgynous elegance that is in itself perhaps an unconscious political statement about gender identity. Modernity is made of this uncomfortable, uneasy stuff.[50]

The kind of alliance between subject, author and critic that is generated by these texts is, as I see it, a constitutive aspect of their relevance to the contemporary project of women's self-representation.

The narratives I speak of cannot, however, be read simply as stirring stories. They are not 'models' conducive to replicability either as actual social communities or within representational structures. They are more usefully regarded instead as specific historical examples. Such representations are 'spaces' that are 'really temporalities, moments in time when certain possibilities coalesce', as Lauren Barlant explains. The 'success' and achievements they celebrate must ultimately be 'framed as failure'[51] because of the rigid and contingent conditions within which alone they operate. (It is for this reason that an account like Veena Oldenberg's, of the lives of Lucknow courtesans, becomes suspect when it unproblematically conflates the professional traditions of the women of this Indian town with the lifestyle and attitudes of the present-day New York hooker; the differences between the community consciousness of the one and the individualism of the other are made negligible, as are periods and places and contexts.)[52]

As is to be expected, my chosen texts are not – as perhaps they cannot be –

sharply disjunct from the contemporary Indian discourse of women, but retain elements of the latter's ideological structures. As Susie Tharu points out, 'the discourses of our time will constitute our world as much as they do our subjectivities', but it is necessary, all the same, that a 'historically informed analysis' be sensitive to the 'subversions, elaborations, hybridizations, transformations, realignments or reappropriations that do take place within oppositional discourses'.[53] Therefore the discriminations that these feminist texts perform are worth noting. Even as we grant that they operate with a utopian bias, we must recognize that they do not create utopian contexts that ignore the tensions of reality (as commercial advertisements do); while they mark what may be described as the brief truces that women seemingly wrest out of history, they do not offer them in the form of a resolution of the conflict between tradition and modernity (as television programmes do); they do reproduce the dialectic of struggle, but not by representing women as unrelentingly external to the social process (as contemporary journalism does). The discriminations that they perform in these respects must be viewed as significant political advances in the self-representation of women. If I designate these representations as 'real' it is in the sense of this political utility that I use the term.[54]

But feminism, as Mary John reminds us, is a 'politics before it is an epistomology', and therefore is not simply a question of 'what is being said' but also of 'who speaks for whom'.[55] My chosen texts derive from a variety of contexts and occupy a range of genres, but I offer them primarily as consciously and radically feminist works that register the voices of women, thus marking the contemporary moment of feminism in India.[56] It is in the process of the creation of selfhood that self-cognition occurs, identity is taken on, and a politics is initiated.

NOTES

1 Kumkum Sangari and Sudesh Vaid, eds, *Recasting Women: Essays in Colonial History*, New Delhi, Kali for Women, 1986, p. 17.
2 Kumkum Sangari, response to Susie Tharu, 'Women Writing in India', *Journal of Arts and Ideas* 20–1, March 1991, p. 57.
3 Jacqueline Rose, 'The State of the Subject (1): The Institution of Feminism', *Critical Quarterly* 29, 4, Winter 1987, pp. 9–15, esp. p. 11.
4 Susie Tharu, 'Response to Julie Stephens', in Ranajit Guha, ed., *Subaltern Studies VI: Writings on South Asian History and Society*, Delhi, Oxford University Press, 1989, p. 127.
5 Rose, 'The State of the Subject', p. 11.
6 Ipshita Chanda, 'Birthing Terrible Beauties: Feminisms and "Women's Magazines"', *Economic and Political Weekly*, 26 October 1991, Review of Women Studies (WS), pp. 67–70, esp. p. 67.
7 Women constitute 49 per cent of the adult Indian population, and of these 42 per cent belong to the 25–44 years age group, the prime target audience for most advertisers. The percentage of working women has also been growing. See Adite Chatterjee and Nandini Lakshman, 'Cashing in on Women Power', *The Best of Brand Equity* (supplement issued by *The Economic Times*, n.d.), pp. 24–6, esp. p. 24.
8 Chatterjee and Lakshman identify 'growing literacy, changing consumption patterns

and the changing status of women' as the significant causes (ibid., p. 25).

9 Television has a reach of 41 per cent among women viewers, as compared to 44 per cent among men (ibid., p. 25).

10 Ibid., pp. 24–6.

11 Chanda, WS p. 67.

12 Similarly the government of India in its last annual budget (1992) raised the income-tax exemption level for women as a benevolent gesture of encouragement towards working women.

13 See Chanda, WS p. 67.

14 Chanda also calls attention to the function of 'inoculation' which women's magazines also perform (ibid., p. 67).

15 See the examples in the article 'Winning over the Trendy Teens' by Nandini Lakshman in *Brand Equity* (*Economic Times*), 1 April 1992.

16 In one popular textile advertisement an elegant woman joins a men's billiard game and stuns all present with a brilliant performance that outshines theirs. The advertisement ends with her shy, silent, smiling, modest, gracefully 'feminine' refusal of their acclaim. Thus it is up to the the 'achieving' woman herself to maintain her traditional status and behaviour.

17 In 'Cashing in on Woman Power', the authors cite the example of an advertisement for a computer course in which the girl declares her wish to pay her father back the money he has spent on her (p. 26). Another advertisement for a business magazine profiles a woman vice-president of a large hotel chain who has 'shown environmental concern way beyond the pale of her profession'.

18 The advertisers of the toilet-cleaner Harpic specifically label its user 'the new woman'. The Duncan tea campaign celebrated *aaj ki nari* ('today's woman').

19 See Jug Suraiya, 'The Chips are down for Post-modern Hindi', *The Times of India*, 19 June 1990. The point is also discussed in the context of television by Prabha Krishnan and Anita Dighe, *Affirmation and Denial: Construction of Feminity in Indian Television*, Delhi, Sage, 1990, pp. 112–3.

20 In the context of regional cinema, Tejaswini Niranjana discusses the invocation of Rajasthani clothes and settings to signify the 'Indian'. See 'Cinema, Femininity and the Economy of Consumption', *Economic and Political Weekly*, 26 October 1991, WS pp. 85–6, esp. p. 85. Similarly several advertisements – for clothes, soft drinks, cigarettes (a new brand of which is named Jaisalmer) – exploit the romantic aura of Rajasthan in their visual images.

21 Gurcharan Das, 'The Modern Indian', *The Sunday Times of India*, 6 September 1992.

22 Niranjana, WS p. 86.

23 For extended discussions of the terms and concepts 'tradition' and 'modernity' in the context of women and social change in India see Sangari and Vaid, *Recasting Women*; Lata Mani, 'Contentious Traditions: The Debate on SATI in Colonial India', *Cultural Critique* 7, Fall 1987, pp. 119–56; and Geetha Kapur, 'Contemporary Cultural Practice: Some Polemical Categories', *Social Scientist* 18, 3, March 1990, pp. 49–59.

24 Arvind Rajagopal, 'Uses of the Past: The Televisual Broadcast of an Ancient Epic and its Reception in Indian Society', Ph.D. dissertation, University of California, Berkeley, 1992.

25 For a lengthy discussion of the representation of women in the television serials of the epics see Prabha Krishnan, 'In the Idiom of Loss: Ideology of Motherhood in Television Serials', *Economic and Political Weekly*, 20 October 1990, WS, pp. 103–15.

26 Draupadi appears in the court when the Pandavas lose her in a game of dice to the Kauravas. She demands to know whether her husband Yudhishter was already a slave when he lost her, 'a complicated legal point', as Iravati Karve describes it. In the television version the famous disrobing scene figures prominently. Krishna

intervenes to save Draupadi eventually, but the scene retains its titillating effect. Mriganayini is a tribal woman whose beauty and musical prowess greatly charm the king; but she uses her influence with him to effect reforms in the kingdom for the benefit of the people rather than for personal power or gain. Her individualism is framed as feminist self-assertion.

27 Ania Loomba, 'Overworlding the third world', *Oxford Literary Review* 13, 1–2, 1991, pp. 164–93, esp. p. 167.

28 Uma Chakravarti, 'Whatever Happened to the Vedic *Dasi*? Orientalism, Nationalism and a Script for the Past', in Sangari and Vaid, *Recasting Women*, pp. 27–86.

29 Iqbal Masood, 'The Sherni, the Superindentent and the Other Woman', *Manushi* 47, July–August 1988, pp. 43–44, esp. p. 44.

30 For examples of Doordarshan's censorship of scenes from films telecast by it see Amit Agarwal, 'Cut it out, Doordarshan!' in *The Times of India*, 15 April 1990. Doordarshan edits out scenes of 'cabarets, "mujras", rapes, and strong abuse words'. It also avoids showing 'anything against any particular caste, creed, religion or country, or against the government of the day'. Prabha Krishnan cites the example of a group which protested to the high court, in February 1989, that 'the religious feelings of Hindus would be upset if the epic carried insinuations against Sita, showed scenes of her banishment, or showed a washerman cast aspersions on Sita's character', in the *Ramayan* serial. 'The telecast of the epic was allowed when lawyers for the producers gave their assurances on these points' (Krishnan, WS, p. 115, n. 11). More recently, there have been doubts expressed about the historical accuracy of the serial, *The Sword of Tipu Sultan*, and protests against the 'revivalist' overtones in another serial, *Chanakya*.

31 Madhu Kishwar, 'Axed', *The Illustrated Weekly of India*, 7–13 August 1988.

32 Amit Agarwal quotes Doordarshan officials who explain that it is pressure from women's groups, and from politicians representing religious and regional constituencies, that makes them cautious about what they telecast. News reports about women's protest against late-night 'adult' films on TV are included in Ramala Baxamusa, ed., *Media Reflections on Women's Movement in India* (Monograph published by Research Centre for Women's Studies, SNDT Women's University, Bombay, 1991).

33 See Maithreyi Krishnaraj, 'Introduction', in Krishnaraj, ed., *Feminism: Indian Debates 1990* (Monograph published by Research Centre for Women's Studies, SNDT Women's University, Bombay, 1991), p. 12.

34 Nandita Gandhi and Nandita Shah, *The Issues at Stake: Theory and Practice in the Contemporary Women's Movement in India*, New Delhi, Kali for Women, 1992.

35 Richard Fox and T.J. Jackson Lears, eds, *The Culture of Consumption: Critical Essays in American History, 1880–1980*, New York, Pantheon, 1983, p. xii; quoted in Bruce Robbins's introduction, 'Grounding Intellectuals', in Robbins, ed., *Intellectuals: Aesthetics, Politics, Academics*, Minneapolis, University of Minnesota Press, 1990, p. xx.

36 Ibid.

37 Other newspapers and magazines have also, recently, begun to recognize and address women as subjects and readers. *The Times of India*, 17 September 1992, advertised a special feature on 'Woman: The New Spirit'. The copy headline read: 'Reach out to the woman of the times. Through "The Times".' A popular English woman's journal, *Femina*, has been running a series of advertisements through 1992, addressed to the 'woman of substance'.

38 See the 'Media Reports' on journals and newspapers in regional languges and English in Maithreyi Krishnaraj, ed., *Women and Violence: A Country Report* (Monograph published by Research Centre for Women's Studies, SNDT Women's University, Bombay, 1991).

39 Judith Butler, 'Contingent Foundations: Feminism and the Question of "Post-modernism"', in Butler and Joan W. Scott, eds, *Feminists Theorize the Political*, London and New York, Routledge, 1992, p. 13.
40 Kankana Das, 'Woman Power', *Sunday*, 8–14 March 1992. Less moderate articles attacking feminists have appeared in prominent dailies like the *Times of India* and news magazines like *India Today*.
41 *Nathabati Anathabat*, written, enacted and directed by Saoli Mitra, performed in Bombay and Delhi in December 1991; Sheba Chachi's photographs entitled *Feminist Portraits*, part of an exhibition of works by Indian and other Asian photographers, *An Economy of Signs*, commissioned by The Photographers Gallery, London, which toured the UK in November 1991, and was displayed in Bombay in September 1992; Mudupalani, 'Radhika Santwanam', extracts translated and published in Susie Tharu and K. Lalitha, eds, *Women Writing in India*, vol. I, Delhi, Oxford University Press, 1991; *Mirch Masala*, directed by Ketan Mehta, 1989, and *Rihayee*, directed by Aruna Raje, 1991; *We Were Making History*, life stories of women in the Telengana people's struggle, by members of Stree Shakti Sanghatana in Hyderabad, Delhi, Kali for Women, 1989.
42 Iravati Karve, *Yuganta: The End of an Epoch*, Hyderabad, Disha, 1991.
43 Sheba Chachi, in 'Looking beyond Finalities', *The Economic Times*, 10 November 1991.
44 Mudupalani, 'Radhika Santwanam', translated by B.V.L. Narayanarow in Tharu and Lalitha, eds, *Women Writing in India*, p. 120; see also editors' headnotes, pp. 116–18.
45 Introduction by editors, *We Were Making History*.
46 Raja Rao, *Kanthapura*, Delhi, Oxford University Press, 1974.
47 Vasantha Kannabiran and K. Lalitha, 'That Magic Time: Women in the Telengana People's Struggle', in Sangari and Vaid, *Recasting Women*, p. 183.
48 Tharu and Lalitha, 'Introduction', *Women Writing in India*, pp. 1–12.
49 Vishwapriya Iyengar, in 'Looking beyond Finalities' (see n. 43).
50 Shuddhabrada Sengupta, '*Nathabati Anathabat*: An Act of Female Resistance' (review), *The Economic Times*, 13 December 1991.
51 Lauren Berlant, 'National Brands/National Body: *Imitation of Life*', in Hortense J. Spillers, ed., *Comparative American Identities: Race, Sex and Nationality in the Modern Text*, London and New York, Routledge, 1991, p. 123.
52 Veena Oldenberg, 'Lifestyle as Resistance: The Case of the Courtesans of Lucknow', in Douglas Haynes and Gyan Prakash, eds, *Contesting Power: Resistance and Everyday Social Relations in South Asia*, Delhi, Oxford University Press, 1992, pp. 23–61.
53 Tharu, 'Response to Julie Stephens', p. 128.
54 My formulation of the 'real' and the functionalism with which I endow representation echoes Marianne Moore's manifesto in 'Poetry'. Moore says of poetry's affects: 'these things are important ... / because they are/ useful'. My sense of the 'real' as that which mediates between the literal and the imaginary is expressed by her in the famous phrase 'imaginary gardens with real toads in them'. 'Genuine' poetry is 'raw material ... in/ all its rawness and/ that which is on the other hand/ genuine'. See *Collected Poems*, New York, Macmillan, 1951, pp. 40–1.
55 Mary E. John, 'Postcolonial Feminists in the Western Intellectual Field', *Inscriptions* 5, 1989, pp. 49–73, esp. p. 63.
56 The 'voices and actions' of women in such a context, as Stephen Heath notes, turn them into the 'subjects of feminism, its initiators. [T]he move and join from being a woman to being a feminist is the grasp of that subjecthood'. See his 'Male Feminism', *Dalhousie Review* 64, 2 (1986), p. 270, cited in John, 'Postcolonial Feminists', p. 64.

INDEX